Anonymus

Deputy Keeper of Public Records in Ireland

Twentieth report

Anonymus

Deputy Keeper of Public Records in Ireland
Twentieth report

ISBN/EAN: 9783742811189

Manufactured in Europe, USA, Canada, Australia, Japa

Cover: Foto ©Suzi / pixelio.de

Manufactured and distributed by brebook publishing software
(www.brebook.com)

Anonymus

Deputy Keeper of Public Records in Ireland

THE

TWENTIETH REPORT

OF THE

DEPUTY KEEPER

OF THE

PUBLIC RECORDS IN IRELAND.

(2ND MAY, 1888.)

Presented to both Houses of Parliament by Command of Her Majesty

DUBLIN:
PRINTED FOR HER MAJESTY'S STATIONERY OFFICE.
BY
ALEXANDER THOM & CO. (LIMITED),
And to be purchased, either directly or through any Bookseller, from
EYRE and SPOTTISWOODE, East Harding-street, Fetter-lane, E.C., or 32, Abingdon-street,
Westminster, S.W.; or ADAM and CHARLES BLACK, 6, North Bridge, Edinburgh; or
HODGES, FIGGIS and Co., 104, Grafton-street, Dublin.

1889.

CONTENTS.

REPORT, .   **PAGE** .   3

APPENDIX.

I. Request from Chief Justice for removal of Records of the Queen's Bench and Common Pleas Divisions, . . 19

II. Warrant for removal of Records of Queen's Bench and Common Pleas Divisions, ... 19

III. Order by Lord Lieutenant and Privy Council as to custody of Records deposited in Office of Clerk of Crown and Peace, co. Kildare, ... 20

IV. Report of Sir Bernard Burke, Ulster, Keeper of the State Papers, ... 21

V. Warrant for the removal of the original Charter of the Hospital and Free School of King Charles the Second, Dublin, ... 34

VI. Certificate of Retainer, Probate Division, . . . 35

VII. Calendar to Christ Church Deeds, ... 36

VIII. Index to Deputy Keeper's Reports, Sixteenth to Twentieth, inclusive, ... 123

THE TWENTIETH REPORT

OF THE

DEPUTY KEEPER OF THE PUBLIC RECORDS

IN IRELAND.

TO THE MOST NOBLE THE MARQUIS OF
LONDONDERRY, K.G.,

LORD LIEUTENANT-GENERAL AND GENERAL GOVERNOR OF IRELAND.

MAY IT PLEASE YOUR EXCELLENCY,

1. The Queen's Bench and Common Pleas Divisions of the *Queen's Bench.* High Court of Justice, Ireland, having become amalgamated under the Chief Justice of the Queen's Bench Division, in accordance with the Act 50 and 51 Victoria, chapter 6, the Lord Chief Justice addressed a request to the Master of the Rolls, pursuant to the *Appendix I.* 14th section of the Public Records (Ireland) Act, 1867, that the records of the Queen's Bench and Common Pleas Divisions of the High Court of Justice in Ireland for the years 1866–1876, *Appendix II.* inclusive, should be transferred to this Department. A Warrant in accordance therewith was signed, and the records removed here at the same time as the ordinary accruing increment.

2. On the application of Mr. Jeremiah Mara, Clerk of the *Kildare, Clerk* Crown and Peace for the County of Kildare, pointing out the *of the Crown,* inadequacy of the space at his disposal for the keeping of the *&c.* records of his office, and the great convenience it would be to the public were the older ones transferred to this Department, application was made to the Lord Lieutenant and Council for an order under the 5th section of the Public Records (Ireland) Act, with a view to bringing the records in question under its *Appendix III* operation, and subsequently an order was made by the Lord Lieutenant and Council on the 2nd of January, 1888, bringing the records in question under the Act, with the intention of their being ultimately transferred to this Office.

A 2

Record and
Writ Office,
Chancery.

3. There were received into this Department during the year 1887 the following records from the Record and Writ Office, Chancery Division:—

Records.	Vols.	Bds.	Dates.
Affidavits,	27	—	1886
„ (Answering) to Cause Petitions,	2	—	1886
Attorneys' Licenses Registry Books,	5	—	1843-1884
Cause Petitions,	6	—	1844-1862
„ Entry Book,	1	—	1886
Certificates : Landed Estates Court,	1	—	1884-1887
Chancery General Hearing Books,	2	—	1845-1863
Common Notices,	16	—	1886
Consents,	1	—	1864-1887
Dead Roll,	—	1	1886
Deeds of Submission, Masters' and Bank Certificates,	1	—	1886
Hearing Book, Court of Appeal,	1	—	1885-1886
Lord Chancellor's Orders,	7	—	1843-1887
„ Chamber Fiat Book,	1	—	1886
Masters' Orders,	16	—	1886
Motions : Landed Estates Court,	8	—	1886
Notices : Landed Estates Court,	6	—	1887
Notices of Motion,	2	—	1886
Orders to vacate Recognizances,	—	1	1886
Patent Roll,	—	1	1886
Petitions,	16	—	1886
Petitions of Appeal and Answers,	2	—	1886
Receivers' Accounts,	17	—	1883-1886
Recognizance Roll,	—	1	1886
Recognizances,	—	1	1886
Registry of Service of Orders and Notices (Landed Estates Court),	2	—	1863-1886
Reports,	5	—	1886
Rolls Motions,	1	—	1885-1886
Rolls Orders on Petition,	1	—	1886
Rolls Orders,	7	—	1885-1887
Rolls Petition Hearing Book,	1	—	1886
Rule Books,	2	—	1886
Side Bar Orders,	3	—	1886
Pluries Fieri Examinations,	—	6	1886
Writs of Summons and Plaint Books,	16	—	1886-1886

4. From the Queen's Bench Division:—

Records.	Vols.	Bdls.	Dates.
Abstracts, ...	—	6	1863–1876
Affidavits, ...	—	78	1846–1876
„ (Indexes), ...	6	—	1847–1876
„ Judgment Mortgage, . . .	—	6	1869–1875
Attorneys' Apprentices: Enrolment of Indentures,	—	1	1840–1867
„ „ Indentures Book, . .	1	—	1866–1872
Attorneys, Roll of, ...	—	1	1851–1864
„ struck off the Rolls: Book of, .	1	—	1857–1876
Bills of Sale, ...	—	52	1863–1876
„ Entry Books, ...	2	—	1863–1876
„ (Indexes), ...	2	—	1863–1876
Certificates of Sums Due: (Indexes), . .	2	—	1875–1876
Certiorari: Copies of Decrees Removed by, .	1	—	1865–1874
Cognovits, ...	—	10	1866–1876
Commissions for Affidavits Book, . . .	1	—	1864–1877
„ „ (Index), . .	1	—	1864
Consents, ...	—	3	1869–1873
Court Books, ...	44	—	1867–1876
Defences and Abstracts, ...	—	7	1866–1867
Defences, ...	—	87	1867–1876
Judges' Reports and Coroners' Certificates, .	—	17	1866–1875
Judgment Books (Final), ...	11	—	1866–1876
„ Pleadings, ...	—	85	1866–1876
„ Rolls (Civil), . . .	—	40	1866–1876
„ „ (Debt), . . .	—	24	1866–1876
Memorials, ...	—	8	1865–1874
„ (Roll), ...	—	1	1868–1869
Pleas, ...	—	35	1866–1876
„ (Indexes), ...	11	—	1866–1876
Poor Law Decrees Index, ...	1	—	1850–1864
Postea, ...	—	4	1850–1876
„ (Index), ...	1	—	1861–1867
Requisitions, ...	—	4	1855–1860
„ Books (Court Duties), . .	2	—	1866–1875
Rule Book (Alphabet for), ...	1	—	H. 1855
Rule Books, ...	44	—	1866–1876
Satisfactions, ...	—	2	1866–1876
„ (Index), ...	1	—	1861–1871
Suggestions, ...	—	1	1854–1876
„ (Index), ...	1	—	1854–1876
Summonses to Settle Issues Book, . . .	1	—	1854–1876
Warrants of Attorney to enter Judgments, .	—	8	1866–1873
„ „ (Index), . .	1	—	1867–1871
Warrants of Attorney: Affidavits to Register,	—	2	1869–1873
„ „ (Index), .	1	—	1849–1864
Writs (Returned), ...	—	82	1866–1876
„ (Indexes), ...	2	—	1866–1876

Crown Office, Queen's Bench.

5. From the Crown Office, Queen's Bench Division:—

Records.	Vols.	Bdls.	Dates.
Affidavits, ...	—	2	1843–1894
Certiorari; Writs of (returned), . . .	—	1	1864–1892
Court Martial Orders, . . .	—	1	1843–1844
Informations, Depositions, Inquisitions, &c., Certified Copies grounding Applications, . . .	—	1	1843–1894
Mandamus Writs, Returns, Pleadings, . . .	—	1	1888
Presentments, City of Dublin, . . .	—	1	1843–1892

Common Pleas Division.

6. From the Common Pleas Division:—

Records.	Vols.	Bdls.	Dates.
Abstracts, ...	—	13	1458–1870
Acknowledgments of Deeds by Married Women, . .	—	94	1835–1864
" " Entry Books of,	3	—	1848–1873
" " Index Books,	3	—	1879–1883
" " Affidavit File,	—	1	1867–1870
Affidavits, ...	—	73	1846–1873
" (Indexes), ...	11	—	1858–1874
Attorneys' Apprentices Indenture Rolls,	—	2	1830–1847
Awards on Submission, . . .	—	1	1834–1859
Case Judgment (Pleadings), . . .	—	117	1834–1870
" Rolls, . . .	—	44	1859–1870
Cognovits, ...	—	1	1849–1871
Commissions for Affidavit Roll, . .	—	1	1871–1876
" " Enrolment of,	—	1	1848–1871
" (Special), . . .	2	—	1873–1873
Commissioners' Names Books, . .	2	—	1834
Caveats, ...	4	1	1888 and 1888–1870
Court Books, ...	54	—	1843–1873
Debt Judgment Roll, . . .	—	1	1846–1860
Defences, ...	—	43	1846–1875
Demurrer Book, ...	1	—	1882
Interlocutory Judgments, . . .	—	4	1843–1870
" Book, . . .	1	—	1844–1874
" Roll, . . .	—	1	1843–1869
Judgment Books (Final), . . .	54	—	1843–1876
Judgment Mortgage Affidavits, . .	—	4	1879–1880
Memorials, ...	—	3	1848–1878
" Roll, . . .	—	1	1858–1870
Orders, ...	2	—	1873–1880

Records.		Vols.	Bdls.	Dates.
Patents,	.	—	7	1848–1876
„ (Books),	.	6	—	1844–1875
Plaints,	.	—	96	1844–1879
„ (Indexes),	.	11	—	1844–1876
Requisitions,	.	—	1	1873
Rule Books,	.	14	—	1846–1879
„ (Rough)	.	3	—	1848–1880
Satisfactions,	.	—	3	1845–1873
„ (Book),	.	1	—	1844–1865
Sid for Rule Books,	.	6	—	1849–1878
Stay File,	.	—	1	1831–1864
Suggestions,	.	—	1	1871–1877
Warrants of Attorney,	.	—	1	1844–1875
„ (Index),	.	1	—	1800–1877
Writs (Returned),	.	—	21	1848–1875

7. From the Exchequer Division :—

Records.		Vols.	Bdls.	Dates.
Abstracts,	.	—	1	1846
Affidavits,	.	—	8	1860
„ (Index),	.	1	—	1608
Cre Judgment Rolls,	.	—	2	1648
Cognovits,	.	6	—	1446
Commits,	.	—	1	1845–1848
Defences,	.	—	3	1864
Final Judgment Book,	.	1	—	1840
Interlocutory Judgments,	.	—	1	1866
Judgment Pleadings,	.	—	8	1864
Kennrials,	.	—	1	1845–1848
Kennrial Roll,	.	—	1	1844–1847
Plaints,	.	—	6	1840
Postens,	.	—	1	1840–1848
Rule Books,	.	8	—	1800–1848
Rule or Court Books (Rough),	.	16	—	1849–1864
Satisfactions,	.	—	1	1846–1848
Sheriffs' Oaths,	.	—	1	1800–1867
Summons and Plaint Index Book,	.	1	—	1844
Warrants of Attorney,	.	—	1	1846–1848
Writs (Returned),	.	—	8	1849

Record Tower, Dublin Castle.

Appendix IV.

8. From the Record Tower, Dublin Castle, there have been transferred the records as set out in the following list. In Appendix IV. will be found the report of Sir Bernard Burke, the Keeper of the State Papers, Ireland.

Records	Vols.	Bdls.	Date
Books of Entries (Civil):—			
Affidavits of Service of Orders of Council,	3	–	1842 1849
Kilkenny Confederates,	5	–	1844–349
Shipping,	1	–	1623–1626
Barrack Correspondence,	–	6	1643–1703
Chief Secretary's Office—Machine Copies of, Letters,	–	16	1760–1801
Correspondence (General and other Officers'),	–	9	1696–1775
Military Certificates,	–	7	1604–1774
„ Commissions,	–	1	1714–1803
„ Contracts,	–	6	1718–1768
„ Notifications,	–	16	1787–1767
Miscellaneous Documents (Index to),	–	–	–

Irish Land Commission (Diocesan Registries.)

9. From the Irish Land Commission (Documents from the Diocesan Registries of the late Established Church of Ireland):—

Diocese.	Records.	Bdls.
Ardagh,	Maps and Terriers,	1
Ardagh, Kilmore, & Elphin,	Glebe Title Deeds,	1
Armagh and Clogher,	Glebe Title Deeds,	1
Cashel, Emly, Waterford and Lismore,	Glebe Title Deeds, and Patents and Titles,	3
Cashel and Emly,	Maps and Terriers,	1
Clonfert and Kilmacduagh,	Glebe Title Deeds,	1
	Dalkling Papers,	3
Cloyne,	Maps and Terriers,	1
Cork, Cloyne and Ross,	Glebe Title Deeds, &c.,	4
	Patents, Titles, &c.,	1
Derry,	Glebe Title Deeds, &c.,	1
Derry and Raphoe,	Glebe Title Deeds, &c.,	1
	Patents, Titles, &c.,	1
Down, Connor & Dromore,	Glebe Title Deeds, &c.,	1
	Patents, Titles, &c.,	1
Down and Connor,	Glebe Title Deeds, &c.,	1
Dublin and Glendalough,	Maps and Terriers,	3
Elphin,	Glebe Title Deeds, &c.,	1
	Maps and Terriers,	1

Diocese.	Records.	Bdls.
Ferns	Maps and Terriers, ...	1
Kildare, ...	Maps and Terriers, ...	1
Killaloe and Kilfenora, .	Glebe Title Deeds, &c., ... Building Papers, ... Patents, Titles, &c., ...	2 4 1
Kilmore, Elphin & Ardagh,	Glebe Title Deeds, &c., ... Building Papers, ...	2 1
Kilmore, ...	Maps and Terriers, ...	1
" (Deanery of), .	Leases, ...	1
Leighlin, ...	Maps and Terriers, ...	1
Limerick, Ardfert and Aghadoe,	Glebe Title Deeds, ... Building Papers, ... Patents, Titles, &c., ... Maps and Terriers, ...	3 1 1 1
Meath, ...	Glebe Title Deeds, &c., ... Building Papers, ...	1 1
Ossory, ...	Glebe Title Deeds, &c., ... Maps and Terriers, ...	1 1
Ossory, Ferns & Leighlin,	Glebe Title Deeds, &c., ... Building Papers, ... Patents, Titles, &c., ... Maps and Terriers, ... Maps—Unions of Parishes, ...	1 1 1 1 1
Raphoe, ...	Glebe Title Deeds, &c., ...	1
Tuam, Killala & Achonry,	Glebe Title Deeds, &c., ... Building Papers, ...	2 2
Waterford and Lismore, .	Maps and Terriers, ...	1
Waterford, Down & Chapter of,	Leases and Deeds, ...	1

10. From the late Consistorial Court of Dublin:—

Consistorial Court, Dublin.

Records.	Vols.	Bdls.	Dates.
Marriage Licenses, Bonds and Affidavits, ...	—	7	1818-1845
Affidavits to obtain Licenses, and Flats, ...	—	85	1846-1879
Miscellaneous Bonds, ...	—	2	—
Affidavits for Licenses, and Flats, Diocese of Kildare, .	—	2	1846-1876

11. From the Office of the Registrar of Judgments:—

Registrar of Judgments.

Records.	Vols.	Bdls.	Dates.
Memorandums—Registration of Judgments, . . .	—	12	1856
" Registration of Satisfactions, . .	—	1	1857-1863

Registrar in Lunacy.

12. From the Office of the Registrar in Lunacy :—

Records.	Vols.	Bdls.	Dates.
Affidavits, ...	3	–	1843-1848
Petitions, ...	6	–	1844-1848
Reports and Accounts, ...	8	–	1843-1848

13 Report, Appendix II.

13. And from the Offices of the Land Judges, Chancery Division, there have been transferred 2,000 Deeds Boxes of the late Landed Estates Court, portion of some 4,500 included in His Honor's warrant of last year. The necessity for putting up fittings to receive them has been the sole cause of the delay in completing this large transfer, but it is expected it will be concluded in the course of the current year.

Blue Coat School, Dublin.

Appendix V

14. The Governors of the Hospital or Free School of King Charles II., near Dublin, commonly known as the Blue Coat School, having applied to the Master of the Rolls for permission, under the 16th section of the Public Records (Ireland) Act, 1867, to deposit their original charter here, His Honor issued his warrant of permission giving them the necessary authority to do so.

Carte Papers.

15. Upon the recommendation of the Master of the Rolls the Lords of the Treasury sanctioned the purchase by this Department of copies of the papers selected by the late Dr. Russell and Mr. Prendergast, Commissioners appointed by the Lords of the Treasury in 1865, from volumes 47, 48, 49, 50, 51, 52, 53, 59, and a portion of volume 60 of the Carte Papers in the Bodleian Library. These copies were made by Mr. Harper (since deceased) transcriber to the Commissioners, in the expectation that the suspension of the Commission would be only temporary, and comprise 579 documents, all of the "Ormonde" collection of the Carte papers, which, added to the copies (4,945) previously furnished to this Department, form a total of 5,524 papers, the complete list of papers selected by the Commissioners being 7,697. This addition has been bound and deposited in our library in sequence to the former volumes, and the titles of the additional papers have been added to the catalogue.

Probate Division.

Appendix VI.

16. No records were removed during the past year from the Probate Division of the High Court of Justice in Ireland, the President of that Division having certified that the records are required for the current business of the Division. There are at the present time nearly ten years accretion of Wills, copies of Wills, and other testamentary documents unremoved to this Department, notwithstanding that arrangements were made in 1861 by the then Master of the Rolls, in concert with the Lord Lieutenant in Council and the High Court of Judicature, by which certificates are issued by this Department, in cases where

the records have been transferred, in order to obviate the necessity of searches being made in the Public Record Office by officers from the Principal Registry. During the past year twenty-seven certificates have been issued in compliance with requisitions received from the Probate Office.

17. Twenty-seven deeds affecting the rights of the Crown, Crown Deeds including twenty-four conveyances of Quit and Crown Rents, have been received and deposited during the year.

18. On the 5th of May Mr. John Lopdell, Senior Second Class Vacancies and Appointments Clerk, sent in his resignation on the ground of ill health. He had been in this Department from its foundation, having been transferred here from the Common Pleas Office in 1868. A ¹ Report, s. 17. pension in accordance with his services has been granted him by the Lords of the Treasury.

Mr. A. J. Fetherstonhaugh, University Student and Scholar of Trinity College, Dublin, was appointed to fill the vacancy thus caused, on the 28th day of November, 1887, and entered upon his duties on the same day.

The vacancy caused by the retirement of the late Mr. Thomas M'Ghee in 1886 still remains unfilled.

The post of Sixth Workman Searcher was filled on the 9th day of June, 1887, by the appointment of Mr. Charles Wright, who was, however, unable to attend until the 20th of the same month.

19. A set of queries was received from the Royal Commission Royal Commission, Civil on Civil Establishments, and duly replied to. Establishments.

Intern.

20. Six bays have had galvanised iron shelving substituted for Iron Fittings. the old wooden fittings, and four of these, on the sixth floor, have been covered with corrugated galvanised iron sheeting to preserve the records from the dust and mortar which accumulate owing to the continued fall of the rendering from the roof. Six vaults C, D, E, F, G, and H have been fitted with iron racks to receive the Deeds Boxes of the late Incumbered and Landed Estates Courts. Galvanised iron drawers have been fitted to a portion of the fittings in Bay 4 R, to hold the "Usher's Box" collection of deeds and other instruments hitherto preserved in vault D in wooden drawers.

I annex a diagram showing the changes made in the deposits and the new work done during the year.

Sorting and arrangement of papers.

21. Much progress has been made in the work of sorting, bundling, and covering with paper the records of the late Incumbered and Landed Estates Courts, removed here during 1886. The affidavits have been arranged in bundles of uniform size and covered with paper, making 165 bundles. The Draft Conveyances from the collection of the late Judge Longfield

(1850–1860) have been sorted under the initial letters of their titles into 25 bundles. The like has been done with the Draft Conveyances of Judge Hargreave (1850–1865), making 40 bundles, as well as to other Draft Conveyances, comprising 38 bundles. The Abstracts and Statements of Title of Judge Longfield and the Registrar have been flattened and arranged in dictionary order, making 48 bundles. Petitions and Copy Petitions have been arranged under their letters, and made into 94 bundles; Duplicate Rentals into 8 bundles; Consents and Claims arranged in order of date; Certificates of Appearances placed in numerical sequence; and Schedules of Incumbrances, Paymaster's Certificates and Declarations of Title wrapped in paper, these latter series forming 77 bundles.

Cause Papers, Probate Division. 19 Report, s. 22. 22. The Cause Papers of the Probate Division from letter E to end have been arranged in the dictionary order of their titles, comprising 1,194 causes.

Admiralty Records. 23. The miscellaneous papers removed in 1874 and 1875 from the Court of Admiralty are in process of being arranged in dictionary order of their titles, with a view of making them accessible by means of an exhaustive index.

Christ Church Deeds. 24. Four hundred and thirty-three of the Deeds, Leases, Papal Bulls, &c., of the Christ Church Collection have been separately covered with brown paper, labelled, and placed in tin boxes.

Dublin Marriage License Bonds. 25. The Dublin Marriage License Bonds (1840–1852) have been stamped, flattened, and arranged in bundles.

Church Papers. 26. Twenty-five bundles of Church Papers of the Diocese of Cloyne and 5 bundles of the Diocese of Limerick have been flattened, as also 10 bundles of Rural Deans' Reports and 17 bundles of Visitation Papers.

Bookbinding and Repairing. 27. In the bookbinding and repairing department 8 volumes of transcripts from the Cause Papers, 3 Parochial Registers, 14 Diocesan Registers, 8 Will and Grant Books, and 2 volumes of Landed Estates Rentals have been bound. Five Hundred sheets of Marriage License Bonds, 20 of Landed Estates Affidavits, and 15 of Chancery Reports have been repaired, as also 94 Membranes of Rolls and 7 Wills, besides other incidental work.

Indexing and Calendaring.

Fiants, Elizabeth. 19 Report, s. 27. 28. Considerable progress has been made in the compilation of the Index to the Fiants of the Reign of Queen Elizabeth, which it was at one time hoped might have been completed in time to have been printed in this Report, but it has proved to be a work of greater magnitude and labour than was anticipated.

Receivers' and Guardians' Accounts. 19 Report, s. 62. 29. The combined Index to the volumes of Receivers' and Guardians' Accounts, Chancery, commencing in April, 1843, has been drafted down to the year 1856.

30. A copy has been made of the volume of the Index to Prerogative Wills and Grants for the years 1847, 1848, and 1849, with the intention of placing it in the Search-room for reference, in lieu of that removed here from the Probate Registry, which had become worn out and in parts almost indecipharable from constant use. *Prerogative Wills.*

31. The combined Index to the volumes of Chancery Petitions mentioned in my last Report, has been engrossed after having been carefully compared with the volumes from which the Index was compiled, and is now in the hands of the binder. *Chancery Petitions. 19 Report, s. 83*

32. A very full and accurate Index Nominum to the Crown Rental for 1013 was made by Mr. George Battersby, late of the Quit Rent Office. This he was kind enough to present to the Department, and, after having been compared with the original and engrossed, it has been prefixed to the volume, the value of which, as a reference in respect to questions of title, is thereby much enhanced. *Crown Rental, 1013.*

33. The Index to Writs de lunatico inquirendo, transferred here from the Hanaper Office, has been completed to the year 1664, and the entire volume transcribed afresh. *Writs de Lunacy. 16 Report, s. 39.*

34. Draft Indexes have been formed to the Will and Grant Books of the Diocesss of Meath (1647-1731) and Ardagh (1762-1802 and 1839-1853), and where Wills are of record in these books that do not appear in the Indexes to the original Wills of those Diocesss, the Indexes have been amended by their insertion. These Indexes have been compared and are ready for engrossment. *Meath and Ardagh Diocesss.*

35. A volume of Grants of Administration, Diocese of Killala and Achonry (1800-1857) has also been indexed. *Diocese of Killala and Achonry.*

36. Of the Draft Indexes made to the Administration Bonds, those for the Dioceses of Cloyne, Connor, Down, Killala and Achonry, Tuam, and Waterford and Lismore have been compared, and those for Ardagh, Ardfert, Clogher, and Clonfert compared and engrossed. *Administration Bonds Index. 19 Report, s. 83.*

37. A consolidated detailed index has been prepared for the Records of the Incumbered and Landed Estates Courts to page 110, and the consolidated Index for the Queen's Bench has been extended to page 501, for the Common Pleas to page 407, for the Law Exchequer to page 408, and for the Equity Exchequer to page 211. The following detailed indexes have also been extended—Record Tower Collection to page 274, Custom House Collection to page 335, Testamentary to page 53, Chancery, volume 2, to page 413, and Miscellaneous General Collections to page 201. *Detailed Indexes.*

38. A Calendar to the ancient Bulls, Grants, Leases, and other muniments belonging to the collection deposited here in 1872 by the Dean and Chapter of Christ Church Cathedral was formed by Mr. M. J. M'Enery of this office under instructions from the *Christ Church Calendar.*

16 Report, s. 27. late Deputy Keeper. A portion of it comprising the earlier documents, which are of more general historic interest, has been compared with the original deeds and printed. (Appendix VII.)

Appendix VII. The Deeds, the calendar of which is now printed, were copied into the "Novum Registrum" of Christ Church Cathedral in the last century by Dr. Lyon, who has also in many instances given copies of the seals then attached, many of which are not now in existence. It is proposed on some future occasion to print the remaining portion of the calendar of the Christ Church Collection comprising the leases together with the documents preserved with them.

Index to Reports. 39. An Index has been formed to the 16th, 17th, 18th, 19th, and 20th Reports of the Deputy Keeper of the Public Records in Appendix VIII. Ireland, which will be found in Appendix VIII.

Proceedings under the Parochial Records Acts.
38 & 39 Vic., c. 59, and 39 & 40 Vic., c. 58.

Reports of Custodians. 40. The reports for the year 1887 furnished by the parochial officers having charge of their parish registers under orders of retention from His Honor the Master of the Rolls, have been returned with great exactness. Out of 471 parishes the reports of none are wanting. In my last Report I mentioned that complaints were made of damp affecting the records, but it has been satisfactory to learn that the measures taken to obviate this evil proved completely successful in the cases reported last year, and that the number of complaints this year has been reduced to five, and those of a very slight nature.

St. Luke's, Cork. 41. St. Luke's Church, Cork, was destroyed by fire in the early part of the year, and as the parish registers were kept in the vestry, under His Honor's retention order, I communicated with the Incumbent, and in reply was informed that the records were quite uninjured, the portion of the building in which they were not having suffered from the fire.

Portarlington Registers. 42. Amongst the annual Warrants for the removal of parochial records to this Department, was one for the parish of St. Michael, Portarlington, on the resignation of the Very Rev. John Wolseley, Dean of Kildare. When executing it, the volume of Baptisms returned in the Inventory, dated 16 December, 1875, as comprising 1810-1819 and 1841-1848 was not forthcoming, and on application being made to the Dean he stated that he had not got it, and was therefore unable to forward it. An instance (one of many) of the unsatisfactory working of the Parochial Records Acts.

Collection of Parochial Records. 43. A practice has been adopted during the past year of obtaining the assistance of the parochial officers to forward to this Department per parcels post the registers of the parishes whose records became attachable by the Warrant of the Master of the Rolls, instead of sending an Officer to collect them. The latter practice was doubtless most advisable when the parishes whose records were to be transferred were numerous, but as they are now few and much scattered the cost per parish had become very considerable. Of course, the new practice depends largely for its success on the co-operation of the clergy concerned,' but that has hitherto been afforded most ungrudgingly, and I have on behalf of the public to return them my most grateful thanks. This change in the mode of collection has resulted in a decided saving to the public funds, and has proved so far very satisfactory.

44. The registers of 25 parishes became attachable by His Honor's Warrant during the year. Of these 15 have been transferred to this custody, and 10 remain in local custody by virtue of His Honor's retention orders. The three tables subjoined show the changes in places of deposit and custody of Parochial Records during 1887.

I. Parishes, the records of which have been transferred to the Public Record Office in the year 1887 :—

Parish Church or Chapel.	County.	Vols.	Baptisms.	Marriages.	Burials.
Ashfield, ...	Tyrone, . .	3	1785-1887	1745-1845	1853-1887
Kanow, ...	Wexford, . .	7	1807-1883	1847-1887	1800-1883
Clayton, ...	Dublin, . .	2	1863-1876	—	1843-1876
Cookson, ...	Armagh, . .	3	1806-1883	1806-1883	1806-1884
Bealaway, ...	Raphoe, . .	3	1853-1877	—	1846-1877
Emlaugh, ...	Kilkenny, . .	4	1818-1818	1817-1853	1818-1873
Drishmoen, ...	Tuam, . .	2	1806-1886	—	1867-1886
Drimtern, ...	Tuam, . .	2	1863-1876	—	1863-1876
Fuddell, ...	Armagh, . .	3	1822-1887	1822-1844	1837-1887
Ellerim and Donaguore, .	Connor, . .	3	1833-1877	1832-1844	1843-1887
Kommell, ...	Clonfert, .	1	1833-1836	1833-1844	1830-1865
Dighni, ...	Killala, .	2	1841-1887	—	1843-1887
Kilmurry, ...	Limerick, . .	3	1764-1883	1784-1813	1783-1866
Eslan, ...	Connor, . .	1	1843-1887	1843-1863	1844-1887
St. George, C.K., . .	Dublin, . .	1	1834-1883	—	1833-1883
St. Helens, Portarlington,	Queen's County,	1	1848-1883	—	—
Zalaid, ...	Tipperary, . .	3	1781-1844	1781-1844	1804-1843

II. Parish, the records of which have been returned from the Public Record Office of Ireland to the former custody of the Incumbent during the year 1887 :—

* St. Bridget, Dublin.

* Taken up temporarily during building of aisle

III. Parishes in which the Parochial Records have been retained under Retention Orders in 1887 :—

Armagh.Tc.
Ballymore.
Carrickfergus.
Carrickmacross.
Castlecomer.
Castletownarra.
Dunleckney.
Falls (Upper).
Glenavy.
Holywood'ck.
Inch (Down).
Innismurra.
Killesher.
Killasnaghan.
Longhgall.

Newmarrock.
Neville (Upper).
Rathfarnham.
Ross (Ross).
St. Bridget.
St. Catherine (Dublin).
St. Mark (Gleaney).
St. Patrick (Waterford).'
St. Peter (Dublin), for St. Kevin, St. Stephen, and Holy Trinity, Rathmines.
Taughboyne.
Tullaghobegley.
Tyran.

Fees 1887. 45. The amount of Fees received during the year was £660 5s. 6d., being an increase of £83 15s. over the receipts of the previous year.

TABLE OF FEES, 1887.

Date.	Inspections.	Tracea of Maps.	Attendances.	Folios at 1s.	Folios at 6d.	Total.
						£ s. d.
January,	314	3	—	156	1,645	63 10 6
February,	143	—	—	64	1,692	63 17 4
March,	174	5	—	800	1,649	64 11 5
April,	171	4	1	64	1,711	63 27 6
May,	163	3	—	156	1,374	57 6 4
June,	171	—	1	431	2,645	67 16 6
July,	179	1	—	6	1,789	60 1 6
August,	174	1	—	60	1,371	63 1 6
September,	111	2	—	70	724	95 7 6
October,	164	6	—	615	1,397	60 14 4
November,	191	3	—	219	1,691	67 14 9
December,	148	—	—	200	715	38 1 4
Total.	**1,899**	**64**	**2**	**1,685**	**19,964**	**660 5 6**

Fees remitted. In addition to the above, fees have been remitted to the amount of £39 18s. 6d. for work of a similar nature done for Public Departments, which would otherwise have been a charge on the public.

Donations. 46. I beg to acknowledge donations of twelve volumes of Record publications by the Right Honorable the Master of the Rolls in England, one volume by the Deputy Clerk Register of Scotland ; Records of the Anglo-Irish Families of Ball from the compiler, the Rev. William Ball Wright, M.A.; a History of the Wolfes of County Kildare, from the author, Major R. Wolfe, and a Historical Sketch of Dublin Castle, by Mr. W. J. Bayly, from the author.

47. The literary searches during the year 1887 included the Literary Searches. histories of the families of Goldsmith, Gillman, White, Deane, Vigors, Aylmer, Steele, Nye, Ellis, Nash, Webb, Von Bilra, Hanna and Hannay, Lyndon, Cox, Myhill, Cottingham, Barnwall, Usher, Langrishe, MacCoughlan, Desminiéres, and O'Toole; and materials for Histories of the Parish of Donagheloney, the County Kilkenny, 29th Regiment of Foot, Parish of St. Audoën's, Christian Antiquities of the County Dublin, Meath Hospital, Dublin, County Sligo, Kingdom of Meath, Parish of Glenarm, and Wilson's Hospital, County Westmeath.

Dated at the Public Record Office,
Four Courts, Dublin, this 2nd
day of May, 1888.

J. J. DIGGES LA TOUCHE,

Deputy Keeper of the Public Records in Ireland.

I humbly certify to your Excellency that this Report is made by the Deputy Keeper of the Public Records in Ireland, under my direction, pursuant to the Statute.

A. M. PORTER.

Master of the Rolls.

APPENDIX.

APPENDIX I.

Pursuant to the Public Record (Ireland) Act, sec. 14, I hereby request that the Records of the Queen's Bench and Common Pleas Division of the High Court of Justice in Ireland for the years 1866 to 1876, both inclusive, may be removed to the Public Record Office forthwith.

Dated this 6th of September, 1887.

M. MORRIS, C. J.

To the Right Honorable the Master of the Rolls.

APPENDIX II.

Warrant under sec. 14 of 30 & 31 Vic., cap. 70.

WARRANT for the removal to the PUBLIC RECORD OFFICE OF IRELAND of the RECORDS of the QUEEN'S BENCH and COMMON PLEAS DIVISIONS of the High Court of Justice in Ireland for the years 1866 to 1876, both inclusive, and RECORDS over twenty years.

Whereas the Right Honorable Sir Michael Morris, Baronet, Chief Justice of the Queen's Bench of Her Majesty's High Court of Justice in Ireland, has requested by letter dated the 6th day of September, 1887, that the Records of the Queen's Bench and Common Pleas Divisions of the High Court of Justice in Ireland for the years 1866 to 1876, both inclusive, may be removed to the Public Record Office of Ireland pursuant to the third proviso of the fourteenth section of the Public Records (Ireland) Act, 1867. And, whereas there would appear to be certain records, books, and documents of the aforesaid Queen's Bench and Common Pleas Divisions of the age of twenty years, from the making thereof, still remaining unremoved to the Public Record Office. And, whereas it appears to me to be to the public advantage that the said records should be removed to the said Public Record Office. Now, I, the Right Honorable Andrew Marshall Porter, Master of the Rolls in Ireland, do hereby, with the approbation of the Right Honorable the Lord Baron Ashbourne, Lord High Chancellor of Ireland, testified by his countersigning these presents, under and by virtue of the provisions of the Public Records (Ireland) Act, 1867, and of all other powers and authorities enabling me in this behalf, appoint you John James Digges La Touche, Esquire, LL.D., the Deputy Keeper of the Records in Ireland, or in your stead some or one of the officers of the said Public Record Office, to attend the several offices of the Queen's Bench and Common Pleas Divisions of the High Court of Justice in Ireland, and in my name to receive and take

B 2

charge of all the Records of the said Divisions of and for the years 1806 to 1870, both inclusive, and also of all the records, books, and documents of the aforesaid divisions of the age of twenty years from the making thereof, according to the specification and description of the same set out in the schedule hereunto annexed.

And for so doing this shall be your sufficient warrant.

Given under my hand this fifteenth day of September, one thousand eight hundred and eighty-seven.

A. M. PORTER, M.R.

Approved and countersigned by me,
ASHBOURNE, C.

APPENDIX III.

By the LORD LIEUTENANT and PRIVY COUNCIL of IRELAND.

LONDONDERRY—

Whereas by section 5 of the "Public Records (Ireland) Act, 1867," it is provided that it should be lawful for the Lord Lieutenant with the advice of the Privy Council in Ireland, to order that Records belonging to Her Majesty deposited in any office, court, place, or custody in Ireland other than is thereinbefore mentioned should be thenceforth under the charge and superintendence of the Master of the Rolls; and thereupon the provisions of that Act should extend to all such Records, and to the persons then having the charge or custody of the same, as fully as if such office, court, place, or custody had been named and included in that Act. And, whereas, it has been represented unto Us by the Deputy Keeper of the Records that there are at present deposited in the Office of the Clerk of the Crown and Peace for the County of Kildare, in the Courthouse at Naas, in the County of Kildare, Records belonging to Her Majesty which have accumulated since the year 1798; and that the said office does not afford due accommodation for the same, or for their proper arrangement and safe preservation, and that consequently the said Records are liable to suffer damage and loss. And, whereas, it appears to Us necessary and desirable to provide for the safe custody and proper arrangement of the aforesaid Records, and of other similar Records which may be from time to time deposited in the said Office of the Clerk of the Crown and Peace for the County of Kildare. Now We, Charles Stewart, Marquess of Londonderry, the Lord Lieutenant-General and General Governor of Ireland, by and with the advice of the Privy Council in Ireland, in pursuance of the powers vested in Us as aforesaid, do hereby order that all Records, as defined by section 5 of the aforesaid Act, belonging to Her Majesty, and which have been for over twenty years deposited in the Office of the Clerk of the Crown and Peace for the County of Kildare, shall be henceforth under the charge and superintendence of the Master of the Rolls: and we do hereby further, by and with the advice aforesaid, order that all Records defined as aforesaid which have been deposited

In the said office within the last twenty years or which shall hereafter be deposited therein, shall, so soon as same shall have been deposited for over twenty years, be from thenceforth under the charge and superintendence of the Master of the Rolls.

Given at the Council Chamber, Dublin Castle, the 2nd day of January, 1888.

Edward Saxe-Weimar, General.   Ashbourne, C.

Meath.   Arthur James Balfour.

Arthur Kavanagh.   John Monroe.

J. G. Gibson.   Ion T. Hamilton

APPENDIX IV.

To the Right Honorable the Master of the Rolls.—The Twentieth Report of Sir Bernard Burke, C.B., Ulster King of Arms, Keeper of the State Papers in the Record Tower, Dublin Castle, dated 2nd February, 1888.

Sir,—I have transferred during the past year nine volumes of Civil Books of Entries, being the remaining part of the Council Office collection of books, which will be found catalogued in the Supplement to the Eighth Report of the Public Record Commissioners (1819), pp. 227 and 228. They comprise:—

Shipping, ... 1630–1688, $\frac{A}{17}$

Kilkenny Confederation, 5 Volumes:—

  1. Orders on Process, . . . 1644–1649, $\frac{A}{17}$
  2. Arrears of Assessments, . . 1645–1649, $\frac{A}{17}$
  3. Arrears of Assessments, . . 1645–1649, $\frac{A}{17}$
  4. Assessments and Assignments, . 1647–1648, $\frac{A}{17}$
  5. Assessments and Assignments, . 1648–1649, $\frac{A}{17}$

Affidavits of Service of Orders of Council,
                      1661–1668, $\frac{A}{17}$

Affidavits of Service of Orders of Council,
                      1663–1669, $\frac{A}{17}$

Affidavits of Service of Orders of Council,
                      1682–1688, $\frac{A}{167}$

These nine Volumes have been duly indexed by this Department, as stated under the heading "Work done." A minute description of their contents, with extracts therefrom, is added to this report.

Work done during the Year 1887.

I. The Index to the Unregistered Miscellaneous Papers, 1821–1876, alluded to in my last (19th) Report, pp. 39 and 40, has been sorted in dictionary order, and transcribed into three large volumes. The Papers to which this Index refers fill 705 Cartons, and the number of entries contained in the three volumes amounts to more than ten thousand.

II. Eight books of entries of the Council Office Collection have been indexed in slips (one Volume, $\frac{V}{1}$, was indexed in 1886), each index sorted in dictionary order, and duly transcribed into its respective volume. The following are the books:—

SHIPPING, ...   1630–1638

KILKENNY CONFEDERATION :—

ARREARS OF ASSESSMENTS,   .   1645–1649. 2 Vols
ASSESSMENTS AND ASSIGNMENTS, 1647–1649. 2 Vols.
AFFIDAVITS OF SERVICE OF ORDERS
   OF COUNCIL,   .   1661–1668. 3 Vols.

III. There is a valuable and interesting collection of documents and letters, transferred to this office from the Chief Secretary's Office in 1859. A few are dated in the 17th century, but the series refers principally to the years intervening between 1701 and 1834. A general Index was formed to the collection in 1860, but it has been found insufficient. I have accordingly directed to be made a more minute description of the contents of the headings—"Miscellaneous Letters;" "Correspondence; Irish Miscellaneous;" "Letters to Mr. Pitt," and others, and similar references. This Index is in course of preparation ; slips have been made up to 1787.

IV. Suitable Indexes have been made (and bound in one volume) to the following :—

BARRACK CORRESPONDENCE,   . 1703–1793. 5 bundles.
MILITARY COMMISSIONS,   . 1715–1763. 1 bundle.
MILITARY CONTRACTS,   . 1710–1760. 6 bundles.
MILITARY NOTIFICATIONS,   . 1702–1767. 15 bundles.
MILITARY CERTIFICATES, MIS-
   CELLANEOUS,   .   1684–1774. 4 bundles.
MILITARY—GENERAL and other
   OFFICERS' CORRESPONDENCE, 1686–1776. 5 bundles.

V. CHIEF SECRETARY'S OFFICE, Letters from 1760–1831, 50 bundles have been catalogued.

VI. A draft index has been also made to OFFICIAL PAPERS, 1851–1866, Carton 557 A.

I may add that the Papers of the Royal Commission (Irish Land Acts, 1886–7), contained in two large tin boxes, have, by order of the Government, been transmitted to this department.

TRANSFERS.

The following books of entries and papers have been transferred from this Department to the Public Record Office, 13th December, 1867 :—

I. The Nine Volumes of the COUNCIL OFFICE COLLECTION described in the first part of this report.
II. MILITARY CERTIFICATES, MISCELLANEOUS, 1681–1774, Cartons 43 and 44.
III. MILITARY COMMISSIONS, 1715–1763, Carton 44.
IV. MILITARY—GENERAL and other OFFICERS' CORRESPONDENCE, 1686–1776, Cartons 45, 46, and 47.
V. BARRACK CORRESPONDENCE, 1703–1793, 5 bundles. Tin box 5.

VI. MILITARY CONTRACTS, 1710–1760, 6 bundles. Tin box 5.
VII. MILITARY NOTIFICATIONS, 1702–1767, 15 bundles. Tin box 6.
VIII. CHIEF SECRETARY'S OFFICE, COPIES OF LETTERS FROM, 1760–1831, 50 bundles.

The Searches required by the Chief Secretary's Office during the past year have been very frequent, and have occupied a considerable portion of time.

The COUNCIL OFFICE COLLECTION calls for a more complete description.

The nine volumes of the Council Office Collection already mentioned comprise three series or classes of MS. books.

THE FIRST VOLUME refers to "Shipping, 1630–1638."

THE SECOND SERIES consists of five volumes of the period of the Civil War, being Books of the Kilkenny Confederation from 1641 to 1649. These records were briefly noticed in my Eighteenth Report, dated 1st of February, 1886. A further description of them is given in this my present report.

THE THIRD SERIES consists of three volumes of the Reigns of King Charles II. and King James II. They comprise Affidavits of Service of Orders of the Council, and commence in 1661, and end in 1688.

The volume entitled "Shipping, 1630–1638," covers the period during which Sir Adam Loftus, and Richard Earl of Cork, were Lords Justices.

Then come the Letters and Orders of Wentworth, Lord Deputy, afterwards made Lord Lieutenant and Earl of Strafford.

The Orders and Letters concern principally the guarding of the coasts against pirates, Turkish and other sea rovers, with Instructions to the Commanders how to carry out the Orders of the State, with various Orders for furnishing the ships with stores.

Great alarm had spread through the whole of Ireland (and England too) by the sack of Baltimore by a pirate fleet from Algiers, in June, 1631. Since that time they had frequented the coast, and sounded the harbours.

On the 11th February, 1631-2, the Lords Justices and Council excuse themselves for the Turks' surprisal of Baltimore by saying it was in the night, and they were gone in the morning with all their prisoners, their stay not being beyond twelve hours. They had made prisoner at sea of a fisherman of Dungarvan, one Hacket, and employed him to steer them into Baltimore, and Hacket showed much disloyalty, as he might have steered them (if he would) into some other harbour where they might have been captured.*

The Lords Justices add that they have had intelligence from Sir Vincent Gookin (a settler, it may be stated, at Court-mac-Sherry, in the Munster plantation), who had his information from a captive lately escaped from the Turks, that the Turks intended another expedition the following summer with such a number of ships as would enable them, by dispersing their forces, to take different towns at once.

The planters (the Lords Justices continue) may by this terror be chased away, and the fishers of pilchards, who in some years have made £15,000, in some £20,000. Mr. Counter had his wife and

* Hacket was convicted and hanged for this crime, see Smith's History of the County of Cork.

seven sons captured by the Turks, and carried from Baltimore to Algiers, and was about to claim relief for his loss.   Signed at the head, Adam Loftus, Canc., R. Corke.   And by the following Privy Councillors :— Lord Primate, Ld. Wilmot, Ld. Moore, Ld. Clanaboye, Ld. Kilmallock, Ld. Ranelagh, Ld. Dillon, Ld. Balfoure, Ld. Caulfuild, Ld. Esmonde, Ld. Ch. Justice, Mr. of the Wards, Ld. Ch. Baron, Sir Wm. Stewart, Sir J. Erskin. ⚓, pp. 41–46.

On 20th July, 1636, Sir Adam Loftus, Canc., and Sir Christopher Wandesforde, Lords Justices, inform the President of Munster that the Turkish Fleet of eight ships had within these twelve days surprised some ships in the harbour of Bristol, and taken prisoners 200 men. And that the Turks had forty ships divided into squadrons of eight or ten dispersed into different parts.   Signed at the head as above, and at foot by the following of the Council :—Ld. Primate, Ld. Chief Justice of Chief Place, Ld. Dillon, Ld. Bishop of Meath, Ld. Chief Baron, Sir Robt. Meredith. ⚓, pp. 215, & 16.

In May, 1632, the Lords Justices inform the Privy Council of a Biscay-ner pirate at the mouth of the Harbour, as it were in their very face, who had chased two merchant ships.   They impute it to the delay of the Commanders of the two King's pinnaces, the Fifth and Ninth Lion's Whelps, who linger over in England.   And they have no hopes until the ships are in the hands of those resident in Ireland, when it would be otherwise. ⚓, pp. 56–59.

On 24th July, 1632, Lord Chancellor Loftus and Richard Earl of Cork, Lords Justices, inform the Council at White Hall, that no sooner had the Biscay-ner departed than Nutt (who seems to have been a notorious pirate) took his place, by reason of the absence of the two pinnaces appointed to guard these coasts.   Nutt last night chased two barques with passengers, who being near Howth Head thought to escape to land, but he reached them with his shot, and made prisoners of them in view of our very good lord the Lord Baron of Howth, and divers others, who also saw seventeen boat loads of plunder brought to Nutt's ship.   Dated, Castle of Dublin, 23rd July, 1632, (and signed) Adam Loftus, Chancellor, and Richard Earl of Cork. ⚓, pp. 64–66.

In 1638, in Wentworth's time, there is a letter of the Lord Deputy and Council, that the ship called the Zutphen, of Amsterdam, lately at Killybegs, broke bulk there contrary to law, endeavoured to bribe the Customs Officer, sold much merchandise there, broke into houses and took what they would at their own prices, and threatened to burn the town, and so terrified the Lady Coatch (Coach) and Mrs. Hamilton, both dwelling near Killybegs, that Lady Coatch in her terror crossed the mountains barefoot, and Mrs. Hamilton was so terrified that she miscarried of a child, and was in danger of her life.   Dated, 20th January, 1637–8.   (Signed), at head, Wentworth.   At foot, R. Dillon, Wm. Parsons, Chr'. Wandesforde, Geo. Radcliff. ⚓ (p. 282).

I now proceed.

THE KILKENNY CONFEDERATE RECORDS.

The Books of the Kilkenny Confederation are only a fragment of the great body of records and papers of that celebrated body seized by Colonel Solomon Richards, in or about the month of February, 1654.

On 20th February in that year he was directed to make inquiry after all the records, books, papers, &c., of the late General Assembly of the Confederate Catholics in Ireland, and of all Courts established by them, and to send such as he could collect, by some trusty officer from garrison to garrison, to the Commissioners of the Commonwealth at Dublin (⚓,

p. 30.) The Records thus seized were duly transmitted. They comprised all the nominations and appointments to the various public offices, created by the Confederate Catholics; but of all these valuable records the accompanying books of public accounts only remain. During the Cromwellian era they were used at the Court of Transplantation (called the Court of Claims and Qualifications of the Irish) at Athlone. They were sent to Athlone on 1st April, 1655 (⅟₁₆), and the Court of Transplantation there having ended on 24th June, 1655, they were sent to the Court at Mallow for hearing the claims of the Old English (Catholic) inhabitants, who had been forcibly expelled from Cork, Kinsale, and Youghal in 1648 by the Earl of Inchiquin, then Commander of the English or Protestant forces for the safety of those garrisons, notwithstanding their constant loyalty. On 24th September, 1655, the Court at Mallow, being over, " Captain Edward Tomlins, comptrouling the Trayne was ordered to prepare a close wagon to send to Mallow for these records to be brought back to Dublin : And the Lord Henry Cromwell was to order a sufficient convoy for guarding the same on their way " ($\frac{A}{n}$ 170).

And by order of 10th of October, 1655, Mathew Doyle, wagon master, being appointed to convey the records of the late Courts of Athlone and Mallow to Dublin, the Governors of Kilmallock and Callan were to furnish four horse soldiers as a convoy between those towns, and none of the guard on the way to depart from his duty, but constantly to attend the guarding of the wagons (Ib. 189). And by order of 12th November, 1655 (the records being arrived), Mr. Enoch Colberne was to take charge of all the records, papers, &c., lately come from Athlone and Mallow to the Castle of Dublin (Ibid, 218).

At Dublin the books and papers were carefully indexed. Mr. Nicholas Coombes, Nicholas Browne, and Thos. Warren " being persons appointed to alphabett the Bookes of the Supreame Council at Kilkenny," were on 29th of May, 1654, ordered respectively salaries of £100, £55, and £50 for the work ($\frac{A}{n}$ 7). And John Smith, for his pains in making catalogues of Books taken at Waterford and Kilkenny, was on the same date to be paid six pounds sterling out of the Treasury at Waterford. Signed, Chas. Fleetwood, Miles Corbett, and John Jones. (Order Book of Council Office. Vol. 10. Late Landed Estates Record Office.) Equal use was made of these Records at the Restoration by the Court of Claims, and it was a common order that the Books at the King's Inns be searched for proof of nocency. They hence got to be called THE BLACK BOOKS. Thus on the 16th June, 1670, William Cooper was ordered to be paid Fifty Pounds (£50) for having had " the keeping and had now delivered up as ordered the Books of Discrimination (commonly called the Black Books), with the Kilkenny Books, Rolls of Association, Proceedings of the Supreme Council, Books of Claims, and Decrees of Athlone, and Transplantation Books " (Auditor General's Records).

It is impossible to exaggerate the historical loss of all these records.

After the closing of the Court of Claims, 4th January, 1669-70, the muniments of Evidence used before the Court which sate in the Court of Wards at the King's Inns (where now the Four Courts stand) were sent to a Chamber in the New Custom House, then on the south bank of the Liffey, just east of Essex's Bridge, a large heavy-corniced brick building, pourtrayed in Brooking's Map of Dublin, 1728. From thence they were removed to the Elephant in Lower Essex-street. And there, on Sunday afternoon the 15th April, 1711, a great fire broke out, and did irreparable damage.

Dr. Richard Stone, Her Majesty's Surveyor-General of Lands, reports

that the office contained the Strafford, the Down, the Civil, and Gross
Surveys, with the Books of Distribution, Claims, Reports, Decrees, Final
Settlements, Inquisitions, and Surveys taken upon the Dissolution of
Abbeys and Monasteries in Ireland, all which (says Dr. Stone) are
likewise consumed, excepting some Reports and Rough Books of Distri-
bution, &c.

Strafford's Survey (he adds), which contained the admeasurement of
the Province of Connaught, and some part of Munster, is altogether
entirely lost, together with all other papers and books thereto belonging.

The Civil and Gross Surveys are also lost excepting some scraps which
when put in order may be of use." He enumerates the Maps of Dr.
Petty's Down Survey severally lost and saved or injured in part. (Pub.
Record Office. Vol. I. E. 3, 73.)

Considering this great destruction of records, it is well to have even
these books of public Accounts of the Kilkenny Confederate Catholics.

With this view I have made a few selections to indicate the nature
of these Books.

VOLUME ENDORSED " ORDERS ON PROCESS, 1644-1649." $\frac{A}{14}$

This book is long and narrow, over one feet in length, and only three
inches wide.

The Kilkenny Confederates had their established Courts of Justice,
and this book regards the processes served and some other proceedings
in court.

The first page has three entries, which are given as a specimen.

Hugh Donegan,
Plff.   23rd May, 1644.
Gerald Grace,   Pcess (process) on sight, or notice. Call
James Brenagh   for the fee for both.
Defts.

Copy—Mathew Walsh,
Plff.   23rd Aug., 1634.
Thomas Comerford,   Pcess, on sight or notice. Or to give
Def.   present satisfaction. Bill entd.

Laurence Conway,
Plff.   24th August, 1644.
Thos. Shertall, Esq.,   Pcess. on sight or notice. Bill entered.
Deft.   Call for the fee of both.

11th Sept., 1645.

Edward Comerford &   The Defts. are required forthwith on sight
Jon. Fitzpatrick,   hereof to restore the mare and garron they
Plffs.   took from the plffs. and to satisfie them for
John Nash, Sub-sheriff, their damages thereby sustained according as
and Robt. Kenrick,   they shall agree ; or to appear before the said
Dfts.   Resident Commr, at Grace's Court in
Kilkennie to-morrow at Ten of the Clock, in the forenoon, to answer
the plffs. bill. Otherwise on default order shall pass against them.

Signed, Thomas Cantwell : George
Gern [   ] Peter Shertall.

Call to Edwd. Comerford for 1s. 2d. being the remainder of
2s. 6d. for the fees. Affidavit against both, 12th Sept., 1645.
Call for the fee, being 10d. wh' Comerford promised me to pay with the
1s. 2d. above on Tuesday next or before. A p. 86.

Hence it appears that the Court was held at Grace's Court, where the Assize Court and Court of Jail Delivery is held to this day, every Commission stating that the Court is to be held "at Grace's Old Castle," though the present Courts and Borough Jail must have been built in comparatively modern times. This volume like the rest of the series contains loose scraps of paper verifying the service of process, some of them sworn before George Blancheville.

There is also a Ger. Blancheville whose name, jointly with Edmund Shee and Peter Roth, appears to many orders on these flying slips, all three being probably Resident Commissioners for the County of Kilkenny, spoken of above.

The next volume is a book of public accounts containing the sums assessed on each "Horseman's Bed," a well known measure of land in the seventeenth century. On the first page is the following as the first Entry:—

"July 10th, 1847. Bar-de-Gouran—
Mr. Edmund Archdeacon [Archdekan] of Cloghla, collector of £3 10s. per Bed imposed per order of this date and payable to the Treasury on or before 14th of July, 1847, oweth out of the said Barony, being 16½ Beds, the sum of £57 15s. 0d."

On the opposite side seem to be credited payments :—

    Deb. s 17th July, 1647, G. Shee, 40 0 0
    Deb. ac 23rd July, 1647, G. Shee, 0 0 0
    Deb. 29th July, 1647, G. Shee, 4 10 0

The next (and only other) entry on this page is as follows :—

"July 10th, 1647. Bar-de-Ida, &c.
Mr. Piers Butler of Annaghs, Collector of £3 10s. 0d. per Bed imposed by Order of this date and payable into the Treasury, oweth out of the said Barony, being ¼ beds the sum of £42 10s. 0d."

On the opposite page :—

"Deb. ac., 22 July, 1647, G. Shee, £39 0s. 0d., Assigned by Order of 27th July, 1649, to Mr. Edmund Murphy, £2 18s. 5d."

On a loose or flying slip of paper attached to the above entry by a red wafer is the following entry :

"Delinquents of the Tax of £3 10s. 0d., imposed per bed in the Barony of Ida, Igrin, and Ibercon. Inprimis Mannerow 2 acres, 3s. 4d., Richard Butler, proprietor, Balljuliaga, 5 acres, 7s. 6d., Ellinor Baron, proprietor.
"Gillaghmore, 2 acres, 4s. 7d., Patrick Den and Thos. Wailsh, proprietors.

                   Witness my hand, 22nd July, 1647.

              "PIERS BUTLER."

Among the many loose slips attached by red wafers or by pins now black with age, are the specifications of lands wasted by the Civil War. At p. 15 are two slips as follows :—

A note of all the waste lands in the Baronies of Ida, Igrin, and Iverkon for the £3 per Bed per order of xth October, 1647.

	£	s	d
Lickerstown,	0	3	4
Ballinla,	} 1	10	0
Ballyvarin and Moumster,			
The 2 acres of Fearred Murry,	0	3	0
Ellen Walsh, one acre,	0	1	8
Laragh,	0	4	0
Edward Barron for Court Proban,	0	3	9
	2	5	7

              THOMAS FORSTALL.
              EDMOND FITZGERALD.

A list of such lands as are waste without habitation in the Barony of Iverke at the levying of three pounds per Horseman's Bed by Order of 9th Octobris, 1647.

		£.
Portnaboly, Mr. John Leonard, proprietor,	. .	xx.
Cornaghmartin, Mr. John Leonard, proprietor,	. .	xv.
Mr. Thomas Wailshe's land in Aglishe, .	. .	v.
Far Grants lands in Aglishe, .	. .	v.
Ballitarmey, Wm. Grant, proprietor,	. .	xliii.
Madogestown, Mr. Walter Wailshe, proprietor,	. .	x.
Barre macnicoll, the Lord Marques of Ormonde, proprietor,		x.
Carrig ne gaye, Captayne Robert Wailshe, proprietor, .		v.
The Treyna, due on Closeconeigu Ex. Gaage ovin discharged by order of this Courte, bearing date 3rd July, 1645, ...	.	viii.
Grange, Mr. Piers Wailshe, Corone, proprietor, .	.	xx.

Edwd. Grant, } Collectors.
R. Butler,   }

Jurat, Edwd. Grant,
Coram, 16th Nov., 1647.
    Ger. Wailshe.

VOLUME ENDORSED " KILKENNY CONFEDERATES.

ASSESSMENTS AND ASSIGNMENTS, 1648–1649." A.

Another Volume of public Accounts of the same nature identically as the last, with flying slips attached by pins or wafers.

At page 10 is the following on a loose or flying slip attached by a wafer:—

A List of the Delinquents in the Barrony of Cranagh, of fifty beeves imposed by Order of 12° Octobris, 1648.

Kesfoord, Mr. Edmund Shee,	.	.	£1 0 0
Ould towne, Harry O'Shee,	.	. .	0 8 8
Richard O'Meragh,	.	.	
The third of Damagh,	.	.	0 11 1

Thomas Shee

On a flying slip at p. 26 is the following:—

The humble peticon of the poore tenants of the Abbey of Kells and Blacke Rothe. } To the Right worshipful the resident Commissioners for the county of Kilkenny.

Humbly sheweth unto your worships that your poore petitioners are tenants unto James Butler of Dangin from yeare to yeare, at the fourth sheafe and other casualties, and that they have paid their last yeare's rent thereout, and that now they are charged with the fourth parte, which they humbly conceive is due of the said James, who utterly refuseth to pay the same, by means whereof the Collectors of the fourth parte have cessed troopers on yo'. petitioners as delinquents, to their utter undoinge, if not by your wisdoms soone relieved.

The premises considered and forasmuch as they are liable to all the cess and presse, without anie cuntribution from their said landlord. That yo'· worships may be pleased to compell their said landlord to pay the same, or if you thinke [fit] to direct yo'· warrant unto the Collectors to cease the said troopers on him, as hereby yo'· peticoners may not be further molested. And they shall ever pray, &c.

Kilkenny, 17th } By the Commiss'· for the Army of the
July, 1645.   }   countie of Kilkenny.

We require the above named James Butler to appeare personally before us to-morrow morninge and make answer to this petioon.

MOUNTGARRETT.   GEO. CANTWELL.
                   C. BRYAN.

Endorsed

The Humble peticon of the poore tenantes of the Abey of Kells.

___

AFFIDAVITS of the SERVICE of ORDERS of COUNCIL.

From these Kilkenny Confederate Public Accounts I pass to the Books of Affidavits of Service of Orders of Council.

This series contains a body of Evidence shewing the great unsettlement of Ireland at the Restoration, the parties out of possession (the old proprietors) hoping and striving to recover possession.

First comes the petition of Lady Grace Talbot (otherwise Lady Grace Calvart, daughter of Calvart, Lord Baltimore), wife of Sir Robert Talbot, eldest brother of Colonel Richard Talbot, afterwards made Duke of Tyrconnell and Lord Lieutenant of Ireland by King James II., concerning the Tythes of Larabrien, not then finally restored to the Established Church, being an inducement to the Bench of Bishops in the Peers House in Ireland to pass the Act of Settlement. Sir Robert himself was at this time in prison for debt incurred for his fellow-sufferers and fellow-claimants before the King and Council.

30th Nov., 1661.

The Lady Grace Talbott in } James Ford made faith that on
y'· behalfe of her husband,   the 16th day of July last hee repaired
Sir Robert Talbott,   to y'· Deft.'s dwelling house or usuall
              Plttff. ;   place of abaode in Maynooths, in the
Wm. Brereton, Clke,   Co. of Kildare, purposing to shew
              Deft.   him the Lords Justices' Order dated

15th July, 1661, and not meeting him, shewed the said Order to the Deft.'s wife, and delivered a coppy thereof, and Deponent did then see the Deft.'s wife deliver the coppy to one of the servants, and heard her tell the said servant to deliver it to the Deft., by which order the Deft. was desired to permitt the said Sir Robert Talbott, or the Pltff. in his absence, to receive and enjoy the tythes mentioned in the said Order. Provided that if His

Majesty should think fitt to restore the said Tythes to the Church in such case the said Sir Robert Talbott should be answerable to the Incumbent of the Parish of Laughbrien for such profitts as he should receive out of the said Tythes in the meantime, and leave the possession thereof to the Incumbent.

Yet the said Deft. doth not permitt the Plitta. to enjoy the Tythes aforesaid, for that severall of the persons to whom the said Plitta. sett part of the said Tythes tould Deponent that the Defendc. ant would not suffer them to pay the money due by them for the said Tythes to the Plitta., and Deponent was tould that the said Deft. did take some parts of the Tythe-hay belonging to the said parish into his owne possession.—Jur., M. B. *

Then follows the petition of Thomas Preston, third Viscount Tara, and of his aunt, Miss Mary Warren, daughter of Anthony Warren, of the King's County. The grandfather, General Thomas Preston, second son of Christopher, fourth Viscount Gormanston, was made General in command of the Leinster forces of the Confederate Catholics from 1642 to 1650, and was created by King Charles II. Viscount Tara by patent dated at Ennis in 1650.

He retired in 1650 to France, and was ordered by the King of France to command some French forces in Catalonia. He died in 1654, and was succeeded by Antony, second Viscount Tara. After his father's death Antony, Lord Tara, retired to Bruges, and must there have died, leaving his widow, Lady Tara, surviving, and his son Thomas, third Viscount, a minor.

At the Restoration (as appears by the "coppie of a letter writt with the King's owne hand," in the Carte collection) the King addressed the following to the Earl of Orrery, one of the Lords Justices :—

" White Hall, 4th of August, 1663.

" My Lord Orrery,—

" When I came first to Bruges, in Flanders, and was far from being in a good condition, I found my Lord Taragh there who invited me to his house, where I lodged near a month, till I could provide another place for myself, and during the whole time of my aboad in those parts he gave me frequent evidence of his good affection and dutie to me, which I resolved to have requited if he had lived.

" And therefore since hee and his wife are dead, I must particularly recommend his children to you, and likewise their aunt, Miss Warren, who was there likewise at Bruges, to your care that they may be out of hand put into the possession of ye severall lands which belong to them ; of which you are to advertise the other Lords Justices, to the end that you may all give effectual orders to the Commissioners to that purpose, and let them know I expect a good account of this business.

" Yor. very affectionate frend,

" CHARLES, R"†

On 28th of April, 1663, Thomas Lord Viscount Tarragh, son of Antony Preston by Margret Warren, recovered with Mary Warren by Decree of Innocence in the Court of Claimes 1,923 acres, Irish plantation measure, in the King's County. Before this Decree, on 29th of November, 1661, the Lords Justices endeavoured to restore Viscount Tarragh and his aunt to their lands, " but the Adventurers or Souldiers

* Mathew Barry was at this time Clerk of the Council, and these initials probably signify his name.
† C. P. xlii., 191., endorsed " Coppie of a letter writt with the King's owne hands."

in possession were not to be disposed of so easily, as appears by the following :—

> "29th Nov., 1661.
>
> "Lord Viscount Tarragh and Mary Warren, . . Plffs.
> "Captan Richard Dane and others, ... Dfts.

George Arthur made faith that on 20th November, last., has shewed Colonell Edward Warren, holding Ballybrittar, in the King's County, the Lord Justices' Order of 14th Novr., 1661. Also to George Sankey, holding BallymacWilliam, and on 23rd of the s⁴ month to Captain Richard Dane, holding Tubberdaly (and deponent enumerates other tenants of the lands of the Estate of the Lord Viscount Tarragh and Mary Warren), by which Order they were not to disturb the tenants of the said Lord Viscount and Mary Warren. But they forced the said tenants to pay notwithstanding the said Order.

"On 4th March, 1641-2 (in the same suit) Edmond Rourke made faith that by warrant of the Lords Justices of 18th of February, 1641-2, he attached the Deft., and desired him to come along with him, which has refused to doe, but took the Deponent by the shoulder and violently thrust him downe a payre of stone stairs, and but that the Deponent saved himself with his hands has had fallen down, and would have been in danger of his life."

> "Jer: M. R."

But nothing could avail ; and in compassion to " the wants and sad condition of Miss Warren, and the orphans of the late Lord Tarragh," the King ordered her a weekly allowance till they should be restored to their Estate. On 13th of January 1663 (when they had only re-received twenty-four weeks allowance) he again interfered, probably with no better success. For in 1682 it was again in arrear, and Ormonde " hoped it would be paid in consideration of the reception she gave the King and all of us " at Bruges, in her sister's house.*

On 5th June, 1649, Ormonde assumed the command of the Confederate Catholic forces, and with them were united for a short space of time Inchiquin's Protestant Regiments.

But in 1650, owing to the opposition of the Catholic Hierarchy, Ormonde was forced to dismiss his Protestant forces, and in December, 1650, he and Inchiquin embarked for France. But already in July, 1647, when Ormonde surrendered Dublin and its adjacent garrisons to the Parliament, the King's forces for the greater part turned over to the Parliament, Ormonde after the Restoration excusing them as being the only means they then had of living. Others, however, remained faithful to the Royal cause, and as Cromwell had divided all the lands of the Transplanted Catholic Irish among his own forces, the Protestant Royalists found that the only things left for them was the house property of the Irish in cities and borough towns, and the four Counties of Leitrim, Donegal, Wicklow, and Longford, which had been set aside for those Regiments that had betrayed the Munster garrisons to Cromwell. But the betrayers of the Munster garrisons not having actually received possession of the four counties, these and the city and borough house property of the Irish were seized by the Protestant Officers who served the King before 5th June, 1649, called shortly, the " 49 Officers."

In the following extract appears the first motion for obtaining possession of this house property :—

7 June, 1662

Alexander Pigott, Esq., made faith that on the 6th of this inst. June hes demanded of Edmund Goddericke, Under Sherriff of the County of Dublin, by the Order of the Lords Justices of the 4th of February of

---

* C. P. ccxix., 289. Ormonde to Arran, London, 20th September, 1682.

this year, the severall forfeited houses in the Borough of Swords allotted by H.M. Declaration and Instructions to the Officers who served H.M. in Ireland before the 5th of June, 1649, in payment of the said Officers' Arrears.

But the said Under Sheriffe refused.

The following petition of the Antient Inhabitants of Galway against the New Corporation gives a good instance of the unsettlement of affairs at the Restoration, and shews the violence and contempt of the Crom-wellians in possession against even so high a body as the Lords Justices and Council of Ireland :—

The 17th of February, 1661.

Sir Thomas Blake and others of the ould Inhabitants of the Towne of Gallway, in the behalfe of themselves and others of the said Towne. . . Plt̃fis. ;
John Eyre, Mayor, and Edward Eyre, Recorder, on the be-halfe of themselves and others of the Protestant Inhabitants of the towne of Gallway, . Defend̃ts

Martin French made faith that on or about the 8th day of February Inst. he shewed to Gabriel King, of the Towne of Gallway, Alderman, and John Warde, an attested coppy of an Order of the Rt. Hon̄ble the Lords Justices and Council, dated the 24th day of February Inst., and delivered unto each of them coppies thereof : And that thereupon the said Warde in a contemptuous manner threw the coppy of the said Order soe delivered unto him into the gutter.

That on or about the same day hee repaired to the dwelling-house of Paul Dodd, Alderman, situate in the said Towne of Galway, purposeing to shew him the attested coppy of the said Order, but that not meeting him hee left a coppy thereof with his wife, who upon delivery thereof threw it from her, and bade him wipe it to his taile, and cuffed the deponent about the facr. And the deponent verily believes were it not that hee immediately runn away from her, she had further abused him.

The deponent above deposeth that on or about the same day hee repaired to the respective dwelling-houses of John Murry and Robert Breck, Sherriffes of the said towne, and to the respective dwelling-houses of George Cashier, Wm. Jones, John Strain, and Henry Blood wick, purposeing to shewe them respectively the attested coppy of the Order aforesaid, but that not meeting them, nor any of them, he shewed the same at their houses, and left coppies thereof with their wives or servants to bee delivered to them. By which said Order the Mayor, Recorder, and Sherriffs, and the other persons complained of in the paper annexed to the Plaintiffs' petition, Intitled 'The particulars of the oppressions done to the ould Natives of Gallway by the present Magistrates and Inhabitants of the said towne,' required foorthwith by themselves or their Agents sufficiently instructed and authorized to appeare and answer the said Petition and the said paper annexed ; And he further deposeth that soone after that hee had left a coppy of the said Order at the house of the aforesaid John Murry, with one of his maid-servants, hee the said Murry mett the deponent departing the said towne of Gallway in the streetes of the said towne. And that then and there hee gave the deponent on his head two blowes with his rodd of office, in that the deponent did not give him (as hee said) the said attested coppy of the Order, which said coppy was sealed upp in a cover with other papers to bee sent to Dublin, and threw his (deponent's) hat into the gutters, and committed him to the dungeon, where hee was kept for two houres or thereabouts, stripped naked to his shirt and drawers. And that all his cloathes, shoes, and stockens were scourched by the jailer and constable, and the said cover wherein the said attested coppy was sealed upp, togeather with other papers, was taken from him by direction of the said Murry, but the said papers were afterwards delivered to the deponent by the said Constable and Gaoler, after that the cover soe sealed upp was broken open by Anthony French, and the said attested coppy shewed to the said John Murry by the said Anthony French. Jur.: M. B.

The following is a similar instance of contempt of the Order of Council :—

7 October,
1073.

James Tennant of Athenry made faith that he delivered the Order of the Lords Justices and Council, on 28ᵈ September last to Joseph Ormsby, late Portreeve of Athenry, whereby the Burgesses were ordered not to swear the said Joseph Ormsby into the Office of Portreeve for the ensuing year, but to swear in John Eyre of Eyre Court, Esq. 'And deponent deposeth that when he showed the said Order to the said Ormsby, and delivered him a coppy thereof, the said Joseph Ormsby answered slightingly That "he would doe by the coppy of the said Order as he had done with other papers." Book of Affidavits, 1608–1682, p. 120.

AFFIDAVITS of SERVICE of ORDERS of COUNCIL, 1661–1603.

In the Volume thus endorsed appears the following :—

9 Novʳ 1661.

Edmund Prendergast made faith that since the Proclamation of the 9ᵗʰ January, 1660, prohibiting the destruction of woods, there hath been great waste and destruction committed on the woods of Curraghnemoney and Glenbreedy, in the County of Tipperary, formerly belonging to this Deponent's father, by the hands of Philip Gibbon, John Hogan, Phillipp Daly, Thomas Dean, Thomas Mullaly, and David Mahery, with divers others, and [they] do still continue destroying the said wood, contrary to the said Proclamation.

And the deponent deposeth that about the 7ᵗʰ of March last hee shewed the said Proclamation to Thoˢ Morgan, of New Castle, in the said Countie, Tobias Smith of Frehans in the said County, which two are the persons who doe from time to time employ the former persons and others to cutt the said woods. And who upon shewing them the Proclamation aforesaid, tould this Deponent that they did not value the said Proclamation but would still continue the cutting of the said woods and that they would not leave one tree thereof but one whereon hee thee Deponent should bee hanged.

And he Deponent deposeth that in the month of March last this Deponent showed the said Proclamation to Richard Homerton, who also doth from time to time employ carpenters and others in cutting the said woods . . . . And they and the said other persons aforesaid doe still continue cutting and destroying the said woods, and

G

have made more destruction thereon since the said proclamacion than
hath been done since the beginning of the Rebellion, as this deponent
truly believeth.

Jur.: M. B.

> Attachm^t Dated the 16th day of Novr 1061,
> Signed by the Lords Justices issued against
> the persons above named.

18th Decr 1662.

Edmund Prendergast again made faith that six men (all named)
by appointment of Valentine Greatrakes and Alexander Deane, had
been cutting the woods of Rossmore, &c., in the barony of Iffay and
Offay, in the County of Tipperary, and deponent meeting the said
six men on 4th and 5th of November last carrying barrel staves, hoopes,
and other ware made of the said woods, asked of them by what
authority they presumed to cutt and carry away the said woods.
They made answer that Valentine Greatrakes, their employer, would
beare them out and therefore would continue cutting.

On 22nd of October last deponent caused the Subsheriff at the
Sheriff's Court held at Knockannanony, in the barony of Iffay and
Offay, publiquely to read the proclamation against cutting timber
woods, all the said six persons being present, whereupon the said Thos
Morgan and Stephen Bateman said they did not care for the said
Proclamation, and if the deponent would inform against them for cutting
the said woods they would cropp off his eare.

The Council records of Ireland are in point of fact of such historical
interest that I have been induced to enter thus fully into the nature
of the portion of them transferred on this occasion.

> I have the honor to be, Sir,
>   Your very faithful servant,
>   J. Bernard Burke, Ulster,
>   Keeper of the State Papers.

Record Tower, Dublin Castle,
   2nd February, 1888.

APPENDIX V.

30 & 31 Vic., c. 70, s. 16.

WARRANT for the REMOVAL to the PUBLIC RECORD OFFICE of
IRELAND of the ORIGINAL CHARTER of the HOSPITAL and FREE
SCHOOL of KING CHARLES the SECOND, Dublin.

WHEREAS it is the wish of the Board of Governors of the Hospital
and Free School of King Charles the Second, Dublin, as expressed by
their minutes of the 21st June, 1887, and 20th September, 1887,
that the Original Charter granted by King Charles the Second on the
5th December in the 23rd year of his reign to that institution, and
which was enrolled in Ireland on the 26th January following should
be deposited in the Public Record Office of Ireland.

AND WHEREAS I am of opinion that the said Charter is a fit and proper document to be deposited in the Public Record Office of Ireland, in accordance with the terms of the 16th section of the Public Records Act, 1867. Now I, the Right Honorable Andrew Marshall Porter, Master of the Rolls in Ireland, do hereby permit the said Original Charter of the Hospital and Free School of King Charles the Second to be deposited in the Public Record Office of Ireland, which said Document shall be deemed to be a Public Record in my custody, and shall be subject to the like rules and regulations as other Public Records.

> Dated at the Rolls Chamber this second day of November, one thousand eight hundred and eighty-seven.
>
> A. M. PORTER, M.R.

APPENDIX VI.

PUBLIC RECORDS (IRELAND) ACT, 1867.

I, the Right Honorable Robert R. Warren, Chief Judge of the Probate Division of the High Court of Justice in Ireland, hereby certify to the Right Honorable the Master of the Rolls in Ireland, that, in my opinion, it will be conducive to the due performance of the business of the Probate Division that the Records belonging to said Court, in the Schedule annexed specified, shall not be delivered into the custody of the Master of the Rolls at the end of twenty years from the making thereof.

Dated this 13th of June, 1887.

> ROBERT R. WARREN.

SCHEDULE.

The Wills, Will Books, and other Records of the Principal and several District Registries of the Court of Probate from 11th January, 1858.

> Appearance Books, from 1865.
> Cause Books, from 16th December, 1864.
> Cause Papers (A-Y), from 1865.
> Cause Papers, Rules Office, (A-W), from 1865.
> Caveats, from December, 1864.
> Day Books, from July, 1865.
> Record Books (Records disposed of), from December, 1866.
> Rule Books, from 16th May, 1865.
> Rule Books (Side Bar), from September, 1864.
> Writ Books, from 1866.

APPENDIX VII

CALENDAR TO CHRIST CHURCH DEEDS

The following Calendar is portion of one made under instructions from the late Deputy Keeper of the Records in 1883, to the Original Bulls, Grants, Deeds, Leases, and other documents transferred to the Public Record Office from Christ Church Cathedral in 1872. It comprises the documents, both numbered and unnumbered, entered in the three volumes of the "Novum Registrum," now in the custody of the Dean and Chapter of Christ Church. Of these documents, Nos. 0, 11, 12, 13, 28, 43, 61, 81ᵃ, 91, 218, 243, 331ᵇ, 335, 372, 374, 375, 376, 377, 378, and 370 were not transferred, and are calendared from the copies extant in the "Novum Registrum." Except those cases noted at foot as being in French or English the original documents are in Latin. It is difficult to ascertain the exact dates of many. The probable dates given by Mr. Lyon in the "Novum Registrum," have been adhered to, save where it is plain that a mistake has occurred.

The numbers prefixed to each article and enclosed thus ( ), are those found on the originals and on the copies in Novum Registrum. The preceding current numbers are added for reference.

1. (2.) Earl Richard, son of Earl Gillibert, on behalf of the King, grants to Hamund son of Torkill, Consalo and adjacent lands held by him before the arrival of the English in Ireland; to hold of the King, at a rent of two marks, payable to the Canons of Holy Trinity Church, to supply light before the Holy Cross.

Witnesses—Hervey de Montmorres, Maurice fitzGerald, Gilbert de Bosco Rob', Mailer fitzHenry, Adam de Hereford, Hugh de Clahell, John the bishop, Walter the goldsmith, Aylred the palmer, Roger, brother of Horn, Augustine, Marcus Judeus, Nicholas the clerk, and Richard Gogan.—*Circa* 1174.

2. (1.) Henry II. confirms to Hamund son of Torkill, the land called Kennsalioh, as granted by Earl Richard. Rent, two marks, payable to the Canons of Holy Trinity, to supply light before the Holy Cross.

Witnesses—C. Elyensis, Earl Richard de Strigoll, Richard de Luci, William fitzAudel, Robert fitzBerna[rd]. At Wodestock.—*Circa* 1174.

3. (2ᵇ.) Earl Richard son of Earl Gillibert, grants the land of Hamand son of Torkaill, called Kennsali, for light for the Holy Cross of Holy Trinity Church, Dublin.

Witnesses—Adam de Hereford, John de Clahulle, Robert de Burmigham, Ramund de Karreu, Roger the chamberlain, Walter the goldsmith, Walter Bloet.—*Circa* 1174.*

4. (3.) Alexander de Cestra grants to Holy Trinity Church, the land in the Parish of St. Brigid without the Wall, in Pulle-street, near the Canons' land; his body to the church to be buried and three masses to be celebrated weekly.

Witnesses—Joseph, chaplain of St. Bridget's, G., chaplain of St. Martin's, R., the dean, Cristred de St. John, W. the goldsmith, C. de Wincestria, W. Pollard, D. Bas.—*Circa* 1180.

5. (4.) Pope Urban III. confirms the Provincial Constitutions framed by John Comyn, Archbishop of Dublin, as follows :—

Altars to be made of stone if possible, otherwise a square stone slab should be inserted in the middle of the altar, large enough to sustain five equidistant crosses, and extending beyond the foot of the largest chalice. The covering of the holy mysteries to be white, and spread

.* For grant by Archbishop Laurence, circa 1173, see No. 364 *infra.*

from the upper part of the altar to the ground in front; the chalice to be made of gold or silver in the richer churches, and of tin in the poorer; the host to be delicate, pure, and white, and the wine so tampered with water as not to lose its natural taste and colour; the lavatory of stone or wood to be hollow, so that the post communion washings may pass to the earth. A Baptismal font to be kept in every church with a channel in the same manner through which the ash of old vestments and altar coverings burned is to be passed; vessels used in Baptism are not to be converted to human purposes; no person to be buried unless in a church consecrated by a bishop, and in the presence of a priest; divine service not to be celebrated in chapels built by laymen to the injury of mother churches, without licence of the bishop; no priest, deacon, or sub-deacon to keep a woman in his house, except a mother, own sister, or person without suspicion through age; Simony to be punished by loss of office and benefice. Then follow regulations with regard to Holy Orders and the punishments directed against fornicators, persons refusing to pay tithes, and plunderers.

Dated at Verona, Non. Mar. (7 Mar.) 1186.

6. (5.) Pope Urban III. confirms to Holy Trinity Church the Rule of its foundation, and the churches of Holy Trinity, St. John the Baptist, St. Michael, St. Michou, the mill and garden near the bridge, the garden near St. Patrick's, the garden near the new ditch, the lands near the church of St. Brigid, Rechen, Port Rochran, Rathchillin, Consali, Trianchochair, Triancillidaria, Lealuan, Cellestra, Danouanach, Clalmaddon with its church, Maginmo, Cilldullg, Farann Amleim, Chualnanim with its church, Kalgnoh, Telachain, Cellsagini Lenin with its church, Celltacan, Ralthealchan, Telachneopscop with its church, Dromming, Feranmochagan, Lonhtignahi, Tirodran, Farannucharan, and Ferannuroulb; freedom from tithes of crops, and nourishment for its beasts; free asylum for refugees; no brother to depart without licence; power to elect priests to their churches and present the same to the bishop, divine offices to be celebrated during a general interdict with closed doors and without ringing the bells, those excommunicated or under interdict being excluded, burial to be permitted in the church except to persons under same condition, no arrest, murder, or theft, to be committed in the close of the church. Priors to be elected by the brethren or the majority thereof, and to have first voice in the election of Archbishop of Dublin.

Dated at Verona by the hand of Albn, Cardinal priest and Chancellor, vi. Non. Jul. (2 July) 1186.

7. (11.) M[alchas], bishop of Glyndelah, reciting a deed of Raymond Gros, patron of Kilkulin, institutes the Canons of Holy Trinity, Dublin, into the said Church, saving the life interest of Robert de Curks, paying one pound of incense yearly.

Witnesses—Will., archdeacon of Dublin, Cornelius, archdeacon of Kildare, Gregory, archdeacon of Glyndelach, Augustine, dean, Simon, prior of St. Thomas.—Circa 1190.

Calendared from "Novum Registrum."

8. (144.) Pope Celestine III. confirms to Columbanus, prior of Holy Trinity Church and his brethren, their rule, lands and privileges as in No. 6. supra.

Dated at St. Peters, Rome, by the hand of Peter. Cardinal deacon of St. Nicholas in carcere Tulliano li. Kal. Feb., 1° Celestine III. (31 January, 1192.)

Only a fragment of this Bull remains, but it is exemplified in No. 383, and is a duplicate of No 6 in every respect except name of Pope.

9. (6.) Ronulph Wterol grants to Holy Trinity Church, a house near land formerly belonging to Helias FitzPhilip, and extending to the land of Wm. Germund.   Prior R. to deliver seisin.

Witnesses.—Roger the chaplain, Master Wm. Utrel, Richard de Cogan, Robert de Garsal, Ralph de Oalieburne, of the King's household, Richard the innkeeper, Wm. Duf, Adam the artisan, Nicholas the deacon.—*Circa* 1200.

10. (7ª.) John de Curci grants to the Church of Holy Trinity, Inlalochaculin, Lescumalcig, Ganimore, and Balemeiadiman.

Witnesses.—John, archbishop of Dublin, Hamo de Maci, Wm. de Curci, Adam the chamberlain, Amauris de Obada, William de Marisco, Osbert Trussel, Macrobius the archdeacon, Cristinus the dean, Roger the chaplain, John Cumin, James the butler, Henry, prior of Lilishula.—*Circa* 1200.

11. (8.) Philip de Nugent grants to Holy Trinity Church, meadow in Lispobel, to build a house there near the river on the western side, with common of pasture of his entire holding of Lispobel.

Witnesses.—Adam the parson, brother of Philip, William de Rolde, Elias Pirrou, Richard de [   ], Jordan Loccard, Roger Brun, Elias de la Mun, Audoen Brnn, Robert the money changer.—*Circa* 1200.

12. (9.) William Mareschall, earl of Pembrock, grants leave to his wife Joanna (*recte* Isabel) to alienate the advowson of Kilcolyn, for the soul of Earl Richard her father and other kindred.—*Circa* 1200.

Calendared from " Novum Registrum."

13. (10.) Joanna (*recte* Isabel), Countess of Panbrock, for the salvation of the soul of Earl Richard her father, and Wm. Mareschall her lord, grants to Holy Trinity Church, the church of Kilcolyn, granted to her by her lord ; one half of the tithes to sustain a Canon, the other for providing linen cloths for the Canons.   Walter her chaplain to hold the perpetual vicarage, at five marks yearly, during his life, and maintain the church.

Witnesses.—Simon, bishop of Meath, S., abbot of St. Thomas, Osbert, prior of the Hospital of St. John without the New Gate, Dublin, Wm., the archdeacon, Helias de Mus, Master Peter Malveisin, Audoen Brun, Master Ralph, Wm., Baron de Nas, Thos. fitz Anthony, Richard de Cogan, Philip fitzRobert, Robert the money-changer, Gilbert de Livet, Wm. de Insula.—*Circa* 1200.

This abstract is made in part from " Novum Registrum," as only a fragment of original remains.

14. (12.) Joanna (*recte* Isabel), Countess of Panbrok, grants to the Church of the Holy Trinity, Dublin, the church of Kylculyn.—*Circa* 1200.

Calendared from " Novum Registrum."

15. (13.) John, archbishop of Dublin, on inspecting the deeds of Wm. Mareschall, earl of Panbrok, Ysabelle, his wife, and Reymond Gros, confirms to the Church and Canons of the Holy Trinity, Dublin, the church of Kylkulin.

Witnesses.—William, archdeacon of Dublin, Elyas de Muhs, Audoen Brun, Elyas, the canon, Master Peter, Master Danyole, William the clerk.—*Circa* 1200.

Calendared from " Novum Registrum."

16. (14.) Richard of Castlemartin grants to Holy Trinity Church, Dublin, the chapels of Castlemartin and Kilgo.

Witnesses.—W., prior of Konal, O., prior of Kilkenny, W. Crass, seneschal of Leinster, sir Henry de Breiboek, sheriff of Dublin, and Robert his brother, David Schurlag, Wm. le Boring, Wm. de Insula, Hugh de Cirencester, John de Kynet.—*Circa* 1202.[*]

17. (15.) Similar to No. 16, *supra*, adding 7 acres of land.

18. (16.) John Harold grants to Holy Trinity Church, half a mark from land held by Ralph White in St. Werchurgo's parish, between the lands formerly belonging to David Latimer and Thomas la Martre, and half a mark from land held by Richard fitzSavar in St. Andoen's parish, between the lands of Richard fitzBernard and Richard, the baker.

Witnesses.—J., archbishop of Dublin, William, the archdeacon, Elias de la Mua, Walter Comin, Master Peter, Turstin de Ballimor, Adam fitz Simon, Robert de Balsford, Thomas Norman, Bartholomew fitz Archdeacon. Walter de Lived, Robt. the clerk.—*Circa* 1206.

19. (17.) Agreement, concerning the lands between Portmirnoc, the Monks' Grange, and the town of Kelsal, which Helias Cumin holds in fee of Holy Trinity, that, by consent of John, archbishop of Dublin, the Canons of Holy Trinity, Helias Cumin, and the Abbot and Chapter of St. Mary, near Dublin, one half of the lands next the Monks' Grange shall belong to the Canons, and the half near the town of Kelsa to Helias Cumin.

Witnesses.—J., archbishop of Dublin, Meiler, the justice, Adam de Hereford, Richard Tirel, Walter Alaman, Eustace, the constable; Matthew fitzGriffin, Jordan Cumyn, Robert Cumin, Geoffrey de Marreis, Helias Harrold, John Evesko, official, Adam fitzSimon, Robert de Bedeford.—*Circa* 1206.

20. (18.) The Archbishop of Tuom and his suffragans testify that J. Papiron, the Roman Legate, coming to Ireland, found a Bishop in Dublin, and another Church in the mountains called a city and having a *chore-episcopus*, and considering that Dublin should be Metropolitan, gave a pall to the Bishop there, and divided the diocese so that one part should belong to the metropolis, and the other to him who ruled in the mountains, intending that at the decease of the latter his portion should revert to the metropolitan; this intention would have been put into effect at once but for the insolence of the Irish who had power in that land: King Henry having heard of the Legate's intention, granted the mountainous portion to the metropolitan, and so did King John, to John, archbishop of Dublin. The church in the mountains was held in great reverence from the earliest times on account of St. Kayrwyn, who lived as hermit there, but for nearly forty years it has become so deserted and desolate as to be used as a den for robbers, and more homicides are committed there than in any part of Ireland.—*Circa* 1211.

21. (19.) Pope Innocent III. takes into his protection the Prior and Canons of Holy Trinity, Dublin, and their possessions, especially the church and house of Holy Trinity, St. John the Baptist, within the walls of Dublin, St. Michean and Kilcolin.

Dated at the Lateran, xiv. Kal. [.] 19° Innocent III. (1216.)

22. (30.) Philip de Porthich, grants to Holy Trinity Church, his land in Oxmantown, lying between the land of Jordan the artisan, and the land of Farend, the son of Cristin, after his decease. He leaves his body to be buried with that of his wife in the church, should he die in

[*] For grant by King John, 1202, see No. 354 infra.

Ireland, and, with his body, his horse and arms; ten shillings and ten sheep towards the building of the church; also one cow and one heifer, and during his life a sheep at the Nativity of St. John the Baptist.

Witnesses.—Master Philip de Bray, then official, W., archdeacon of Dublin, Master R. de Gusulhal, G. de Livet, R. de Plutun, H. Le Noble, Ingilbricht, Turkill de Ozmantown, Fintan.—*Circa* 1218.

23. (20.) And, Brun and Richard de Bedeford grant to Holy Trinity Church, land near the water-course of Aucmelich, on the north side of Ozmantown Bridge, Dublin, as a site for St. Saviour's Church.

Witnesses.—Wm., archdeacon of Dublin, Peter Malvasin, Elias de Muha, Bartholomew de Camera, Gilbert de Lyvet, Gilbert Burel, Robt, the money changer, Wm., the money changer, Bartholomew fitz Archdeacon, Wm. le Bas, Alan de Dedeford, Adam his brother, Richard Black, Wm. do Barri, William Benedict, Henry de Stanford.—*Circa* 1218.

24. (21.) William de Hastam grants to Gillefintan, land, with common of pasture, lying between the bounds of Holy Trinity land and William's domain, on the north of Killinassach grove; rent, 2s. 4d.

Witnesses.—R., prior of Holy Trinity, W., archdeacon of Dublin, Andoen Brun, Helias de Mus, Peter Mauvesin, Hugh de Chernesfend, Adam de Chernesfend, Nicolas Curain, Peter Costard, Robert de Crauford, Walter Wranch, Nicholas Kauchun, Ralph Heyrun.—*Circa* 1218.

25. (22.) William de Eastam grants to Holy Trinity Church, land, held in fee of the Archbishop of Dublin.

Witnesses.—Roger, son of Sir W. de Estam, Nicholas Comin, William Tyrun, Fintan, Malbride, Sir Gilbert de Valle, Wm. de Valle, Hyngelbricht, Walter Wranch.—*Circa* 1218.

26. (24.) Robert de Grendun grants to Thomas, chaplain of Kildare, the church of Galmor's town, for his life.

Witnesses.—Robert de la Berei, Henry Mansell, Benedict de Kildare, William de Aleshope, Thomas de Bosco, Peter, then chaplain of the Castle of Kildare.—*Circa* 1218.

27. (23.) Robert de Grendun grants to Holy Trinity Church, the advowson of his chapel of Galmor's town after the decease of Thomas, the chaplain.

Witnesses.—H., archbishop of Dublin and Apostolic Legate, G., bishop of Kildare, Augustine, then archdeacon, Richard Kadel, Peter and Thomas, chaplains.—*Circa* 1219.

28. (24b bis.) Robert de Grendun having contested the right of presentation to the chapel of Galmor's town alleged by the Prior and Convent of Holy Trinity Church to belong to the mother church of Kylkoli, it is agreed that during the said Robert's life they shall present a proper parson whom the Archbishop shall receive, and who shall pay half a mark yearly to Kilcoly Church by way of pension, and the right of both parties after Robert's decease to be reserved.

Witnesses.—H., archbishop of Dublin, Thomas fitz Anthony, seneschal of Leinster, Walter Purcell, Robert de la Bere, William, archdeacon of Dublin, Elias de Muta, Master Wm. de London, Master Philip de Bray, Master Peter, Master Robert de Bedeford.—*Circa* 1219.

29. (25.) H[enry], archbishop of Dublin, approves of the erection of St. Saviour's Chapel near Dublin Bridge, provision being made for the chaplain.

Witnesses.—Wm., archdeacon of Dublin, Master Wm. de London, Master Philip de Dray, Master Peter Mulvain, Audoen Brun, Master Robt. de Bedeford, Master Ralph de Dristoll, Ralph de Mora, R. de Kardif, H. de Gloucester, J. the Welshman.—*Circa* 1219.

30. (26.) H[enry], archbishop of Dublin, grants to the Prior and Chapter of Holy Trinity, land, held by Gilbert Comin, at a rent of three marks, to build a gate at the entrance of the church; the anniversary of his obit to be celebrated for ever.

Witnesses.—W., dean of St. Patrick's, Dublin, Master Philp, precentor, W. archdeacon of Dublin, Gilbert de Livet, Ralph de Mora, Robert the money changer, Ingolbricht, citizens of Dublin.—*Circa* 1220.

31. Adam de Stanton grants to Holy Trinity Church, land in Kilbrenin, and land held by John Bedoll, the church of Kildenal with the chapels pertaining thereto, the mill of Kilbrenin, and tithes of the expenses of the house of Kildenal in bread, ale, flesh, and fish: provided a cell be built on the said land and canons kept resident there.

Witnesses.—Hubert, prior of Athboll, Master John, archdeacon of Kessel, Wm., parson of Athissel, Richard le Sauvage, Thomas de Sernesfeld, Michael de Hubreschi, Wm. White of Kessel, Humphrey Bisot, Wm. Stanton, Roger St. Stephen, John Bedell.—*Circa* 1220.

32. (27.) Pope Honorius III. grants to the Prior and Canons of Lanthony, near Gloucester, the churches of Dunade, Colon, and Drumin. Dated at Verolli, iii. Knl. Maii. (29 April, 1222).

33. (29.) C[ornelius], bishop of Kildare, A[ugustin], archdeacon of Kildare, and W., prior of Cunal, delegates to try a suit between the Prior and Canons of Holy Trinity and the Abbot and Convent of Saint Mary, near Dublin, with reference to the tithes of Crinach, Baliokeran, Tyodran, and Andrew Harang's town, in the parish of Kilculin, award the said tithes to the Prior and Canons, and command R[adulphus], archdeacon of Meath, that the Abbot of St. Mary's who has been excommunicated for his disobedience and contumacy is to be shunned.—*Circa* 1222.

34. (28.) Henry, archbishop of Dublin, ordains that the Prebends of St. Patrick's, Dublin, the chapels pertaining to them, and the churches of their Common Fund, be free from senage and procurations as well to the Archdeacon as the Dean, and that the Canons may have pleas "de humilia sua" as well of clergy as laity, and of those who dwell in the sanctuaries of the Prebendal Churches; and that the Dean of St. Patrick's or other Canon whom the Chapter may assign may have pleas of churches and chapels belonging to the Common Fund, and that two parts fall to the Archbishop's use, and a third part, which the Archdeacon was wont to receive, to the use of the Common Fund of St. Patrick's; also that the Archdeacon should not have power to suspend the churches or chapels of the Prebends or Common Fund, or their chaplains or clergy without the Archbishop's consent.

Witnesses.—Reginald de Cornill, Gerv. de Cornill, John de London, Humfrey de Erlonde, Master John de Merlebury, Master Hugh, Sir Philip the chaplain, Warren de Finnakre and Roger de Felda, clerks, Reginald the chaplain, Master John de Stafford, and William de Lychafeld.—*Circa* 1222.

Calendared from "Novum Registrum."

35. (31.) Hugh de Lacy, earl of Ulster, grants to Richard White, the land of the Cross of Holy Trinity, Dublin, in Lechkachel, to hold as he holds from the Prior and Convent of Holy Trinity.
Witnesses.—Lord Thomas, bishop of Down, W., prior of St. Patrick's, Down, Robert de Mandevill, Robert Talebot, Henry the Welshman, Ralph Pel de Lu, Thos. fitz Bishop, Wm. Sancmolls, Wm. de Stokes, Rich. de Petruponte, Nicholas de Dunmal:—*Circa* 1224.

36. (33.) Pope Honorius III. commands the Priors of St. John and St. Thomas, Dublin, and of Kuml, Kildare diocese, to determine the dispute between the Prior and Canons of Holy Trinity, Dublin, and W., archdeacon of Dublin, with reference to Rathfarnan church and its tithes.
Dated at the Lateran, xvii. Kal. Maii 9° Hon. III. (15 April, 1225.)

37. (34.) Pope Gregory IX. confirms to the Prior and Canons of Holy Trinity Church, Dublin, their customs, privileges, immunities, and possessions.
Dated at Perugia, vi. Kal. Maii, 3° Greg. IX. (26 April, 1229.)

38. (35.) Pope Gregory IX., reciting that having quashed the election of L[uke], dean of St. Martin's, London, to be Archbishop of Dublin, on account of its irregularity, and commanded R., bishop of Chichester, H., bishop of Rochester, and R., bishop of London to direct the proper parties to provide a pastor: Wm. of Kilkenny and Richard of St. Martin's, proctors of the said Dean, having brought letters from the said Bishops, stating that in pursuance of the Papal mandate the chapters of Holy Trinity and St. Patrick's had again chosen the said Luke; confirms the re-election.—*Circa* 1230. *This document is much damaged.*

39. (7') Turphin, brother of Cristin parson of St. Nicholas', Dublin, grants to Holy Trinity Church, his land in Sutor st., lying between the land of Wydo de Redinges and that of David la Warre, and extending from the street to land held by William de Flamestade from Dublin City.
Witnesses.—Richard Mutun, Edward the palmer, Walter de Nounham, Wydo de Radinges, William White, Hosbert de Kerdif, Robert cum coifa, Benedict the grocer.—*Circa* 1230.

40. Wm. de Glesneyvin and Juliana his wife grant to Holy Trinity Church, land in Kensale.
Witnesses.—Sir Richard de Pheypo, Sir Jordan Lokard, Sir Almaric de Houethe, Sir Simon Murydach, knts., John le Ware, Elyas Burell, Roger Owen, Richard Olof, Wm. de Flamstede, Wm. the clerk, Wm. Depingge, Robt. Passelewe.—*Circa* 1230.

41. Luke, archbishop of Dublin, awards to Holy Trinity Church a stone house in Dublin, which formerly belonged to Adam FitzSymon, bequeathed to it by Robt. Pollard. Rent 20s. and half a mark for the sick, payable to the Hospital of St. John without the New Gate, Dublin.—*Circa* 1230.

42. (36.) Luke, archbishop of Dublin, in a dispute between the churches of Holy Trinity and St. Patrick's, Dublin, with reference to the election of Archbishop of Dublin, awards, that when the See is vacant, the Prior and Canons of Holy Trinity and the Dean and Chapter of St. Patrick's shall assemble in Holy Trinity Church, and in due form proceed to unanimously elect a pastor. Other disputes between the said Churches and the nuns of Grace Dieu are arranged, and the said Churches are bound in £200 to abide this award.—*Circa* 1230.

43. (37.) Geoffrey do Tureville grants to the Canons of Holy Trinity, Dublin, a rent of thirty shillings, payable by Maurice de Striguil from land in the Strond lying between the house formerly belonging to Roger Palmer and the house of William Tailloburc, two marks being assigned for ever for a priest to celebrate mass at the New Altar of the B. V. M. and 3s. 4d. for a refection for the Canons on the vigil of the Epiphany. Said rent to be free from a landgable of 2s. 6d.

Witnesses.—Thomas le Corner, Wm. de Flambestede, Richard de Tureville, Maurice de Striguil, Gilbert de Wisa, clerk, Randulf de Muchelesbulle.—*Circa* 1230.

44. (38.) L[uke], archbishop of Dublin, confirms to the Prior and Canons of Holy Trinity Church, Dublin, the grants of his predecessors, L[aurence], J[ohn], and H[enry]—viz., the Grange called Kyldull beyond the bridge, with Ballmachkanel, Machduma, the Grange of Glasnevyn with its church, Dunconach with its tithes, Kyllaxtre with its tithes, the lands of Hamund Mascturkyl, the Grange called Telachken with Calgach and Klonken, Kyllmi, Kyltuc, Rathmalhan, Telach, Drummig, Ballihogan, Torroderan and Baliokaran with their tithes, Baliorolf and Stacloeb, the mill near Dublin Bridge with its tithes and lands on both sides of the bridge and its garden, the lands near St. Michenn's Church, the stone house opposite the door of Holy Trinity, lands in St. Bridget's parish stretching to the City Wall beyond the garden of Earl Hascald, a rent of 12s. 8d. payable by the Prior and convent for tenements held by Arnkin and Bridoch, opposite the stone chamber of Holy Trinity, land near Fineglas, the churches of Klonken and Kylkolln with tithes both great and small, the church of Rafernan with its appurtenances issuing from the holdings of Rafernan and Dunnavet, as in the deed of Walter le Bret more fully contained, the churches of St. John of Bodastret, St. Michael, St. Michenn, St. Paul and Ratchobel, provided the benefices be converted to their own use and not assigned vicariously.—*Circa* 1230.

45. (39.) Pope Gregory IX. directs the Bishops of Laighlin, Ossory, and Meath to recall to the property of the Prior and Convent of the Monastery of Holy Trinity, Dublin, whatsoever goods they shall find to have been illegally alienated from them.

Dated at Anagni, v. Non. Oct., 7° Greg. IX.   (3 October, 1233).

46. (41.) Pope Gregory IX. having learned from the Petition of the Prior of Holy Trinity, Dublin, that several of the Canons had fallen into the bonds of excommunication, some for laying violent hands on themselves and others, some for the detention of property, and others for disobedience or conspiracy ; that some had entered the Monastery by means of simony, and that others had taken Holy Orders and celebrated the divine offices while excommunicated ; grants power to the Prior to subject the various offenders to punishment with full power of dispensation : those guilty of the more heinous excesses to be sent to the Holy See for absolution, and those guilty of simony to give up to the Prior whatever they possess.

Dated at Perugia, viii. Id. Nov. 8° Greg. IX.   (6 November, 1234.)

47. (42.) Sir Gilbert de Lyvet grants to Holy Trinity Church the land on which his great stone hall is built with its loft and cellar on the west and the portico on the north, without the King's Gate, next the house which was Yngelbrichte's, land on which a stone house containing his kitchen is built as the porch extends next the land of

Robert the money changer, and land with an oven, opposite his stone house lying between the land of Robert the money changer and land which belonged to Leticia Fair, from the street to the middle of the Auemleliff Water, rent one mark payable to Vincent Mainwrench, to be held in frankalmoign, except there be an heir of the said Gilbert and his wife Sibilla, in which case, rents of the same value will be provided in lieu thereof and the premises will belong to the heir. His wife is to possess the premises during her life should she survive him, and their bodies are left to be buried in Holy Trinity Church should they die in Ireland.

Witnesses—L. archbishop of Dublin, W. dean of St. Patricks, O. de Turoville, archdeacon of Dublin, Master T. chancellor of St. Patricks, Sir G. de Marisc' and W. his son, Sir W. de Rideloford, Sir Eustace de Rupe, John the innkeeper, Robert the money changer, Ralph de la Morv, Thomas le Corner, Richard Mult', Edward the palmer, Robert Pollard, Ralph de Stanes then provost of Dublin, Wm. Fitz Robert then clerk, Walter Tailor, Guido of Cornwall, Robert cum ocipha.— *Circa,* 1234.

48. (43.) The Prior and Convent of Holy Trinity grant to Robert Pollard of Dublin, land in the Lormory in Castle st. between the land which belonged to Gilebert de Lavet and that which belonged to Audoen Bron, and extending from the street to the land held by Jordan Ohampencis from the hospital of St. John without the new gate ; Rent four shillings; the Prior and Convent to get a preference in case of sale, and should they not accept, the assignees to be subject to the said rent.

Witnesses—Gilebert de Lavet, mayor of Dublin, Thomas le Corner, Edward the palmer, Ralph the porter, Walter the tailor, Robert de Bristoll, and Wm. de Lenno then provosts of Dublin, Adam Eulyn, Mathias fitz Daniel, Philip son of Dame Letice, Wm. fitz Roger.— *Circa,* 1235.

49. (40.) Gregory IX. commands the Bishop of Leighlin and the Dean and Archdeacon of Kilkenny, in the diocese of Ossory, to hear a dispute between the Prior and Convent of Holy Trinity, Dublin, and the Treasurer and others of Dublin diocese concerning lands, tithes, and other matters.

Dated at Perugia, Non. Mar., 8° Greg. IX. (7 Mar., 1235.)

50. Walter Fitz Yvo grants to Holy Trinity Church, land held by his father in the parish of St. Nicholas within the walls, Dublin, situate between the land of Bartholomew the goldsmith and that formerly belonging to Bridok, but now to the said church, and extending from the street to the land of David Duncopuke ; Rent, a pair of white gloves.

Witnesses—Sir O. de Lyvet, Robert the money changer, Ralph de la More, Ingellby, Thomas le Corner, Wm. de Flamsted, Ralph de Stanton, then provost of Dublin, Thomas le Poitevin, one of the bailiffs, Robert, chaplain of St. Olaves. (*In dorso*—In 1335, Thos. Fankoun, skinner, held the ground aforesaid then built upon.)—*Circa,* 1286.

51. (45.) Luke, archbishop of Dublin, confirms to the Prior and Canons of the Holy Trinity, Dublin, the church of the Holy Trinity with its cemetery, Klunken, with the chapel of Karobranan, Kylbekenot, Killeny, Telach and the chapel of Stachlorgan.

Witnesses—R. dean of St. Patrick's, Dublin, G. archdeacon of Dublin, Master Maurice de St. Columba, Master R. de St. Martin, Eustace the clerk, W. the clerk.—*Circa*, 1240.

Calendared from the Novum Registrum.

52. (44.) The Dean and Chapter of St. Patrick's, Dublin, ratify the collation to the Prior and Canons of Holy Trinity, Dublin, by L[uke] archbishop of Dublin, of the church of Clunken with the chapel of Karrobrenan the churches of Killekenet, Killeni, Tylach and Tachlorgan chapel with their chapels, lands and tithes, both great and small, for ever.

Witnesses—J. precentor of St. Patricks, Dublin, Master T. de Craville, chancellor, R. Lutarel, treasurer of St. Patricks, Dublin, Geoffroy de Tureville, archdeacon of Dublin, Master M. de St. Columbn, Master W. de Culne, Masters [   ] and Eustace, canons of St. Patricks, Master J. de Chippenham.—*Circa*, 1240.

53. (40.) Pope Innocent IV. confirms to Holy Trinity Church, the churches of Clainkain, Kilbek [enat], Killenni, Telach, Balisendan, Rathfernan, Kilkuly, Dunnaveth, Kildenal, and Drummlan.

Dated at Lyons, xvii. Kal. April 2° Innocent IV. (16 Mar., 1245).

54. (76b.) An Inspeximus by J[ohn] and G[eoffrey] bishops of Kildare and Ossory, S. and N., abbots of the B. V. M. and St. Thomas, Dublin, and R. Walens', preceptor of the Knights Templars in Ireland, of the following deed :—

Luke, archbishop of Dublin, grants to the Prior and Canons of Holy Trinity, and the Dean and Chapter of St. Patrick's, Dublin, the cantred of Oconnah.

Witnesses—R., bishop of Meath, S., bishop of Waterford, J., bishop of Kildare, G., elect of Ossory, Sir Walran, John de Craville, Richd. Clement, Robt. de Bemiver. *In dorso*—For this we have the land of Babiscndan ; *and in a modern hand*—On this side is Brea.—*Circa* 1246.

55. (49.) Richard Bland of Ulster grants to Holy Trinity Church, one-third of his land in Clonskellan, in the holding of Naas.

The Canons are to be put in possession of the land when he acquires it by means of their advice and assistance, and should he fail to acquire it, the land of Mocles called Holy Cross, which he holds of them in Ulster, is to be mortgaged to secure the repayment of their losses and expenses, together with all his goods should they require it.

Witnesses—Master H. de Atherda, Walter Tailor, Richard Olof, Constantine the chaplain, Robert Archer, Hugh the clerk, Elias de Kenturc, Melbride O'Bren, Robert, H., and Gilbert, carpenters.—*Circa*, 1247.

56. (47.) A fine made on the morrow of All Souls, 32 Henry III., before Master Robert de Shardel, Walleran de Wellesagh, Walter Folyot, Robert de Ben', justices itinerant, witnesseth that Richard Bland of Ulster, having agreed to convey to the Prior and Convent of Holy Trinity, Dublin, land in Clomkallan and Clonnarry, provided he could recover them from John Fitz [   ] at a rent of five marks, payable to him, until a like rent should be provided for him in Ulster. The Prior complains that Richard having recovered the said lands and put them in seizin thereof, now deforces them from the same.

It is agreed that the said Richard shall acknowledge the lands to belong to the said Prior and Convent, the Prior releasing to him two hundred pounds, finding a canon to say mass in the church fo'

ever, and necessaries for the said Richard, with three horses and two boys, when he should come to their house, together with ten marks.
Morrow of All Souls, 32° Henry III. (3 Nov., 1247.)

57. (48.) Richard Blund of Ulster grants to Holy Trinity Church land in Clonscallan and Clonneri; rent five marks and the service of one archer to the Lord of the fee.
Witnesses—Master Robert de Scherdel, Walleran de Wellesloah, Walter Folyot, Robert de Ben', Michael de Reynevill, Justices Itinerant, Thomas de Bristoll, Thomas de Eymnll, Robert fitzNicholas, Richard Horn, Audrew the clerk, Matthew de Stokes, John de Trum, clerk.—Circa, 1247.

58. (50.) Cecilia Nangle on behalf of herself and her daughter Cecilia, the daughter of John of Trim, clerk, for 4 marks, releases to Holy Trinity Church their claim to Ferencosthueth under the will of the said John.
Witnesses—Walter de Gateleye, knt., sheriff of Dublin, Roger de Orumba, Walter de Wellward, Nicholas de Ely, Master John de Notingham.—Circa, 1247.

59. (51.) Nicholas Labonah grants to the Prior and Canons of Holy Trinity Church, land near the red Moor, where Muridach Machboylan dwelt, with tartary in Olonamachgillcgric, the said land lying between Kylmachmoynan and the red Moor.
Witnesses—Philip de Rath, Hugh de Luske, Richard Labonah, Richard de Finsglas, Robert de Balimadnn, Hugh Hurelaud, William de Rath, W. Francis, David Labonch, Walter de Fribeleye, John de Trum, clerk—Circa 1247.

60. (53°.) Roger de Chiltuno grants to Holy Trinity Church, Baliardor, which he held of Baldewin Fichet: the said land lies in breadth between the land which belonged to Sir Richard de St. Michael, and that of Adam the Forester, and in length between the land of the said Richard and Olincolin; Rent three marks, payable to the heirs of Baldewin Fichet, and a pair of white gloves to Roger and his heirs; four shillings is reserved for royal service.
Witnesses—Sir John Harold, Sir Robert de Turville, Randolphe fitz John, Andrew the clerk, William Lissebon, Geoffrey de Radmlshean, Robert fitz Sylvester, William le Bas, Thos. de Adgo, Richard Stachcunil, Adam the forester, Milo Chevre, Peter the miller, Wm. the clerk.—Circa 1247.

61. (53°.) Duplicate of No 60 supra.
Witnesses—Sir John fitz Geoffrey, Justiciary; Sir Robert de Scardolowe, Justice Itinerant, Sir G. Welward, chancellor, Sir Walleran de Wellesley, Sir S., abbot of St. Mary's, near Dublin, Sir John Harold, Sir D. de St. Michael, Sir John le Ware, mayor of Dublin, Richard Holof, Milo Chevre.—Circa, 1247.

62. (54°.) Matthew, son of Baldewin Fichet, grants, for two marks, to Holy Trinity Church, Baliardor, as in the deed of Roger de Chilton. Rent, forty shillings, and a royal service of four shillings.
Witnesses—Sir John Harould, Sir John Laghelen, Sir Robert de Turville, knts., Richard de Stagonil, Milo Chevre, Peter the miller, Thomas de Adgo, Roger de Kilgoban, Andrew de Rabo, Walter de Ulster, Jordan Horth, Edulf, Jordan Gudlac, John de Trum.—Circa, 1247.

63. (54.) Similar to No. 62 *supra*, save that the rent is forty-four shillings, and no service is reserved.
Witnesses as in No. 62 *supra, omitting Sir John Harould and adding William the clerk.*

64. (55.) Robert, prior of Holy Trinity, Dublin, and the Convent thereof, and Nicholas de St. Edward, prior of the Hospital of Jerusalem in Ireland, and the brethren thereof, agree to afford each other mutual aid in emergencies and matters concerning their houses.
Saturday before Feast of SS. Simon and Jude, (24 Oct.) 1248.

65. (56.) Pope Innocent IV. commands the prior of St. Thomas, Dublin, and the Dean of Kildare to hear the complaint of the Preceptor and Brethren of the Hospital of Jerusalem in Ireland against Thos. de Eymele, clerk, Sir Richard de Haddefore, knt., and others (not named) of Armagh, Kildare, and Dublin city and diocese, concerning the churches of Dumbenghi, Dunlar, and Keren.
Dated at Lyons, vi. Non. Jul, 6° Innocent IV. (2 July, 1248.)

66. (57.) Pope Innocent IV. directs the Bishop of Kildare to compel the Archdeacon of Dublin and his co-arbitrators, in a dispute between the Prior and Convent of Holy Trinity, Dublin, and the Prior and Convent of Lanthony, diocese of St. David's, concerning tithes, &c., to make their award.
Dated at Lyons, v. Non. Jul, 6° Innocent IV. (3 July, 1248.)

67. (58.) Pope Innocent IV. directs the Archdeacon and Chancellor of Dublin Diocese to hear the complaint of the Prior and Convent of Holy Trinity, Dublin, against the Abbot and Convent of Saint Mary near Dublin, Hugh de Tyrel, knt., and certain others of Dublin, Kildare, and Ossory diocese respecting money, tithes, &c.
Dated at Lyons, iv. Non. Jul, 6° Innocent IV. (4 July, 1248.)

68. (145.) Pope Innocent IV. commanding [   ] to hear a dispute between the [Prior and Convent] of Holy Trinity and [   ] with reference to money.
Dated at Lyons, iv. Non. Jul, 6° Innocent IV. (4 July, 1248.) *Very much obliterated.*

69. (59.) Margery Cumyn grants to the Prior and Convent of Holy Trinity, Dublin, her land of Kansale during her life; rent, 100 shillings Irish, payable at the Monastery of St. Augustine, Bristol.
Witnesses—S. Longespeye, Meyler de Rupe, Robt. de Ullycote, G. fitz Philip, Adam de Napece, Walter de Vilo, Richard de Cerney, Wm. de Wynecote, Robt. de Ullycote.—34 Henry III. (1249-50)

70. (60.) Pope Innocent IV. directs the Priors of Genal and Olpatrik, Dublin and Kildare dioceses, and the official of Meath, to determine the dispute between the Prior and Convent of Holy Trinity, Dublin, and the Prior and Convent of Lantony, of the first order of St. Augustine, concerning tithes &c., belonging to Foners and Kilherd, should they consider the appeal of Holy Trinity against pleading before Master Richard of Louth, clerk, in conformity with former letters, to be valid.
Dated at Lyons, iii. Non. Sep., 8° Innocent IV. (3 Sept. 1250.)

71. (61.) Henry de Pencost releases to the Prior and Canons of Holy Trinity, all his right to the chapel of Kilengli.
Witnesses—Geoffrey de Appelbi, then seneschal of Kildare, Walcran de Welleslee, Richard the Englishman, W. the Englishman, Robert

fitz Nicholas, Andrew the clerk, Laurence the clerk, Duncan the chaplain, William the clerk, John Torellus.—*Circa* 1250.
Calendared from the "Novum Registrum."

72. (62.) Inquisition taken at Kylkolyn before Master Thos. Kylmore, clerk, and Sir Robert Clinche, Sir Henry Mannings, Sir William le Witc, chaplains, William Bolloc, John Rasel, clerks, Stephen Ram, John Colbi, Ralph the merchant, and Matthew fitz Henry, jurors, finds that Brother John Comyn brought with him to Kylkolyn Sir Nicholas the chaplain and Elias, his brothers, and Milsanda, his cousin, who lived there for eight weeks, at a loss to the Prior and Convent of ten shillings; that Sir Nicholas and Johanna, maid to Brother John, gave scandal by carnal offence, and John wasted the Prior's goods to the value of two shillings to extinguish the scandal; that John sold two crannocks of oats for six shillings, took away twenty hanks of linen thread value five shillings, and half a stone of wool worth tenpence; that Sir Nicholas gave six fleeces of wool for a fat beast for his dinner; that John and Sir Nicholas, his brother, by pompous words and obstructing the victuals of the farm boys, retarded the cultivation of eight acres, at a loss of four shillings and an ox worth five shillings that died; that they gave a cart to Henry Tallon to carry a mill stone, and a piece of iron worth twopence, at tenpence loss to the Prior; and that on the feast of the Purification of the B.V.M. John spitefully refused the parish chaplain to celebrate in the church, whereby two pounds of wax worth sixteenpence were lost, and also that they took away things belonging to Brother Nicholas, and other matters to the value of twelvepence.—24 Feb., 1251.

73. (63.) Pope Innocent IV. directs the Archbishop of Armagh and the Prior of St. John's, without the new gate, Dublin, to do what is right with reference to the petition of the Prior and Convent of Holy Trinity, Dublin, viz., that the decision of the Bishop of Kildare and his collengues in the suit between the Prior and Convent of Holy Trinity and the Prior and Convent of Lantony, concerning tithes, be confirmed.—Dated at Genoa, iii. Non. Jun., 8° Innocent IV. (3 June, 1251.)

74. (65.) Pope Innocent IV. reciting that the Prior and Convent of Holy Trinity, Dublin, having shown by their petition that, in a suit before the Dean of Kildare and other Papal delegates, between them and the Prior and Convent of Lanthony, diocese of St. David's, concerning tithes, &c., the Bishop of Meath, asserting that he was concerned in the matter, appealed to the Holy See, and the appeal was referred to the Priors of de Urso (B. V. M. of Drogheda) and Dundalk, and the Archdeacon of Glendalough, the latter having retired and the two former being objected to by Holy Trinity; directs the Abbot and Prior of St. Augustine's, Bristol, and the Archdeacon of Gloucester, diocese of Worcester, to determine the matter.
Dated at Perugia, x. Kal. Mar. 9° Innocent IV. (21. February, 1252.)

75. (64.) Pope Innocent IV. grants to the Prior and Convent of Holy Trinity, that letters from the Apostolic See or the Legates thereof, for the reception or provision of any one into livings or pensions, shall not be valid except they recite this grant.
Dated at Perugia, iv. Kal. Mar., 9° Innocent IV. (27 February, 1252.)

76. (64b.) Pope Innocent IV. directs the Priors of St. John of Kilkenny and Kenles, diocese of Ossory, to protect the Prior and Convent

of Holy Trinity, Dublin, from being molested contrary to the tenor of No. 75, supra.
Dated at Perugia, iv. Kal. Mar. 9° Innocent IV.   (27 February, 1252.)

77. (68.) Pope Innocent IV. reciting that a dispute between the Prior and Convent of Holy Trinity and the Archdeacon of Dublin, with reference to the church of SS. Peter and Paul, Rathfernan, and other matters having been referred to Peter, rector of Villa [   ] and the Master of Trum Schools, the Prior and Convent of Holy Trinity appealed to the Apostolic See; directs the Dean and Precentor of Lismore, if the contents of the appeal petition be true, to determine the matter.
Dated at Asixi, Id. Maii. 10° Innocent IV.   (15 May, 1253.)

78. (66 ter.) Pope Innocent IV. reciting that the Dean and Chapter of St. Patrick's, claiming a voice in the election of the Archbishop of Dublin, and the matter having been referred to the Archbishop by the Prior and Convent of Holy Trinity, and the said Dean and Chapter, he decided that the Dean and Chapter of St. Patrick's had a voice in the election, from which award the Prior and Convent having appealed; directs the Bishops of Emly and Limerick and the Dean of Limerick, or two of them, to decide the matter within six months if the parties acquiesce in the proceedings, otherwise to remit the trial to the Apostolic See.
Dated at Asisi xii. Kal. Jun. 10° Innocent IV.   (21 May, 1253.)

79. (70.) Pope Innocent IV. reciting that the Prior and Convent of Holy Trinity Church, Dublin, having stated that their church was greatly injured by the composition entered into by them and the Canons of St. Patrick's, in the time of Luke, archbishop of Dublin, with reference to the election of the Archbishop, to which they are bound by penalty and pledge; directs the Bishops of Emly and Limerick, and the Dean of Limerick, to hear the matter, if the parties acquiesce, otherwise to remit the trial to Rome.—Dated at Asisi xii. Kal. Jun. 10° Innocent IV. (21 May, 1253.)

80. (71.) Pope Innocent IV. directs the Prior of Hathisil, in the diocese of Cashel, and the Archdeacon of Cashel, to recall to Holy Trinity Church, Dublin, the pensions, tithes, possessions, lands, rents, manors, houses, and other goods which have been abstracted therefrom. Dated at Asisi xii. Kal. Jun. 10° Innocent IV.   (21 May, 1253.)

81. (67.) Pope Innocent IV. takes into his protection all the privileges, lands, and tithes granted to the Prior and Convent of Holy Trinity, Dublin.—Dated at Asisi vi. Kal. Jun. 10° Innocent IV.   (27 May, 1253.)

82. (69.) L[uke], archbishop of Dublin, with the assent of the Prior and Convent of Holy Trinity, decrees that vicars instituted to Kylcollin Church at the presentation of the Prior and Convent, shall pay forty marks yearly to the Prior and Convent, the residue of the fruits and obventions of the said church remaining with the vicars, except Galmorstown chapel, held by Symon of Kyldare, clerk, from the Prior and Convent, after whose death or removal the fruits and obventions thereof shall revert to the Prior and Convent, and reserving for the mother church the legacies of parishioners, and of those whose bodies

D

are buried there: the said Symon, the clerk, and the Prior and Convent shall maintain this chapel, unless otherwise arranged with the vicar, who has to maintain his church in all ordinary matters, and in a third part of the extraordinaries, to reside there continuously, to cause worthy chaplains to serve in all the chapels except Galmorstown, and, when they have been sufficiently adorned by the Prior and Convent, to maintain them at his own expense.

Done at the New Colony near Dublin, on Saturday before the feast of St. Dunstan. (16th Oct.,) 1253.

83. (52.) Robert de la Roche, knt., brother of Dame Margery, formerly wife of Nicholas Cumin, binds himself to acquit the Prior and Convent of Holy Trinity, Dublin, of 100 shillings which they owed to the said Margery, on the quindene of Michaelmas 37 Henry III. Seal of John FitzGeoffrey, Justiciary of Ireland, affixed.—*Circa* 1253.

84. (72.) Pope Innocent IV. directs the Bishop and Archdeacon of Leighlin to hear the complaint of the Prior and Convent of Holy Trinity, Dublin, against the Dean and Archdeacon of Cashel, and other clerks of the cities and dioceses of Dublin, Leighlin, and Cashel, with reference to tithes, &c.

Dated at the Lateran, v. Id. Jan. 11° Innocent IV. (9 Jan., 1254.)

85. (73.) Pope Alexander IV. directs the Bishop of Ossory to recall as in No. 80 *supra*.

Dated at Anagni, iii. Id. Sep. 1° Alex. IV. (11 Sep. 1255.)

86. (74.) Pope Alexander IV. commands the Priors of St. John of Kilkenny and Kenlis, diocese of Ossory, to recall *as in No.* 80 *supra*.

Dated at the Lateran, xv. Kal. Jun. 2° Alex IV. (18 May, 1256.)

87. (75.) Alexander Noke releases to the Prior and Convent of Holy Trinity, Dublin, his right to land in Gilmaholmog st., near St. Michael's Church, which his father held, receiving two shillings; rent a penny or a pair of white gloves.

Witnesses.—Hamund de Selewde, John del Nass, Wm. Swethaman, Richd. Olaf, Geoffrey the porter.—*Circa* 1258.

88. (76.) Slany, formerly wife of Gillepatrick the butcher, grants to Ralph the cook, of Dublin, the land situate in the suburbs of Dublin, in the Parish of St. Brigid in the Pool, lying between the land formerly belonging to Eustace de Taunton, and that of the Hospital of St. John without the new gate of Dublin, and extending from the street to the Pool water, to be held for ever; Rent twelve pence, payable to the Canons of Holy Trinity, and to her and her heirs a rose.

Witnesses.—Peter Abraham, Mayor of Dublin, Symon Unred and Thos. Wrench, provosts, Elias Durol, Richd. Olof, Thos. de Wyntoun. Stephen de Karlel, Wm. the glassworker, John de Derby, Roger Camico, Walter the clerk, Wm. de Donington, clerk.—*Circa* 1258.

89. (77.) Pope Alexander IV. directs the Bishop of Leighlin, and the Archdeacon of Kildare, to recall as in No. 80 *supra*.

Dated at Anagni, viii. Kal. Ap. 6° Alex. IV. (25 Mar., 1260.)

90. (78a.) Robt., prior of Holy Trinity, Dublin, and the convent thereof, grant to John Cumin, Kensale which Nicholas Cumin, his brother, held before him; the carucate of land once held by Mabilla

Cumin, and a rent of one mark to Elyas Cumin being reserved. Rent eleven marks. Should John or his heirs sell, the Prior and Convent are to get a preference. Covenant against alienation to any other religious house.

Witnesses—Brother Herbert, Sir Waller de Walleslegh, John Cadel, Geoffrey de Travers, Geoffrey del Val, Wm. Cumin.—Circa 1260.

91. (785.) A fine made on the quindene of Michaelmas, 44° Hen. III., at the court of King Edward, before Hugh, bishop of Meath, Walaran de Wellesley, Arnald de Barkeley, and Alexr. de Notingham, Justices Itinerant, between the Prior of Holy Trinity, Dublin, and John Cumin, of Kynsaal. John acknowledges Kynsaal to belong to the Prior, for which the Prior grants him it, except a carucate formerly held by Mabilia Cumyn, for ever. Rent five marks during the life of Margery Cumyn, who holds a third part in dower, and after her death one hundred shillings.

Attached are the objections of the Prior of Holy Trinity, Dublin, to the judgment given by Sir Ralph de Hengham with reference to the wardship and marriage of the tenant of Kynsale manor.

Sir Ralph founded his judgment on the English law, which gave no wardship except in case of tenants by knight's service.

The Prior takes exception that, tenants by various other tenures are subject to wardship and marriage in England, and similarly in Ireland, and quotes cases in proof.—18 Oct., 1200. (*Portion in French.*)

92. (78c.) Roger Oweyn, for fourteen marks, grants to Alan de Wyfford, of Dublin, land in St. Andeou's parish, in the street of Oxmantown Bridge, lying between the land, formerly belonging to William the merchant, and that of Henry Wyne, extending from the King's way on the east to the city wall on the west, for ever; rent four shillings and five pence, payable to the Canons of Holy Trinity, Dublin, and a pair of white gloves or a penny to grantor, preference to be given to grantor in case of sale. Covenants against alienation to any religious house except Holy Trinity.

Witnesses.—Thomas de Wynton, mayor of Dublin, Raymund Poitevin, and Symon Unred, provosts, Elyas Burel, Richard Olof, William de Chester, Richard Mok, Walter Unred, Michael de Kymardin, Walter Man, John le Gros, Henry Barot, Thomas de Cadewelly, William de Donington, clerk.—Circa 1260.

93. (79.) Philip Scadan, of Dublin, undertakes to pay on St. Dunstan's day to the Prior and Convent of Holy Trinity, Dublin, twenty shillings arrears, and the rents for Michaelmas and Easter, 46° and 47° Hen III., of a messuage near that which formerly belonged to William de Flemstede, in the parish of St. Nicholas, Dublin; failing payment, the Prior and Convent to enter into possession.

Witnesses.—Thomas de Wynton, mayor of Dublin, William de Chester, and Walter Unred, provosts, William and Roger, clerks, of the city.—Circa 1268.

94. (80.) Roger, son of Walter Durant, grants to Robert Thurgod, citizen of Dublin, land, with the buildings thereon, in Oxmantown, near St. Michan's churchyard, on the south, for ever; rent three shillings, payable to the Canons of Holy Trinity, Dublin, and, to grantor a pair of white gloves or a penny.

Witnesses.—Thomas de Wynton, mayor of Dublin, William de
Bristoll and Thomas Wrench, provosts, Elyas Burel, Richard Olof,
Vincent the innkeeper, Walter Unrod, Walter Man, Thomas de
Lexinton, Walter Haket, William de Buklewas, William de Donington
the clerk.—*Circa* 1264.

In dorso.—This deed speaks of a shop near the churchyard of Saint
Michan, on the south side, which John Beke now holds viz. in 1304.

95. (81*a*.) John, abbot of St. Mary, near Dublin, and the Convent
thereof, grant to the Prior of Holy Trinity, Dublin, a right of tur-
bary in Balykeyth, sufficient for the Grange of Kylmehyoc.—1268.
Calendared from the "Novum Registrum."

96. (81*b*.) Wm. de Gran, prior of Holy Trinity, Dublin, and the
convent, grant to Henry, son of Henry Marscall, of Dublin, land in the
suburbs of Dublin, upon the river bank in St. Michael's Parish, lying
between the stone house formerly belonging to Wm. Taylkburche on
the south, land formerly belonging to the said Wm. on the north, and
extending from the King's Lane leading to Auenoliffy, to land formerly
belonging to the said Wm., for ever. Rent, eighteen pence.

Witnesses—Vincent the innkeeper, mayor of Dublin, Walter Unred
and Geoffrey de Lyvet, then provosts, Elyas Burel, Richd. Oloff, Thos.
de Winton, Reymund Poitevin, Simon and Lawrence Unred, Laurence
the tailor, Adam de Clana, Simon de Witteneye, Richd. de Lodlow,
baker, Roger clerk of the city.—*Circa* 1270. (*In dorso* :—in
Lowestocks lane.)

97. Inspeximus from Polk, archbishop of Dublin, Philip, prior of
the Hospital of Jerusalem in Ireland, W[arin], abbot of the Monastery
of St. Thomas near Dublin, J[ohn], abbot of the Monastery of S. Mary
near Dublin, the Mayor and Citizens of Dublin, and the Prior of All
Saints, Dublin, of the following deeds :—

(*a.*) Holy Trinity Church admits John Cumyn to free entry of Kensale, held by his brother Nicholas, except Mabilia Cumyn's carucate
and Helyas Cumyn's rent; at a rent of 6½ marks and 26⅞ pence during
Margery Cumyn's life, and 11 marks afterwards.

(*b.*) Grants to him the same premises at a rent of 11 marks.—*Circa*
1270.

98. Robert Herbert, of Dublin, and Margaret his wife, grant to
John Parchiamenarius and Agnes his wife, their land, with the buildings
thereon, opposite the Hospital of St. John, in St. Katharine's parish,
without the new gate, Dublin; situate between the land of Thos. de
la Grave on the east, and that of Thos. de Cromelyn on the west, the
street in front and an old ditch in the rere. Rent, one penny to
grantors or the heirs of the said Margt., 6s. to the Canons of St.
Thomas, Dublin, half a mark to Holy Trinity Church, one penny to
Alice de Lynne, half a mark to Alice de Taunton.

Witnesses—David de Callan, then mayor of Dublin, Wm. de
Bevarleye and Adam Unred then provosts, Thos. de Wynton, Walter
Unred, Hugh de Kerseye, Symon Unred, Robert Mei, Reginald de
Kilmaynan, Robt. Unred, Thos. de la Grave, Thos. de Cromelyn, and
Wm. de Donington, clerk. (*In dorso*)—A.D. 1664. This is known by
the sign of the Swan, next to Mr. Bennett's, Thos. St.—*Circa* 1270.

99. (104.) Richard the forester leases to Holy Trinity Church, land
called Stakyng, between his house and the watercourse at Kylmehyoc

mill, for forty years, from Michaelmas, 1273, at a rent of a pair of white gloves, in consideration of a lease of the tithes of corn of Balyardur, from Holy Trinity Church to John the forester, clerk, his brother, for four years, from the feast of St. Peter ad Vincula, 1271, no rent for first two years, and 20s. afterwards, and in default of payment the term to Holy Trinity Church to be tripled.

Witnesses—Simon of the White Monastery, Roger de Balyardur, Roger Rufus, Philip Bodnam, Simon Thevelach, Walter de Lynns, and Robert Gerard the clerk.—*Circa* 1271.

100. (83.) Adam Schipman of Dublin, grants to Holy Trinity Church land, with the buildings thereon, in St. Martin's parish, lying between the land of Wm. Foucan and the lane leading to St. Martin's Church, and extending from the King's street in front to the lane aforesaid, as fully as his father, Robert Elys, granted the same. Rent, a pair of white gloves worth one halfpenny to Adam, a pound of cumin or three half-pence to Adam de Lychenfeld, and sixpence to Edward Uolet.

Witnesses.—John Gargeht, mayor of Dublin, Robert de Asseburn and Laurence Unred, provosts, Roger Oweyn, Thos. de Wynton, Richard Olof, Roger the clerk.—*Circa* 1272.

101. (84.) Pope Gregory X., bewailing the Greek scession, the blasphemy of the name of Christ, and the occupation of the Holy Land by the Saracens; summons the Archbishop of Dublin, and the Bishops, Abbots, and other ecclesiastics of Dublin Province, to a general council to commence at Lyons on the Kalends of May, 1274; one or two bishops to remain for the episcopal work of the Province. Provisions to guard their interests while absent.

Dated at the Lateran, ii. Kal. April, 1° Gregory X. (31 March, 1272.)

102. (85 bis.) Pope Gregory X. directs the Bishop of Leighlin to recall as in *No.* 80 *supra*.

Dated at Civita Vecchia, xvi. Kal. August 1°. Gregory X. (17 July, 1272.)

103. (82.) Wm., prior of Holy Trinity, Dublin, and the Convent thereof, lease to John de Culna and Avice his wife, during the life of the said Avice, land, with the buildings thereon, in St. Martin's parish, the gift of Adam, son of Robert Elys: the said land lies between the land formerly belonging to Wm. Facun and the lane leading to St. Martin's church. Rent, two pounds of cumin, a pair of white gloves worth one halfpenny, and sixpence; also subject to landgable: covenants for repair, bodies of lessees to be buried in Holy Trinity churchyard, and against selling or mortgaging land.

Witnesses.—John Gargech, mayor of Dublin, Robt. de Hasseburn, and Laurence Unred, provosts, Roger Oweyn, Nicholas de Hasslowe, Thos. de Wynton, Roger the clerk.

Dated, Feast of St. Clement, Pope, 57° Hen. III. (17 Nov. 1272.)

104. (80.) Friar Wm., Penitentiary of the Pope, having learned from the Prior of Holy Trinity Church, Dublin, that some of the canons, for laying violent hands on themselves or others, some for unlawful detention, and others for disobedience, have fallen into the bond of excommunication, and that many entering the church by simony have received

Holy Orders and celebrated Divine offices; grants power to the Prior, provided the injured receive satisfaction, and the crime has not been so enormous as to require the offender to be sent to the Apostolic See, to purge these offenders from the excommunication, and, having suspended those who entered Holy Orders while excommunicated, to dispense with the same at his discretion.

Dated at Civita Vecchia vi. Ides [   ] 1° Greg. X.   1272 or 1273.

105. (146.) Pope Gregory X. directs the Prior of Holy Trinity and [   ], Dublin, to hear the dispute between Master Nicholas de B[   ] and Robert de Kanorsham, clerk, executor of the will of the late Baron of [   ] with reference to money and other matters.

Dated at Lyons, Non. December 3° Gregory X.   (5 Dec., 1274.)

106. (87.) Katerine, wife of John le Grout, bequeaths her body to be buried in the churchyard of Holy Trinity, Dublin, and legacies to the following : to her parish church and chaplain, to Philip, suffragan of the said Church, the chaplain and clerks of the B. V. M. of St. Audoen's church, the Friars Preachers and Friars Minors, Dublin, the infirm of St. John without the New Gate, Dublin, the brethren of the Sac, the Lepers of St. Stephen and St. Laurence, the Recluse of St. Paul, her servant Petronilla, Brother John de Wyflyfford, Brother Adam de la More, John her servant, Juliana, daughter of Thomas Maroschall, Avice, the maid, Sarah, daughter of Walter Man, Katerine, daughter of John Benedict, Alice White, Agnes Everard, Margery Tenwryth, Matilda, daughter of Henry Baret ; to the Holy Trinity Convent a rent payable by Eynulf, rent for land in St. Olave's parish, and her land on the opposite side from the King's way to the Awynlyf Water, and to her husband the utensils with the moveables and immoveables in the house and out of it belonging to her, and she appoints John le Grant her husband, Brother Adam de Mora canon of Holy Trinity, Henry Baret, and Walter Man, executors, and the Prior of Holy Trinity as counsellor.

Witnesses.—Thomas Marescall, Robert le Pochbarer, John le Tannur, Wm. the clerk, John FitzThomas.

Dated 31 Mar., 1275.

107. (90ᵃ.) Pope John XXI. directs the Bishop of Waterford, the Abbot of St. Mary, near Dublin, and the Prior of St. Peter's, Trym, diocese of Meath ; to hear the complaint of the Prior and Chapter of Holy Trinity against Wm. de Salinis, archdeacon of Dublin, and his official, for having usurped the Archiepiscopal jurisdiction, the See being vacant, and, contrary to the canons, caused them to be summoned before the secular courts ; also that the said official, after their appeal to the Holy See, excommunicated various clerks of Dublin City and Diocese, for disobedience, and caused them to be detained in prison.

Dated at the Lateran, x Kal. Maii 1 Innocent V (22 Apr., 1276.)

108. (89.) Pope John XXI. directs the Bishop of Waterford, and the Abbot of St. Mary, near Dublin, and the Prior of St. Peter of Trym, Meath diocese ; to hear the dispute between the Prior and Chapter of Holy Trinity Church, Dublin, and the Chapter of St. Patrick's, Dublin, with reference to the Archiepiscopal jurisdiction, the See of Dublin being vacant.

Dated at Viterbo, iv. Kal. Oct. 1° John XXI. (28 Sep., 1276.)

109. (90.) A Bull similar to No. 108 supra. Dated at Viterbo, vi. Non. Oct. 1° John XXI. (2 Oct., 1276.)

110. (88.) Pope John XXI. directs the Major and Senior Arch-deacons of the church of Meath to hear the dispute between Robert de St. John, rector of Rachlong church, and the Bishop of Connor, respecting money and other matters concerning Rachlong church. Dated at Viterbo, Non. Nov. 1° John XXI   (5th Nov., 1276.)

111. (92.) Master Walter Ythel, proctor at Rome of the sub prior and chapter of Holy Trinity, Dublin, acknowledges the receipt from Manfred Dardaguini, merchant of Lucca, Leonard Tosta, and other members of the Society of the Bettoli of Lucca, of 380 marks, portion of 680 marks, which the said Leonard received at Dublin from the said sub prior and chapter, by the hand of Master Simon de Bokyngham, clerk, and was bound to pay to Masters Walter and Simon aforesaid, or either of them, at Rome. The said Walter authorises Manfred, Leonard, and their company to pay the residue, viz., 300 marks to Sir Fromund, chancellor of Ireland, and 100 marks to the sub prior and chapter, aforesaid ; for the 280 marks he gives an acquittance and shall give another for the residue after the payment thereof. This residue Manfred, for himself, Leonard and their company, binds himself to pay as authorised within four weeks after this document shall be presented to their company in Dublin.

Witnesses—Manfred, rector of the Hospital of SS. Matthew and Peregrinus of Lunata, diocese of Lucca, Signor Gogolino, of Viterbo goldsmith, Baccomeo Accursii Darochi, William Puntassa, and Bindo Galgunetti, citizens of Lucca, Tucio Rolandi and Angelo Henrici of Viterbo, Thomaxinus formerly Potricoli Armanini of Bologna, not. pub.

Dated 27 Jnl., 1279.

112. Claricia, widow of Gilbert Gentyl, grants to Henry Fychet, land in Oxmantown, which belonged to Richard le Lynkerner, and extends from the water of Auemelif on the west, to the highway on the east, opposite the Friars Preachers, and from the land of Edward Colet, to that of William Waleram, her father. Rent 8s. payable to Holy Trinity Church.

Witnesses—David de Callan, then mayor of Dublin, Robert le Decer, and Thomas de Covyntre, provosts, Walter Unred, Roger the clerk, Walter le Marchand and Edward Colet.

Dated at Dublin, Thursday, feast of Nativity B.V.M., 7 Ed. I. (8th Sep., 1279.)

113. (91.) Pope Nicholas III., at the request of the prior and chapter of the Holy Trinity, Dublin, directs the Archdeacon of Leighlin to hear an appeal from the excommunication rashly promulgated by John, perpetual vicar of the church of Baliradri, diocese of Dublin, against William, then prior, Reginald, then official of the said chapter, the See of Dublin being vacant, and Philip de Schitschyr, canon of the said Church.

Dated at Viterbo, Non. Oct. 2° Nicholas III.   (7th Oct. 1279.)
Calendared from " Novum Registrum."

114. (93.) John, son of William de Denheved, with consent of Isabella his wife, grants to Adam de Helmiswell and Mabilla his wife, 1 mark rent payable by the Prior and Convent of Holy Trinity, for Balyardour, being Isabella's proportion of 8 marks, formerly payable by the Prior and Convent for land in Balyardour which they held of Stephen de May, who assigned the rent to John and Isabella for land

in Athskay in the holding of Rathwor, pursuant to a fine levied in the court of the liberty of Trym. Paying a pair of white gloves, or a penny, yearly.

Witnesses—Sir Nicholas do Donheved, Sir William Kadel, and Sir Nicholas de Hovethe, knights, Wlftam do Berneval, Luke le Chamberleng, Ralph le Ohamberleng, Thomas Russell of Cromelyn.—*Circa* 1281.

115. (94.) John do Possowyk, with consent of Anastaso his wife, grants to Adam de Helmiswoll and Mabilla his wife, 1 mark rent as in No. 114 *supra*.

Witnesses as in 114 *supra.—Circa* 1281.

116. (95.) Adam de Helmeswolle, with consent of Mabilla his wife, grants to the Prior and Convent of Holy Trinity, 2 marks rent granted them in Nos. 114 and 115 *supra*. Paying one pair of white gloves yearly.

Witnesses—Sir Robert de Ufford, chief justiciary of Ireland, Robert Bagot, Richard de Northampton, Robert do Lestre, justices itinerant, Henry le Mareschall, mayor of Dublin, Hugh de Kerssy and Laurence Unred, provosts, Henry the clerk.—*Circa* 1281.

117. (103.) Peter Paraventure, for half a mark, grants to Holy Trinity Church, three shillings and four pence rent out of Rochel-street, Dublin, which Master Hugh de Kyngesbyry formerly held.

Witnesses—Sir Robert de Ufford, chief justiciary of Ireland, Sir Robert Bagot, Sir Richard de Northampton, Sir Robert de Lestre, justices itinerant, Henry le Mareschall, mayor of Dublin, Hugh de Carssy and Laurence Unred, provosts, and Henry the clerk.—*Circa* 1281.

118. (96.) John Dunheved, with consent of Isabella his wife, confirms to the Prior and Convent of Holy Trinity, the rent of 1 mark, granted in No. 114 *supra*.

Witnesses—Sir Robert de Ufford, Justiciary of Ireland, Fromund de Brun, chancellor, Sir Robert Bagot, Richard de Exeter, Richard de Northampton, Master Thomas de Chaderworth, Walter Unred, mayor of Dublin.—*Circa* 1281.

119. (98.) John de Posswyko, with consent of Anastase his wife, confirms to the Prior and Convent of Holy Trinity, the rent of 1 mark, granted in No. 115 *supra*.

Witnesses as in 118 *supra.—Circa* 1281.

120. (07.) John Dunheved, with consent of Isabella his wife, grants to the Prior and Convent of Holy Trinity, the rent of a pair of white gloves or a penny, reserved in No. 114 *supra*.

Witnesses—S., bishop of Waterford, then justiciary of Ireland, and others as in No. 118 *supra.—Circa* 1281.

121. (99.) John de Possewyke, with consent of Anastase his wife, grants to the Prior and Convent of Holy Trinity, a rent of a pair of white gloves or a penny, reserved in No. 119 *supra*.

Witnesses as in No. 120 *supra.—Circa* 1281.

122. (101.) Geoffrey Fitzleonis and Johanna his wife grant to the Prior and Convent of Holy Trinity, a rent of 1 mark out of Balyardolf, grantors to participate in the benefit of the vigils and other spiritual matters of Holy Trinity.

Witnesses—Sir Robert Bagot and Sir Nicholas Taf, knights, justices itinerant, Nicholas de Clere, treasurer, Master Robert Walleroud, then official of the Court of Dublin, Henry Mareacall, William de Halvaton, clerk.—*Circa* 1281.

123. (100.) Sir Geoffrey le Bret, knight, releases to Holy Trinity Church, all rights which belong to the lordship of Rathfernan, in respect of Baliardur, granted it by Roger de Chiltoun, Matthew and Walter Fychet, Geoffrey Fitzleonis and Joanna, his wife, John de Possowyk and Anastasa, his wife, John Dunheved and Isabella, his wife.

Witnesses—Sir Robert Bagot and Nicholas Taf, justices, King's Bench, Geoffrey Harold, William Ballygodman, William Burgoys, chaplain, Henry Mareacall, and Robert de Wyleby, citizens of Dublin. *Circa* 1281.

124. (102.) John de Possowyke directs Adam de Helmeswall to act in conformity with his grant, No. 121 *supra*, to Holy Trinity Church.
Dated at Dublin, Wednesday after the conversion of St. Paul, 10° Edward I. (28 Jan., 1282.)

125. (106.) Luke le Chaumberleyn, senior, grants to Holy Trinity Church, land obtained from Richard the forester, in Balyardur, lying between the land of Luke le Chaumberleyn, junior, on the south, and that of Holy Trinity Church on the other sides.

Witnesses—Sir Robert Bagod and Master Thomas de Chaddlisworth, justices of the Bench, Sir Geoffrey le Bret and Sir Ralph FitzJohn, knts., William Balygodman, Nicholas Andrew, Geoffrey Harold, Thomas the clerk.—*Circa* 1282.

126. (105.) Richard the forester, of Balyardur, confirms to Holy Trinity Church, Baliardur, as granted in No. 125 *supra*.

Witnesses—Sir Robert Bagot and Master Thomas de Chaldesworth, justices of the Bench, Sir Geoffrey le Bret and Sir Ralph FitzJohn, knts., Robert FitzJohn, Nicholas Andrew, Geoffrey Harold, Geoffrey Chevere, John Cherere, Thomas Pygot, clerk.—*Circa* 1282.

127. (107 *bis*.) Robert de Trim grants to Holy Trinity Church, Tyrcrony, yielding yearly to the Chief Lords of the fee two shillings and three pence.

Witnesses—Sir Robert Bagot and Master Thomas de Chadesworth, justices of the Bench, Sir Geoffrey le Bret and Sir Ralph FitzJohn, knts., William Balygodman, Nicholas Andrew, Geoffrey Harold, Luke de St. Edmond, clerk.

[*In dorso*] In the holding of Clonken.—*Circa* 1282.

128. (108.) Roger FitzDavid confirms to Holy Trinity Church, Tyrcrony, as granted in No. 127 *supra*.—*Circa* 1282.

129. (100.) Proceedings in the Church of St. Patrick's, Dublin, on Wednesday after the feast of St. Mark the Evangelist, 1282.
The Chapter of Holy Trinity Church was ordered to pay to the Hospital of St. John without the New Gate, Dublin, the arrears of a certain annual pension.
This document is very illegible. Dated 29th Apr., 1282.

130. (110 *bis*.) Henry FitzRye, son of Henry, lord of Penkoyte, confirms the grants from his ancestors to Holy Trinity church, of the advowson of the chapel anciently called Kylengly, but, after the arrival of the English and Welsh in Ireland, Penkoyte, belonging to Kylculyn church, the property of Holy Trinity.

Witnesses—Stephen, bishop of Waterford, justiciary of Ireland, Master Richard de Northampton, elect of Ferns, Fromuud le Bran, chancellor of Ireland, John de Sannford, then escheator of Ireland, Richard de Exeter and Robert Bagot, justices of the Bench, Walter Lenfant, Master Thomas the Englishman, clerk, Augustine de Notingham, clerk.—*Circa* 1283.

131. (111.) Peter of Kylgo grants to Holy Trinity Church, his claim to the advowson of the chapel of Kylgo, appurtenant to Kylkalyn church, belonging to Holy Trinity.

Witnesses.—S., bishop of Waterford, justiciary of Ireland, R., bishop of Ferns, John de Saunford, escheator of Ireland, Robert Bagot and Richard de Exeter, justices of the King's Bench, Walter Lenfant, Master Thomas the Englishman, clerk, Augustine de Notingham, clerk. *Circa* 1283.

132. Henry, son of Henry de Poncoit, grants to Holy Trinity Church, Wallynymertaghe, lying between the land of Roskngathe on the east, the margin of the forest on the west, the wood of Wm. le Preys on the north, and Wernaconnaghtye on the south ; the wood of Wallininduatha, situate between the land and wood of Theobald Butler on the east and west, Kengualassed on the north, and the land and wood of John the skinner on the south; and the advowson of Akeoherlar church, with the land belonging thereto.

Witnesses—Stephen de Failliburne, bishop of Waterford, then Chief Justiciary of Ireland, Sir Robt. Bagod, Nicholas Tafe, and Master Thos. de Chadiaworthe.

Dated at Dublin on the morrow of Michaelmas, 11° Ed. I. (30 Sep., 1283.)

133. (113.) Scholastica, daughter of Vincent Coupun, grants to Holy Trinity Church, land with buildings in St. Nicholas-street, Dublin, lying between the land of Master Richard de Exeter and that of William le Bretun.

Witnesses.—Walter Unred, mayor of Dublin, Thomas de Coventre and Robert de Wylsby, provosts, Henry Mareschal, Robert Turbut, Robert le Decer, William Devaneys, Roger the clerk, Nicholas the clerk—*Circa* 1283.

134. (112.) Holy Trinity Church, in consideration of No. 133 *supra* grants Scholastica and her maid, daily for life, bread and ale from their cellar and meat from their kitchen, with liberty to dwell in the buildings for life at 41 pence rent and keeping them in repair.

Witnesses.—The Mayor and Provosts as in No. 130 *supra*, Master Augustine de Notingham, clerk, Henry Marescall, Robert de Trym, Henry the clerk—*Circa* 1283.

135. (115.) Peter Arborensis, archbishop, and Bernard Humana, bishop, grant an indulgence of forty days to those who, having confessed and being contrite, hear Mass from any canon of the Monastery of Holy Trinity, Dublin, or say the Lord's Prayer and the Salutation of the B V. M., for the benefactors of the said Monastery, and for the souls of the faithful departed, provided the diocesan of the place ratify this indulgence.

Dated at Perugia, 1284, 4° Martin IV.

136. (116.) J. de Loncombe, official of Dublin, the See being vacant, directs W. de Moenes and the other executors of J[ohn], late archbishop of Dublin, to pay Master Thomas de Cheddeworth, chancellor of St.

Patrick's, £100 due him, otherwise to appear before the Dean of Christianity and two chaplains in St. Patrick's Cathedral to answer Master Thomas' petition for payment.

Dated, Feast of St. Juliana Virgin (22 May), 1284.

137. (117.) Adam de la More, prior of Holy Trinity, Dublin, and the Chapter of St. Patrick's, Dublin, inform the Pope of the election of Master John de Saunford in the room of Brother John de Derlington, the late Archbishop of Dublin, and that Audoen do Ymer and John de Exeter, canons of Holy Trinity, Master John de Notingham, Ralph de Stanes and Henry de Rathkenny, canons of St. Patrick's, have been appointed to seek the confirmation of His Holiness to the said election.

Dated on the morrow of the Nativity of St. John the Baptist (25 Jun.), 1284.

138. (114.) Holy Trinity Church, Dublin, and the Dean and Chapter of St. Patrick's agree to appoint an official to represent them when the See of Dublin is vacant.

Dated, the Feast of the Apostles Peter and Paul (29 Jun.), 1284.

139. (118.) Pope Honorius IV. informs the Prior and Convent of Holy Trinity, Dublin, that the proctors of the Churches of Holy Trinity and St. Patrick having sought confirmation of the election of John de Saunford, dean of St. Patrick's, to be Archbishop of Dublin, from Pope Martin IV., and, some questions having arisen to postpone for a long time the celebration of this election, John de Saunford resigned, and power to elect was granted to him and the five canons then present as proctors, who re-elected John de Saunford; he now confirms this election.

Dated at St. Peter's, Rome, iii. Kal. Jun 1° Honorius IV. (30 May, 1285.)

140. (120.) Pope Honorius IV. informs the Chapters of Holy Trinity and St. Patrick's, Dublin, that the election in No. 139 supra shall not prejudice in any way the right of either church in the election of Archbishop of Dublin, as laid down by the ordinance of Pope Nicholas III.

Dated at St. Peter's, Rome iii. Kal. Jun. 1° Honorius IV. (30 May, 1285.)

141. (119.) William, son and heir of Walter Man, grants to Walter Unred and Roger de Wyngham, clerk, citizens of Dublin, his land and buildings in St. Andoen's Parish, formerly belonging to William de Chester, and situate between the land which belonged to John de Lang-caster and that of Elyas Clare, from the King's way to St. Andoen's churchyard; rent 20½d., payable to the heirs of Robert the knight; and other land in the same parish situate between the land which belonged to William de Chester on the east, and that which belonged to Andrew de Sparisholt on the west, from the King's way to St. Andoen's churchyard; rent ¼ mark to the pipe of Dublin, 8s. 4d. to the canons of Holy Trinity, 20d. to the canons of St. Thomas, and a rose to the grantor and his heirs, free from all other secular exactions except landgable.

Witnesses—William de Notingham and Robert le Decer, provosts, Henry le Mareschl, Robert de Wylleby, Thomas de Coryntre, Andrew de Sparisholt, and Robert de Esseburne.

Dated at Dublin, Saturday after Feast of St. Luke, 13° Edward I. (20 Oct., 1285.)

142. (121.) John le Decer of Dublin, grants to John, son and heir of Richard de Bakepns, and Petronilla his wife, a messuage and building in Bridge-street, Dublin, lying between the land of Henry Oysel on one side, and that of Henry Moris on the other, and extending from Bridge-street to the city wall; rent 10s., payable to Holy Trinity Church, and to grantor and his heirs one penny.

Witnesses—John Serjant and Nicholas the clerk, then balliffs of Dublin, Henry le Mareschall, Robert de Wylaby, Bartholomew Crek, William Stoyl, and Hugh the clerk.—*Circa* 1285.

143. (132.) Holy Trinity Church, Dublin, and Amabila, late wife of John Comyn, by Nicholas Comyn, her attorney, agree that the latter shall give an acquittance for £3 6s. 0d., for the issues of the manor of Kyncual from John Comyn's death to the recovery of the same, and that the former shall acknowledge the receipt of the rents due from John Comyn's death.

Dated at Dublin, Friday before the Feast of St. Edmund, bishop, 14° Edward I. (15 Nov., 1286.)

144. (123.) Richard, bishop of Ferns, grants an indulgence in the same terms as No. 135 *supra*, as well as to those who by legacy or gift promote the building of Holy Trinity Church.

Dated at Dublin, the Feast of St. Mark the Evangelist (25 Apr.), 1289.

145. (125.) Richard, bishop of Lysmore, grants as in No. 144 *supra*. Dated at Dublin, on Feast of St. Mary Magdalene (22 Jul.), 1289.

146. (127.) Nicholas, bishop of Cloyne, grants as in No. 144 *supra*. Dated at Dublin, Friday before the Feast of the Apostles Symon and Jude (21 Oct.), 1289.

147. (124.) Walter, bishop of Waterford, grants as in No. 144 *supra*. Dated at Dublin, on the morrow of the Feast of the Apostles Symon and Jude (22 Oct.) 1289.

148. (126.) Matthew, bishop of Ardagh, grants as in No. 144 *supra*. Dated at Drogheda, xii. Kal. Apr. (21 Mar.) 1291.

149. (128.) William, bishop of Clonmacnois, grants as in No. 144 *supra*.

Dated at Drogheda, xii. Kal. Apr. (21 Mar.) 1291.

150. (129.) New taxation of the Diocese of Dublin.

Taxation of the Dignities and Prebends of the Church of St. Patrick, Dublin, with their Vicarages.

Archbishopric of Dublin £170 19s. 8d.: Deanery of Dublin £41: Precentor of the Church of Dublin £2: Chancellor 20 marks and Treasurer of the same £7 7s.: Archdeacon of Dublin £10: Archdeacon of Glyndelach, 5 marks, his prebend nothing on account of war: Prebendary of Swerlys 80 marks, and the Vicarage there £2: Prebends of Sir R. de Apryslon, and Master James of Spain, prebendaries of Lusks, 40 marks each, and the two Vicarages there 20 marks: Prebend of Glynmeahane £10: Prebendary of Howth and Kylbarroke [   ]: Prebend of Sir J. of [   ]: Prebend of Master N. of Lescapoune 10 marks, the Vicarage there not sufficient for the charges; Prebend of Rathmighill nothing because waste, 5 marks [   ]: Prebend de Novo Castro 20 marks; Tassngard £5; Maynothe £5 17s. 4d., and the Vicarage there £1; Prebend of Yagdistoune £8; Dunlovane 8 marks; Monamohemoke £5; Tamochane nothing on account of war; Typyr 8 marks; two Prebendaries of Typyrkevyn 1 mark ; Vicarage of Tauelaghte nothing on account of war : Prebend of Stagonyll nothing because waste : Vicarage of St. Keviny not sufficient for the charges.

Common Fund of the Church of St. Patrick, Dublin :—
Church of St. Keviny, portion of Castrocnok, church of Cromylyn, Mon and Rorton (Borton) £90 ; Churches of Arscoll, St. Nicholas within the walls, with its altarage, Braynokystoune and Tamelok, cannot support the charges ; Churches of Kylmacantane and Kylbryde, Rathsal Inchan, church of Donaghmore, Villa frazini, rent of the City of Dublin, Vicarage of Donaghmore and Term Sylloe are all waste.—Total, £460 3s. 7d.

Taxation of the goods, issues, and rents of Holy Trinity Church, Dublin :—
Church of St. Michael, 7 marks ; Churches of St. John and St. Michan, cannot support the charges ; Rent of the City of Dublin, £7 10s. 2d. ; Grange of Glasuevyn in spiritualities and temporalities 7 marks ; Grange of Gorman 7 marks ; Manor and Church of Clunkene, with their members, cannot sustain the charges ; Church of Balysaadan, 8 marks, and yearly rent there 9 marks ; Church of Kylcolyn, with the chapel, rent, &c., £3 1s. 1d.—Total, £35 18s. 11d.

Deanery of Christianity, Dublin :—
Churches of Hull, Dam, St. Olave, and St. James, not sufficient for the charges ; Churches of St. Michael de Poll and St. Catherine not worth the service of a chaplain ; Rent of the Abbot of the house of the B. V M, Dublin £2 1s. ; Rent of the Abbot of the Monastery of St. Thomas, Dublin, £2 ; Temporalities of the same in the town £1, alms of ale therein 2 marks, the issues of the mills there are not sufficient for the keeper about them, and the Abbot receives nothing of the alms of the Lord the King in the Exchequer ; Rent of the Prior of St. John in the city £4 10s. 2½d. ; of the Prior of All Saints in his land near Dublin 2 marks, and in the city £2 1s. ; and of the Abbess del Hoggys in the city £1 ; the Prior of St. Catherine, near the Salmon Leap, receives nothing of the rents in the city.—Total, £15 5s. 6¾d.

Deanery of Tauby :—
Church of Coulok £2 ; and vicarage there, 1 mark ; Chapel of Isolde's Town, the Hospitallers are rectors ; Portion of the tithes of the monks at Clonachlagh and their temporalities there 12 marks ; Church of Leucane (Monastery of St. Thomas) £5 ; and the vicarage there 1 mark ; Church of Balithermot, the Hospitallers are rectors ; Church of Kylmahud 4 marks ; Temporality of the Prior of St. Catherine ½ mark ; Church of Kylmatalwey 2 marks ; Chapel of Kynturk not worth the service of a chaplain, Temporality of All Saints there 10 marks ; Temporalities of the monks at Kylmatalwey not sufficient for the charges ; the Prioress of Leasnolyn at Clonachlagh, Dunsank, and Balegrene, 18 marks ; the Prior of St. John of Dublin, at Palmerstown, 10 marks, but the tithes not sufficient for the service of a chaplain ; the Prior of All Saints at Ballyoolhy, with the chapel, 10 marks ; the monks at Kylnacodrak not sufficient for the charges ; Ballykegh nothing on account of war ; the monks at Coulmyne and Clonlyff, £3 ; Cloghranhydryt   and Aderk 5 marks.—Total, £60 13s. 4d.

Deanery de Saltu :—
Churches of Kyldonane and Tristyldalane (Monastery of St. Thomas)

not worth the service of chaplains ; of Confy (Monasteries of St. Thomas and de Saltu) for two portions £2 ; Rent of the Abbot of St. Thomas at Saltus 4 shillings ; Temporality of the Prior of St. Catherine nothing because waste, and he receives nothing of his rent at Confy ; Churches of Taghto £5 ; Stocumny £5 ; and Straffane £2, but the vicarage there nothing beyond service of a chaplain ; Temporality of the Prior of St. Wolfstan 10 shillings ; Church of Kyldroght (Monastery of St. Thomas) £1, vicarage there no value beyond service of a chaplain ; Donacumper and Donamoro   —Total, £15 14s.

Deanery of Rellymore :—

Temporality and Tithes at Ballyboght not worth service of a chaplain ; Churches of Ballycotalane 6 marks ; Rathsallaghan 2 marks ; and Rathimore, with portions of the villa of Ponceston and Ildryga   ; Chapels of Loghloane and Lewalyuy, Hospitallers are rectors ; Vicarage of Rathmore 4 marks ; Temporality of the Prioress of Lesmolyn in the parish of Rath' ; and of St. John of Naas there, nothing because waste ; Church and Vicarage de Sancto Bosco and Haroldstown Church, nothing because waste ; Rent of the monks at Inchoberstalane and Tithes there 4½ marks ; their tithes at Donneston and Temporality and Tithes at Rathargych' £1 ; Chapel Villa Walenaium nothing because waste ; Churches of Kylpatryk (waste) 1 mark ; Kylbodane and the parish next Kylpatryk nothing ; and Tobird £2 0s. 8d.—Total, £16 1s. 4d.

Deanery of Swerdyn :—

Churches of Nall 5 marks 4s. 6d. ; de Sancto bosco 8 marks, vicarage there not worth the service of a chaplain ; Sauntreff 5 marks ; Balyogary, with the chapel of Palmerston, £13 6s. 8d. (Hosp.) ; Balyrothery 16 marks, and the vicarage there 4½ marks ; Balmadun, with the chapel of Boranceston, 8 marks, and the vicarage there no value beyond service of a chaplain ; Portraghlyn £3 ; Waspaylyston £1 ; Balybaghill £1 ; Donabate 10 marks, and the vicarage there, 4 marks ; Balygriffyn 5 marks ; Balydonegane £2 ; Holmpatryk 2 marks ; Kylsalghne (Monastery of St. Thomas) 7 marks, but the vicarage there not sufficient for the charges ; Clogherans 4 marks, and Balydowyl   ; Temporality of the Monks at Balybaghyll £10 ; the Prior of Holmpatryk 5 marks, the Prioress de Gracia Dei, with the rents there, £2 ; and the Prior of All Saints at Dalydowyl 8 marks ; Chapel of Portmernock, nothing ; Temporalities of Portmernok £3 ; Kiloragh £2 : Glasenhagh, with the tithes there, 9 marks, and the Prior of St. John at Palmerston [   ] Balyakadan   :—Total, £103 18s.

Deanery of Omurthy :—

Churches of Kynnogh chapel [5 marks] ; vill of Bitholoyane, nothing because waste ; Tamalyn £2 8s. ; rent of the Prioress £3 ; and her lands there 2 marks ; Orokeston 1 mark, and the Temporality of the Prioress [   ] ; Malamaste 2 marks, Nicholastown 6 marks ; Inchmaquedryt 2 marks, and the Temporality of the said Prioress there half a mark ; Dullardstown £2 ; Uak 2 marks 4s. 8d. ; chapels of Gryn, nothing because waste ; Glassoly £1 2s. 6d., and rent of the Prioress of Tamalyn there, half a mark ; agriculture of the Prioress there and church of Thoragh, waste ; church of Norragh with the rents of   , 4s. 6d., £3 18s., vicarage there not sufficient for the charges, and Temporality of the Prior thereof, nothing because waste : churches of Ballycollan and Loyston, and Rathknavis, Hospitallers are rectors ; Church of Grane £1 ; and Temporality of the Prioress thereof there, £1 ;

Church of Kyngelano 2 marks, but vicarage there not worth the service of a chaplain; Churches of Cordergrano, nothing because waste; Waastown 2s., 2 marks; Kylka 8 marks, vicarage there			; chapel of Konney 6 marks, and Temporality of the Prioress of Orane there 17s.; Church of Trestyldermote with the rents and mill there 9 marks 3s. 4d., vicarage there			; Chapel of vill of Leys, Hospitallers are rectors; Church of Bethlane 1 mark; Vicarages of Kylka not sufficient for the charges, and Stafonan, Ramoly and Faunteston nothing because waste; Temporality of the Prior of St. J. of Trestyldermote in the said villa, the Prior has not permitted it to be taxed; Rents of the Priors of Conall at Trestyldermote 3s.; Kenlys, Ossory Ds., St. John Dublin there 4s.; and Monks of Dublin at Busroyl waste; Church of Ryban £5; Temporality of the Monks of Balkynglass at Rosnalvan £1; Churches of Tankardstown Slane £1; and Dennbryn 1 mark; Moiety of the church of Monthannock, for the Abbot of St. Thomas £2; Church of the vill of Trenedyn 1 mark, but vicarage there not sufficient for the charges; Chapel of Hubertstown 8s. 8d.; Vicarages of Trestyll £1; Davyston and Galveston			—Total, £60 16s. 2d.

Deanery of Brec:—

Church of Bree £1, but Vicarage there nothing on account of war; Church of Sankyll not sufficient for the charges; Temporalities of the monks at Kylmohennok waste, and of same monks at Karrygbrekane nothing on account of war: chapel there not sufficient for a chaplain; Churches of Kyloowyll £2: de Novo Castro Makyngane £5, and the Vicarage there £2; Delgeney 5 marks; and Glenmondyr 4 marks.— Total £10.

Total of the sums £707 11s.

Sum of the temporal and spiritual papal taxation, except the Churches of Holy Trinity, St. Patrick's, Dublin, and the nuns of Lesmolyn, £258 15s. sterling.

The writer adds:—

Now the writings are written give me what I have deserved.—*Circa* 1394.

151. (130.) Pope Celestino V. informs the Archbishop of Dublin and his suffragans of his election as Pope in the room of Nicholas IV.

Dated at Aquila, viii. Id. Sep. 1° Celestino V. (6 Sep., 1294).

[*Indorso*] This Bull was presented to the Prior of Holy Trinity, Dublin, xi. Kal. Maii, 1295, the see of Dublin being vacant by the death of Master John de Saunford.

152. (131.) Thomas, son of Richard le Blund of Ardraa, citizen of Dublin, grants to John de Leycester, called le Heyward, and Alice, daughter of Geoffrey Calun, his wife, land and buildings in Bridge St., parish of St. Audoen, Dublin, lying between the land of William de Bradone on the south, and the land of Henry Morice, which formerly belonged to William Marcnund, on the north, and extending from the street on the east to the city wall on the west, which land was granted to him by John, son and heir of Richard de Westam; Rent 16s., payable to Holy Trinity Church, a penny payable to the heirs of John Westam, and a rose to grantor.

Witnesses—John le Sarjaunt, mayor of Dublin, John Giffard and Hugh de Carltons, then bailiffs, Henry le Mareschal, Robert de Wyleby, Thomas de Covyntre, William de Bristoll, Roger de Aneeburna, Richard Laweles, William le Graunt, Richard Westam, and John Oadwaly.

Dated at Dublin, Monday, Feast of St. Mark the Evangelist, 23 Edward I. (25 Apr., 1295.)

153. (133.) John, son of John Comyn, having obtained a writ of mort d'ancestor against the Prior of Holy Trinity, for two parts of the manor of Kynsale, they agree that the Prior is to release John of five gales of rent of 100s., to Easter, 26 Edward I., due his Church from the manor, and John is to release the Prior of all damages and waste under the writ.

Dated at Dublin, xi, Kal. Mar. 24° Edward I.   (30 Feb., 1296.)

154. (132.) Pope Boniface VIII. directs the Prior of All Saints, near Dublin, to decide the dispute between the Prior of Holy Trinity, Dublin, and the Dean of St. Patrick's of the one part, and the Bishop of Ferns on the other part, concerning the Archiepiscopal jurisdiction of Dublin when the see is vacant, alleged by the Prior and Dean to belong to them.

Dated at St. Peter's, Rome, Non. Mar. 3° Boniface VIII.   (7 Mar., 1307.)

155. (134.) Edward I. directs John Wogan, Justiciary of Ireland, and the Treasurer and Barons of the Exchequer, Dublin, to restore the Priory of Holy Trinity, Dublin, to the Prior and convent thereof, when they have given security to satisfy the King for having proceeded to elect an Archbishop of Dublin, without having obtained licence. Dated at Westminster, 27 March, 27 Edward I.   This was done by the hands of Richard de Balybrenan, chaplain, Milo Passelewe, John Passelewe, Thomas le Blound of Kynsale.

Dated 27 Mar., 1299.

156. (138.) Pope Boniface VIII. directs the Priors of Dundalk and St. Mary de Urso, diocese of Armagh, and the Archdeacon of Armagh church, to determine the dispute between Holy Trinity church, Dublin, and the Bishop of Meath about tithes and other matters.

Dated at Anagni, iv. Id. Jun. 5° Boniface VIII.   (10 Jun., 1299.)

157. (139.) Pope Boniface VIII. directs the Abbot of the Monastery of St. Thomas the Martyr, near Dublin, and the Priors of the Friars Preachers, Dublin and Dundalk diocese of Armagh, to determine the dispute between Holy Trinity Church and Thomas, dean of St. Patrick's, Dublin, about tithes and other matters.

Dated at Anagni, iv. Id. Jun. 5° Boniface VIII.   (10 Jun., 1299.)

158. (135.) Pope Boniface VIII. directs the Abbot of the Monastery of St. Thomas the Martyr, near Dublin, to revoke anything done to the prejudice of the Prior of Holy Trinity after his departure for Rome on business.

Dated at Anagni, Id. Jun., 5° Boniface VIII.   (13 Jun., 1299.)

159. (136.) Pope Boniface VIII. directs the Prior of St. Leonard's, Dundalk, diocese of Armagh, to determine the complaint of Adam, prior of the Cathedral Church, Dublin, against William de Nunes, priest, of Dublin diocese, for having excommunicated him.

Dated at Anagni, Id. Jun. 5° Boniface VIII.   (13 Jun., 1299.)

160. (140.) Proceedings at the church of St. John the Baptist within the walls of Dublin before the Prior of St. Leonard's, Dundalk, directed by Pope Boniface VIII., to recall to Holy Trinity Church the tithes, &c., aliened therefrom. Master Adam de Furneys, who alleges that he is vicar of Kilkolyn church, having been cited to answer Holy Trinity Church for having unjustly detained Kilkolyn church, the parties appeared by their proctors, John de Horton and Brother Audoen respectively, and were ordered to appear at the church of St. Peters, Drogheda, on the Vigil of All Saints.

Dated at the Church of St. John, Saturday after the feast of St. Luke the Evangelist (24th October), 1299.

161. (137). Enrolment of Deeds, Nos. 44, 14, 12, 7, 15, 160, *supra*, and of the following :—The Prior and Convent of Holy Trinity and Master Adam de Furneys having appeared before the Prior of St. Leonard's, Dundalk, on Saturday, the Vigil of All Saints, 1299, at Dinolek Parish church, by consent, instead of at St. Peter's, Drogheda ; the church of Kylkelyn and the vicarage thereof was awarded to Holy Trinity.

Dated at Dinelok, Saturday, Vigil of All Saints (31st Oct.), 1299.

162. (141 *bis.*) Pope Boniface VIII. directs the Prior of Holmpatrick, Dublin diocese, to cause the award in No. 161 *supra*, to be observed.

Dated at the Lateran, xii. Kal. Feb., 6° Boniface VIII. (21 Jan., 1300).*

163. (142). Pope Boniface VIII. directs the Archbishop, Dean, and Archdeacon of Armagh, to cite the Dean and Chapter of St. Patrick's, Dublin, to appear before them, to defend the suit between them and Holy Trinity Church, with reference to the election of Archbishop of Dublin, which suit had been referred to Matthew, Cardinal Deacon of St. Mary in Portico, who had summoned the Dean and Chapter to appear before him without effect.

Dated at the Lateran, v. Kal. Apr. 6° Boniface VIII. (28 Mar., 1300).

164. (142b.) Roll of proceedings setting out that John de Braybrok, on the feast of S. Francis of the Friar's Minor (16 Jul.), 1300, brought from Rome the bull No. 163, *supra*.

The Dean and Chapter of St. Patrick's submitted that on the vacancy of the see, royal license should be sought by both Chapters (of Holy Trinity and S. Patrick's) to elect ; the former to arrange and conduct the election ; the Archbishop to be enthroned in Holy Trinity ; and the decree of election to be sealed by both Chapters.

The Prior and Convent of Holy Trinity claimed that the grant of Archbishop Luke be confirmed ; restitution of the Church of Rathfernan, exemption from the Archdeacon's jurisdiction, restoration of the chapels of Archbishops Fulk, Luke, and John de Saunford, and of certain bulls in their favour ; also the cope taken from brothers Hugh le Mareschal and Rich. de Notingham, in S. Patrick's, in which W[alter] Calf, bishop of Kildare, was consecrated ; they claimed power to elect their Prior ; as mother church, an annual payment of 3 ounces of gold from S. Patrick's ; the see being vacant, officials to be appointed and account in Holy Trinity, and their seal kept there ; synods to be held in that church ; and canons and prebendaries of S. Patrick's to swear to observe these privileges.

The Dean and Chapter of S. Patrick's consented to admit these claims if, as formerly, equal rights in the election were conceded to them. The Convent refusing, the Dean threatened, as Vicar-General, to visit the Convent. The latter thereupon appealed to Rome, 11 August, 1300, in presence of Sir Hugh the chaplain, dean of Christianity, Nicholas the clerk, provost of Dublin, Master John de Kerdyf, and Master Adam de Stratton, official of the Archdeacon ; and their proctors (Master Peter de Lando and Audoen de Ymar), left for Rome on the Sunday after the feast of S. Luke the Evangelist (18 Oct.)

* For confirmation of ordinance of Pope Nicholas III. by Richard, Archbishop of Dublin, 2 May, 1800, see No. 804, *infra*.

E

The Dean and Chapter, through Sir J. Wogan, the justiciary, compelled the Prior to agree to the compromise directed by R[ichard de Feringe], the Archbishop, 2 March, 1300, to the following effect:—

That the ordinance of Pope Nicholas stand firm; the consecration and enthronisation of Archbishops to take place in Holy Trinity as the Mother Church; that S. Patrick's be called Cathedral, though admitting the precedence of the other; the cross, mitre, and ring of deceased archbishops to belong to Holy Trinity, and their bodies to be buried there unless willed otherwise; the consecration of chrism and oil to belong to Holy Trinity, and its chapter to have equal power in rural churches during vacancy of the see.

The Convent of Holy Trinity having refused to seal this ordinance or revoke their appeal, the prior (Adam de Balscham) deposed the sub-prior, seneschal, sacrist, and precentor, and instituted brother Philip de Braybrok as sacrist. The Convent revoke the institution.

Brothers Gilbert de Winchester, sub-prior, Walter de Clontarf, Henry de Kork, Nicholas de Medlers, precentor, William de Cari, John de Forneja, Philip de Braybrok, John de Balscham, Richard de Nottingham, Elias Was, and Hugh de Sutton, canons of Holy Trinity, accuse the prior of apostasy, simony, perjury, incontinence, and waste, and appeal to Rome, 21 Oct., 1300.

The same day William Canno put to sea from Dublin, and brother Audoen from Ross. Brothers Philip de Braybrok and John de Balscham renounce the accusation and appeal.

The dean visited the convent as vicar-general, and pronounced excommunication against those opposing him; he required the convent to revoke their appeals, called on the prior to account, and directed that Gilbert de Winchester, sub prior, John Pecok, master of the building of the church, and Nicholas de Medlers, precentor, be sent for penance to the monasteries of S. John, Kilkenny, Inistyok and Kells in Ossory, the first to abstain from fish on the sixth day of the week, the others on the fourth, and to receive only bread and water on the sixth day, and all to sit last in choir and at table.

The penitents appealed to Rome in presence of the prior, Baron de Signo, diocese of Florence, notary public, Sir Hugh, dean of Christianity, John de Horton, chaplain, Sir Hugh de Assaford, Sir John de Bothestrete, Gerard Chimberd, merchant, Adam de Cromelyn, sheriff of Dublin, Richard le Blund, J. de Chichester, and the canons—Henry de Kork, William de Cari, John de Furneya, Philip de Braybrok.

Finally the vicar-general, having found the prior's accounts unsatisfactory, deprived him of his office for simony, and excommunicated him; restored the brethren, relieved them from the excommunication of the prior, and appointed officers during vacancy of the prior.

The treasurer (Rich. de Bireford) and barons of the Exchequer appointed as custodian of the priory, Nich. de Campeden, who removed the officer of the vicar. The canons and vicar obtained a writ from the justiciary (23 Nov., 1300) for Campeden's removal, and the vicar again appointed a custodian. The vicar to prevent the oblations, being used to maintain the cause at Rome, came on the feast of S. Stephen (26 Dec.) and took the key of the oblations from the sacrist. He found £8 in the chest, the oblations being valued at £40 yearly. Having obtained permission of the vicar, the convent on 31 Jan. elected Henry de Bristoll, prior, who was confirmed by the vicar.—Circa 1301.

165. (160.) Pope Boniface VIII. confirms the award in No. 161 supra. Dated at the Lateran, xv. Kal. Mar., 7° Boniface VIII. (15 Feb. 1301).

166. (143.) Huguicio de Vercellis, canon of Bruges, sub-deacon and chaplain of the Pope, announces that Adam de Strachon, proctor of Nicholas de Clere, archdeacon of Dublin, obtained a Bull dated at the Lateran, ii. Kal. November, 7° Boniface VIII., directing the Archdeacon of Armagh to determine the complaint of the Archdeacon of Dublin, that the Dean of St. Patrick's installed brother Henry de Bristole as Prior of Holy Trinity contrary to the right of the Archdeacon of Dublin to install priors into monasteries governed by priors in his Archdeaconate, on the understanding that it should not prejudice the Prior and Convent of Holy Trinity.
Dated at the Lateran [ii.] Kal. Nov., 7° Boniface VIII. ([31] Oct., 1301).

167. (147.) Pope Boniface VIII. directs the Archbishop of Armagh to protect for three years the Holy Trinity Church from being injured by robbers and plunderers, saving the rights of litigants; no sentence of excommunication to be promulgated against Bishops, the higher Prelates, or Universities.
Dated at the Lateran, vi. Id. Nov., 7° Boniface VIII. (8 Nov., 1301).

168. (148 bis.) Pope Boniface VIII. directs the Archbishop of Armagh to publish in the Churches that those who detain the tithes and other goods of Holy Trinity Church should produce them and render satisfaction therefor, and having warned them, to publish general excommunication against them.
Dated at the Lateran, iv. Id. Nov., 7° Boniface VIII. (10 Nov., 1601).

169. (149.) Pope Boniface VIII. prohibits all persons from attacking or detaining the Canons, lay brethren, or goods of Holy Trinity for the purpose of obtaining satisfaction in any matter of dispute.
Dated at the Lateran, v. Kal. Dec., 7° Boniface VIII. (27 Nov., 1301.)

170. (154.) Pope Boniface VIII. takes into his protection Holy Trinity Church, and confirms its lands and goods.
Dated at the Lateran, v. Id. Mar., 6° Boniface VIII. (11 Mar., 1302.)

171. (153.) Pope Boniface VIII. confirms to Holy Trinity Church all the liberties, immunities, and secular exemptions granted to them.
Dated at the Lateran, ii. Id. Mar., 8° Boniface VIII. (14 Mar., 1302.)

172. (151.) John de Nevill, for 30 marks sterling, releases to Holy Trinity Church his right to the land in Kyntork, which formerly belonged to William del Raht, and was demised to him for life by the said Church, and to the houses he has built near the Chapel of the B.V.M. in the said Priory.
Dated at York, 10 Jun., 30° Edward I. (1302.)

173. (152.) Fine in the Octave of the Purification B.V.M., 31 Edward I. before Richard de Exeter, Robert de Littlebyr', Master Thomas de Chadderworth, and Thomas de Suyterby, justices, and afterwards recited in the quindene of Easter before Richard de Exeter, William Deveneys, Thomas de Suyterby, and John de Ponte, wherein Henry de Assheborne and Cecilia his wife, release to Holy Trinity Church a messuage in Dublin, for a sparrowhawk.
Quindene of Easter, 1303.

E 2

174. (156b.) The Prior of St. Leonard's, Dundalk, informs the Archbishop of Dublin of his award, as in No. 161, *supra*, and directs him to enforce it.

Dated Tuesday after the Assumption of the B.V.M. (18 Aug.), 1304.

175. (155 *bis*.) R{ichard de Feringa], archbishop of Dublin, in pursuance of No. 174 *supra*, commands the Dean of Omurthy to induct the Prior and Convent of Holy Trinity into Kilkolyn Church.

Dated at Swerdes, vi. Kal. Sep. (27 Aug.), 1304.

176. (156.) The Dean of Omurthy certifies to the Archbishop of Dublin that he has executed No. 175 *supra*.

Dated at Kilkolyn, Monday after the feast of the beheading of St. John the Baptist (31 Aug.), 1304.

177. (157.) Pope Clement V. directs the Bishop, Dean, and Archdeacon of Clogher to revoke anything rashly done by Richard, archbishop of Dublin, against Philip de Braybrok, canon of Holy Trinity, Dublin, whilst absent at Rome on business.

Dated at Bordeaux, Kal. Nov., 1° Clement V. (1 Nov., 1306.)

178. (159.) Henry la Warre de Bristoll, prior of Holy Trinity, Dublin, and the Convent thereof, being entitled to 3½ marks rent, payable by Robert de Notingham of Dublin, for a holding in High-street, parish of St. Michael, Dublin, situate between the holding of John Stakepol, on the east, and that of the said Robert on the west, which formerly belonged to Matilla Stokes and was bequeathed to the Prior and Convent by Elias Burel; reduce the rent to 2 marks for this year, to 20s. during the lives of the said Robert and Matilla, daughter of Robert de Wileby, his wife, and to 2 marks after their deaths.

Dated at Dublin, Sunday after feast of St. Nicholas, 35 Edward I. (15 Dec., 1306).

179. (158.) Pope Clement V. informs the Prior and Convent of Holy Trinity, and the Dean and Chapter of St. Patrick's, Dublin, that the appointment of Archbishop of Dublin vacant by the death of Richard, late Archbishop, was reserved by decree to the Holy See, in ignorance of which brother Richard of Dublin was elected by the Dean and Chapter of St. Patrick's, and Nicholas called "the Butiler," clerk, by the Prior and Convent of Holy Trinity; that he has declared those elections void, and appointed the said Richard to be archbishop of Dublin, and commands both Chapters to receive him.

Dated at Poictiers, vi. Id. Jul., 2° Clement V. (10 Jul., 1307.)

180. (160.) William, Alexander, and Thomas Mareschal, sons and executors of Henry Mareschal, grant to Hugh de Tuyford of Dublin, a holding with houses in St. Michael's parish, Dublin, formerly inhabited by William le Peyntor, granted to Henry by the Prior and Convent of Holy Trinity, Dublin, likewise 2 shops on the east of said holding with a vacant place in the rere, granted to Henry by Richard Peal and extending from the quay near the Ausmeliffy water to the holding formerly belonging to Laurence de Winton, and from that of Robert de Wileby, on the east, to that of John Bowet on the west.

Witnesses—Robert de Notingham, mayor of Dublin, Richard de St. Olave and Hugh de Carleton, bailiffs, Robert de Wileby, John Decer, Geoffrey de Morton, Thomas Colyn, and John Bowet.

Dated at Dublin, 13 Aug., 4° Edward II. (1310).

181. (161.) The Prior and Convent of Holy Trinity, Dublin, reciting that the Church of Kilkolyn belongs to them, that Sir John Wogan, Justiciary of Ireland, on the Vigil of St. Peter ad Vincula, claiming it under the statute of Mortmain, presented a clerk thereto, who was instituted by the Vicar of the Archbishop, pray from John, Bishop of Chichester, chancellor of Ireland, a writ to enquire whether the Vicarage belonged to them since the statute. (*In dorso*)—Sir Edmond le Botiler of Ireland, Richard de Exeter, Justice of the Bench, and William de Bradefeld, Justice of the Bench.—*Circa* 1310.

182. (162*b*.) Philip fitzLys, son of Henry de Pencoyt, grants to Holy Trinity Church, the chapel of Pencoyt, anciently called Kylangly, with the advowson thereof.

Witnesses—Sir Richard de Exeter, Sir Robert Dagod, Sir Wm. le Deveneys, knts. Justices of the Bench, Richard Laweles, mayor of Dublin, Nicholas Golding, and Thomas Hunt, bailiffs, Richard le Blund of Ardlo, Robert de Bristoll, John Plunket and John de Stanes.

Dated 15 Feb., 6° Ed. II. (1313.)

183. (162.) Similar to No. 182 *supra*, *except that it is dated Friday after Feast of St. Valentine* (10 Feb.), 1313, 6°. Ed. II., *and that the names of the Mayor and Bailiffs of Dublin are not among the witnesses.*

184. (107.) Thomas, son and heir of Henry Marechal, formerly citizen of Dublin, grants to Robert de Moenes his fellow-citizen, land and buildings in Bothe strete, parish of St. Michael, Dublin, and situate between the house of Holy Trinity on one side, and the lands which belonged to Alice Peel on the other, which land was granted jointly to Henry Marechal and Robert de Wileby, by John Cyffard, and Cecilia his wife, rendering to Holy Trinity Church 12*s.* yearly and to John le Rydere 10*d.* yearly.

Witnesses—Richard Lawales, mayor of Dublin, Nicholas Golding and Thomas Hunt, bailiffs, John le Decer, John Serjeant, Robert de Notingham, William Douce, Robert le Weder, John Stakepol, Richard de St. Olave, and Wm. de Compton.

Dated at Dublin, 17, Aug., 7° Edward II. (1313).

185. (105.) Inquisition taken at the Naas before Edmond le Botiler, Custos of Ireland, on Sunday after the Feast of St. Bartholomew, Apostle, 7 Edward II., by Edmond de Norragh, John le Reve, Philip de Mone, Thomas le Jostre, William, son of Ralph de Balicotlan, Robert de Kerdif of the Granges, Walter Pauchard, John de Pencoyt, William de Eytele, Stephen de Kermerdyn, Thomas le Taverner, and William Joye, finds that Holy Trinity Church, Dublin, of ancient right possessed the advowson of the Vicarage of Kilkolyn and appropriated it without royal licence, wherefore it is now in the King's hands; should the King grant it to Holy Trinity it will not be prejudicial to Thomas de Kilmaynan, as his claim was derived through the Archdeacon of Glendalough, who had no power to present; and that it is worth £10 per year.—26 Aug., 1313.

186. (103.) Proceedings at the Manor of St. Sepulchre's, Dublin, on 4th Sep., 1313, wherein brother Thos. de Clonard, sub-prior of Holy Trinity Church, Dublin, read to Sir Wm. de Leek, treasurer of the late Archbishop of Dublin, a mandate dated Dublin, Feast of St. John the Baptist, 1313, from Ralph, abbot of the Monastery of St. Thomas the Martyr, near Dublin, and Adam de Stratton, commissary of lord Alexander de Bikenor, treasurer of Ireland, specially appointed collectors of triennial tenths in Ireland by Pope Clement V., commanding the Prior of Holy Trinity, Dublin, and Nicholas de Kyngton, subcollectors for the Chapters of Holy Trinity and St. Patrick's, Dublin, to compel the said Sir William Leek to render satisfaction on the Feast of the Nativity of the B. V. M. next ensuing for triennial tenths for two years last past, which the late Archbishop had neglected to render, and to excommunicate him, to sequestrate all the fruits and obventions in his hands, especially those of the Prebend of Colonia in St. Patrick's Church, until he does render satisfaction, and to certify that the mandate has been executed on the morrow of the Nativity of the B.V. M. Certificate of execution in presence of brother Nicholas de Barton, canon of Holy Trinity, Walter de Schakenester, and Henry de Fyvebury annexed, and publication of proceedings by John de Domenia, clerk, of Winchester diocese, notary public.—4 Sep., 1313.

187 (184 bis.) Edward II. pardons the Prior and Convent of Holy Trinity, Dublin, their appropriation, without licence, in the time of Edward I., of the Vicarage of the church of Kilkolyn, which is of his advowson, since the publication of the Statute of Mortmain, and grants them the same again.

Dated at Westminster, 2 Nov., 7° Edward II. (1313).

188 (32.) T[homas], prior of St. Patrick's, Down, requests the Prior of Holy Trinity Church, Dublin, to present Master John, the bearer, to the chapel of Richard White's town in Letkayl, vacant by the resignation of Master Robert, the late rector.—Circa 1318.

189 (169.) The Spiritual Guardian of Dublin diocese recites a writ from King Edward II., that the Prior and Convent of Holy Trinity Church should have again the advowson of the Vicarage of Kilkolyn, witnessed by Edmond le Botelyr, Custos of Ireland, at Baligaveran, 4 May, 7 Edward II., and directs Roger, chaplain of Athgo, to permit the Prior and Convent to hold the vicarage, and summon any who oppose to appear before him.

Dated at Dublin, the Feast of St. John (6 May, 1314.)

190 (170.) Brother Nicholas de Barton, proctor of Holy Trinity Church, having appealed from the action of Nicholas de Balscot, archdeacon of Glandalough, in placing the Church of Kilcolyn belonging to it, under ecclesiastical interdict, the official of the Court of Dublin directs the Dean of Christianity, Dublin, to cite the Archdeacon before him in the Church of St. Patrick's, Dublin, on Thursday before the Nativity of St. John the Baptist.

Dated at Dublin, vill. Id. Jun. (6 June), 1314.

191 (168.) The official of Glendalough, the See of Dublin being vacant, directs the perpetual vicar of Calvestown, and Roger, chaplain of Kilcolyn, to put Thomas de Warllowe in corporal possession of the vicarage of Kilcolyn, of which he has been deprived by Holy Trinity Church, and to defend him therein.

Dated Friday, morrow of St. Peter ad Vincula. (2 Aug.), 1314.

192 (166.) Thomas de Warylowe, clerk, presented to the vicarage of Kylcolyn church by King Edward, renounces his right, and swears not to disturb Holy Trinity Church therein.

Dated at Dublin the morrow of the Assumption of the B. V. M. (16 Aug.) 1314.

193. (171b.) Maurice, archbishop of Cashel, reciting the deeds
a, b, and c, infra, grants to the Canons of Holy Trinity, the Church of
Kyldenall with its chapels (reserving the services due to the Archdeacon); the Prior and Convent shall have a proper vicar there, and
present to it when vacant.
Dated at Cashel the morrow of St. Michael the Archangel (30 Sep.),
1315.

(a.) Adam de Stancton grants to Holy Trinity Church, the church of
Kyldenall, with its chapels and tithes.
Witnesses—Milo de Stancton, Michael de Abreskyn, Thomas de
Barynscide, Richard de Salvagio, John de Stancton, Hamo Nocte,
Reginald Estyrmistore, William de Wormaley, William de St. Denis,
Master Henry de Stanford.

(b.) Philip, son and heir of Adam de Stancton, ratifies a, supra.
Witnesses—Sir Robert de Ufford, justiciary of Ireland, Sir Fromund,
chancellor of Ireland, Sir Alexander de Notingham, Sir Richard de
Exeter and Master William de Bakepus, eschentors of Ireland, Sir
Michael de Livet, Sir Henry de Rupeforti, Gilbert de Livet.

(c.) Donat, archbishop of Cashel, having inspected (a), supra, in sti-
tutes the Canons of Holy Trinity Church, Dublin, into the Church of
Kyldenal.   Witnesses—H. archbishop of Dublin, E. bishop of
Limerick, L. bishop of Clonmacnois, W. archdeacon of Dublin, Masters
Peter Malveisin, P. de Bray, Daniel, W. de St. Denis.

194. (171.) Similar to No. 193 supra, except that it contains no
provisions with regard to the Vicar.
Dated on the morrow of the Feast of St. Matthias the Apostle (25 Feb.),
1316.

195. (172 bis.) Sir Hugh Hosey, knt., son and heir of Adam de
Hosey, lord of Galtrym, releases to Holy Trinity Church, the Grange
of Gylgorman, granted by his ancestor Sir Hugh Hosey, who received it
from King John.
Witnesses—William, Richard, and Walter Hosey, Robert and John
Passelewe.
Dated at Galtrym, Friday before the Feast of the Nativity, 10°
Edward II. (24 Dec., 1316.)

196. (176.) The official of Glendalough acknowledges the receipt of a
mandate, dated Friday after the Feast of St. Dunstan, bishop and confessor, 1317, from the Bishop of Kildare, the Prior of the Monastery of
St. Mary of Conalle and the Precentor of Kildare, delegates appointed
by Pope John XXII. at Avignon, 1 Dec., 1316, to restore Thomas de
Kilmaynan, as Vicar of Kyleolyn, and to try his case against Holy
Trinity Church, who had deprived him thereof, directing him to cite
the Prior and Convent to appear at the church of St. Brigid of Kildare,
on Monday after the Feast of St. Barnabas the Apostle, 1317, to answer
Thomas's petition; and certifies that he has executed it.
Dated at Dublin, viii. Kal. Jun. (25 May), 1317.

197. (177.) Proceedings in the Church of St. Brigid, Kildare, on
Monday after the Feast of the Apostles Peter and Paul, 1317, before
the delegates and between the parties named in No. 196 supra, and
postponement to Monday after the Feast of the Translation of St.
Thomas the Martyr.—4 Jul., 1317.

198. (180.) Proceedings as postponed in No. 197 supra, on Monday
after the Feast of the Translation of St. Thomas the Martyr, 1317, before

Walter, bishop of Kildare, John, prior of the Monastery of St. Mary of Conal, and Maurice Jak, precentor of Kildare Church, in the cause and between the parties in No. 196 *supra*, the Prior and Convent appearing by Nicholas de Barton, their proctor, instruments on the part of the appellant, and of justification on the other side were produced, and further postponement was ordered to Tuesday after the Feast of St. Margaret, virgin.—11 Jul., 1317.

199. (181.) Proceedings as postponed in No. 197 *supra*, wherein Nicholas de Barton, proctor of Holy Trinity Church, takes exception to the Apostolic Rescript on account of the excommunication of the appellant (Thomas de Kilmaynan) ; further postponement to Tuesday, after the Feast of St. Margaret the Virgin.—11 July, 1317.

200. (102 *bis*.) Nicholas de Barton, proctor of Holy Trinity Church, Dublin (delegates and parties as in 196 *supra*), submits that he is not bound to answer the complaint of Thomas de Kilmaynan, as at the time of obtaining the Apostolic Rescript he had been excommunicated by Master Nicholas de Bray, then official of Dublin, at the instance of brother Adam de Forneys, and he claims expenses estimated at £10. *Circa* 11 July, 1317.

(This would appear to be the pleading in No. 199 supra.)

201. (178.) Proceedings as postponed in No. 199 *supra*, before William de Inchem'Wyther, canon of Kildare, acting as commissary for the Prior of the Monastery of St. Mary of Conall, and Maurice Jacko precentor, wherein a discussion was had with reference to removal of excommunication, and a further postponement was ordered to Tuesday after the Feast of St. James the Apostle.

Dated 19 Jul , 1317.

202. (179.) Proceedings in the Church of the Naas, on Tuesday after the Feast of St. James the Apostle, 1317, before Walter de Tywyrton and William de Inchem'Wythyr, canons of Kildare, between the parties as in No. 196 *supra*, the Prior and Convent of Holy Trinity appearing by Nicholas de Barton, their proctor, postponement was ordered to the greater Church of Kildare, on Monday after the Feast of St. Lawrence the Martyr, to hear a definitive sentence.

Dated 26th Jul., 1317.

203. (173.) Pope John XXII., reciting that on the death of John, archbishop of Dublin, and the elections of Alexander, archbishop of Dublin, then canon, and Walter, precentor of St. Patrick's, the said Alexander came to Rome to promote his election, the matter was referred by Pope Clement to James, Cardinal Deacon of St. George ad Velum Aureum, before whom nobody appeared to oppose the election of the said Alexander, and the said Pope Clement having died, Bartholomew de Eyteleys, rector of Kynneigh, diocese of Dublin, as proctor for Holy Trinity Church, appeared to oppose the election, and the matter having been referred to the same Cardinal, the proctor was permitted to retire, and for three years nobody appeared for Walter, who it is believed was drowned at sea, whereupon the said Alexander resigned all claims upon the See, and that he had appointed him Archbishop of Dublin ; commands the Prior and Convent of Holy Trinity, and the Dean and Chapter of St. Patrick's, to receive him with due obedience.

Dated at Avignon, xiii. Kal. Sep., 1° John XXII. (20 Aug., 1317.)

204. (174.) Like Bull to the people of Dublin city and diocese.

205. (175.) Proceedings in the church of St. Brigid of Kildare, Saturday after the Feast of the Conversion of St. Paul, 1317, before Richard de Hulot, canon of the church, commissary of Walter, bishop of Kildare, and John prior of the Monastery of St. Mary of Conal, papal delegates, and Maurice Jacke, precentor of the Church of Kildare, the other delegate, in an appeal from Brother William de Hasselbourne, abbot of the Monastery of St. Mary near Dublin, papal delegate, by Thomas de Kylmaynan, the appellant, against the Prior and Convent of Holy Trinity Church. The appeal was dismissed with half a mark costs to Holy Trinity Church.—31st Jan., 1318.

206. (183.) The official of the Court of Dublin directs the Dean of Christianity to summon Master Hervieus Bagot, archdeacon of Glendalough, to appear in St. Patrick's Church on Thursday after the Feast of the Epiphany to answer the complaint of the Prior and Convent of Holy Trinity, that they, or their Rector in the Church of St. MacTal of Kylcolyn, have been suspended without citation, monition, confession, or conviction of any crime, fined 40s., and fined for not being present at the Archdeacon's Synod, and the tithes, fruits, and obventions sequestered.

Dated at Dublin [   ].—Circa 1318.

207. (185.) Roger Ontlagho, prior of the House of the Hospital of St. John of Jerusalem in Ireland, and the brethren thereof, grant to the Chapter of Holy Trinity, Dublin, ten pounds of wax yearly for Rathmor church.

Dated at Kilmaynan, xvi. Kal. Jan. (17 Dec.) 1318.

208. (184.) Roger Wtelane, prior of the House of the Hospital of St. John of Jerusalem and his brethren, acknowledge the receipt of the deed (a.) recited at foot hereof.

Dated at Dublin, Friday after the feast of St. Hilary (20 Jan.) 1319.

(a.) Alexander, archbishop of Dublin, with the consent of the Chapters of Holy Trinity and St. Patrick's, Dublin, grants to the Prior and Brethren aforesaid the parish church of Rathmore, with its chapels, tithes, and obventions, for the sustentation of pilgrims and the necessities of the poor, institutes the Prior in the name of his House, and decrees that he should be inducted into corporal possession thereof, the rights of the Archbishop and Archdeacon being reserved, and a proper person presented when the church is vacant.

Dated at Dublin, Monday after the feast of St. Hilary (16 Jan.) 1319.

209 (186.) Thomas de Kilmaynan, perpetual Vicar of Kylcolyn Church, diocese of Dublin, prefers his complaint before the delegates named in No. 190 supra, in his appeal from the Abbot of the Monastery of the Blessed Mary, near Dublin, against the Prior and Convent of Holy Trinity, pursuant to the Apostolic Rescript, as below.

Dated at the church of St. Brigid, Kildare, Monday before the feast of St. Margaret, Virgin. (18 Jul.), 1319.

Pope John XXII. directs the delegates in No. 196 supra, to hear the appeal of Thomas de Kilmaynan, perpetual Vicar of Kylcolyn, from the decision of the Abbot of the Monastery of the B. V. M. near Dublin, who, in a suit between the said Thomas and Richard de Wodehouse, clerk, with reference to the Vicarage of Kylcolyn, admitted the Prior and Convent of Holy Trinity, Dublin, to plead against the said Thomas after Richard de Wodehouse had retired therefrom ; and, should the cause be not terminated within three months, to remit it to the Bishop of Ossory.

Dated at Avignon, xvi. Kal. Maii, 3° John XXII., (16 April, 1319.)

210. (187.) John prior of the Monastery of Conal, one of the delegates in No. 209 *supra*, appoints during his pleasure William de Inchem'Wyther, canon of Kildare, to act as delegate in his stead.

Dated at the Monastery, aforesaid, Saturday after the feast of St. Margaret, Virgin. (21 Jul.), 1319.

211. (188.) Proceedings in the church of St. Brigid of Kildare, Monday after the feast of St. Margaret, Virgin, 1319, before Walter bishop of Kildare and William de Inchem'Wyther, canon of Kildare, between the parties in No. 209, *supra*; the Prior and Convent of Holy Trinity took exception to the Rescript, and the parties were ordered to appear on Monday after the feast of St. James the Apostle.—23 Jul., 1319.

212. (189.) Proceedings as adjourned in No. 211 *supra*, the appellant having submitted that the exception should not be admitted, after argument, the parties were ordered to appear at the parish church of the Nans on Tuesday after the feast of St. James the Apostle to interplead.—30 Jul., 1319.

213. (190.) Proceedings as adjourned in No. 212 *supra*, before Walter de Tywyrton and William de Inchem'Wyther, canons of Kildare; the exception was admitted, security for costs was given, and the parties were ordered to appear in the greater church, Kildare, to hear definitive sentence on Monday after the feast of St. Laurance the Martyr.—31 Jul. 1319.

214. (191. *bis.*) Proceedings as adjourned in No. 213 *supra*, the sub-delegates declared that the exception had been sustained, quashed the Rescript, and condemned the appellant in half a mark costs.

Dated 13th Aug., 1319.

215. (192.) Proceedings in the church of St. Canice, Kilkenny, diocese of Ossory, on Friday after the feast of St. Martin Bishop 13[19], before [   ] precentor of the said Church, sub-dulegate of [Richard] bishop of Ossory, in an appeal between the parties in No. 209 *supra*. On behalf of Holy Trinity Church, the jurisdiction was objected to, as the matter should have been concluded within three months; a question having arisen with regard to the seals of the sub-delegates of the Bishop of Kildare affixed to the process and definitive sentence produced, both parties were ordered to appear at the above church the day after the Epiphany.—16 Nov., 13[19.]

216. (193.) Pope John XXII., directs the Abbot of the Monastery of B.V.M., of Novan, diocese of Meath as in No. 167 *supra*.

Dated at Avignon, v. Id. Maii, 8° John XXII. (11 May, 1824.)

217. (194 *bis.*) Pope John XXII. directs the archbishop of Armagh to hear the complaint of the Prior and chapter of Holy Trinity, Dublin, against Richard de St. Leodgario, archdeacon of Dublin, who has claimed a right of visitation and proxies out of the churches of St. John the Baptist in Bothe-street, St. Michael, and St. Michan, Dublin, and has excommunicated them, for resisting his claim, and sequestered their fruits, rents, &c.

Dated at Avignon, Id. Maii, 8 John XXII. (15 May, 1324.)

218. (195.) Pope John XXII. directs the Archbishop of Armagh to hear the complaint of the Prior and Chapter of Holy Trinity, Dublin,

against Elyas Lanles, rector of St. Audoens, Dublin, concerning the tithes of salmon taken in the fishery of Auynliffi within the confines of St. Michan's parish near Dublin, of the fruits from the gardens near the mill of Drege-streta, and of hay from a meadow near the fishery.
Dated at Avignon, Id. May, 8 John XXII (15 May, 1324.)

219 (197.) Nicholas de Barton, proctor of Hugh, prior of Holy Trinity Church, Dublin, Nicholas de Esoden, Simon de Lodegate, John Dolfyn, Adam Coleby, John Dayaye, canons, and Robert de Mainchester, lay brother, states before Peter de Wylebi, official of Dublin Court, that he appeals to the Apostolic See against the claim of Richard de St. Leodguric, archdeacon of Dublin, with reference to his right of Visitation to the Churches of St. Michael, St. Michan, and St. John of Bothe Strete, Dublin, Dalkey, and Stalorgan, and the sentence of excommunication and interdict pronounced for resistance to the same while an appeal was pending.
Done at the Church of St. Patrick's, Dublin, by John de Domesia, clerk, of Winchester diocese, notary public, in the presence of Master John de Kyngston, canon of St. Patrick's, William Douce and Thomas Hunter, citizens of Dublin, on the 26th day of May, 1325.

220 (196.) Inquisition taken at Dublin before Walter de la Pulle, escheator of Ireland, on Monday the feast of St. Matthias the Apostle 19º Edward II., by Reginald de Bernsvale, Luke de Balynges, Geoffrey de Brandannold, Andrew Tyrel, Thomas le Walers, William Uriel, John le Mareschal of Ratheoul, Gerrard Bossard, William Fynglas, Thomas Wyconbe, John Haket, John FitzMichael of Kyllath, [Richard Derpatrick, Alex. Rathlawe, Jordan, John Huutt], finds that the Church of Holy Trinity, Dublin, was founded by various Irishmen, and its granges, lands, and tenements given by Irishmen unknown, before the Conquest, in free alms to God and the said Church, and the canons serving God there, that there has been no custodiam by reason of a vacancy in the office of Prior, and that none of their lands are held of the King in capita.—24 Feb., 1326.

221 (1985.) Copies of the following deeds :—
(a.) Thomas fitz John, earl of Kildare, grants to the Prior and Convent of Holy Trinity, Dublin, the church of Kilcullyn, with the advowson of the Rectory and Vicarage, the said Prior and Convent keeping a Canon to celebrate daily Mass at the altar before the High Cross of the Church, for the souls of the Earl, his wife, his parents, and the faithful departed (in default, power is reserved to him and his heirs to compel them), by all their lands and tenements within Kilcullyn parish), and sustaining a chantry in the said church.
Witnesses.—Roger Outlay, prior of Kilmaynan, chancellor of Ireland, Adam Bretton, seneschal of the Liberty of Kildare, Sir Peter Legleys, Sir Gerald de St. Michael, Sir John de Welesley, Sir Milo Rochfort, knights, John Barby, clerk.
Dated at Dublin, 1327.

(b.) Release of above to Robert de Gloucetyr, prior of Holy Trinity, Dublin, and the Convent thereof.
Dated at Dublin, 8th Aug., 1327.

222. Edward III., by his writ dated 1st Aug., 3 Ed. III., having commanded the Archbishop of Dublin to induct the Prior and Convent of Holy Trinity Church into the Vicarage of Kylcolin church, as the judgment against them and in favour of Thos. fitz John, earl of Kildare, had been reversed ; Sir Robert de Kykolin, the late view, who had been presented by the said Earl having resigned ; and Wm. de Rodyerd, dean of St. Patrick's, vicar-general of Archbishop Alexander who was then absent, having commanded John de Kyngeston, canon of St. Patricks and spiritual guardian of the Archdeaconate of Glendalough, on the 5th Aug., 1328, to execute the Royal writ ; the said Dean was informed on the 8th Aug. that the writ had been executed and now formally acknowledges receipt of writ and letter of resignation.

Dated at Dublin, Friday before feast of Nativity B.V.M. (2 Sep.), 1328.

223. Edward III. grants licence to Holy Trinity Church to construct a belfry with a stone wall having a crenelle and battlement.

Witness—J. Darcy le [C]hayn, Justiciary of Ireland.

Dated at Dublin 13 Jan., 3 Ed. III (1330).

224. (100.) Edward III. commands John Moris, escheator of Ireland, to restore to the Sub-Prior and Convent of Holy Trinity their temporalities, taken into his hands on the death of Robert de Gloucytr the late Prior.

Witness—brother Roger Owthawe, deputy.

Dated at Dublin 20th April, 5 Edward III. (1331.)

225. (201.) Roger Goioun, prior of Holy Trinity Church and the Convent thereof, ordain that John de Grauntsete and Alice his late wife, may participate in the Masses and other devotions celebrated in Holy Trinity Church as fully as the original founder thereof ; and bind themselves to establish two Canons to celebrate the divine office for John's health whilst he lives and his soul when dead, and for the soul of Alice—one Canon to celebrate daily the Mass of the B. V. M. with special collects for John and Alice his wife, and the other to celebrate Mass before the Holy Cross in like manner ; their anniversaries to be celebrated with the same solemnity as that of the founder, on the Assumption of the B. V. M. and on the 6th June, every Mass book to contain in the margin near the Secreta the Inscription, pray for John de Graunteete and Alice his wife. This ordinance to be entered word for word in the Martyrology, and the gold ring and precious stone with the silver chain presented by the said John, in honour of the Holy Trinity, to be suspended from the Holy Cross.

Dated at Dublin, 9th July 1335.

226. (200.) The Abbot and Convent of St. Thomas the Martyr near Dublin, agree with the Prior and Convent of Holy Trinity, to release their claim to the tithes of Coelaygh in the holding of Kynneigh, lying between the highway from Kynneigh to Adgarran and the Curragh of Kildare, and between the roads called the "Canonbothir" and the "Rathbothir ;" and to the tithes from the increase of animals depasturing thereon, save those of the Abbot. The Prior and Convent to release the other tithes out of Kynneigh.—24th July, 1335.

227. (202.) John, son of William Tuttebury of Dublin, releases to Holy Trinity Church, Dublin, land in High-street, Dublin, opposite St. Michael's Church, inherited from his mother Elena daughter of Eynulph Olyt ; between the land of John Stakepol and that of John le Sherman, and from High-street to land which belonged to Master Walter de Istelep.

Witnesses—Philip Cradok, mayor of Dublin, Roger Grauntcourt and Robert Hony, bailiffs, Robert Tanner, William Douce, Geoffrey Crump, John de Moones, William Walach, John de Balymor, clerk. Dated at Dublin, 19th Dec., 10 Edward III. (1336).

228. (204.) Pope Benedict XII. directs the Archbishop of Armagh to hear the appeal of the Prior and Chapter of Holy Trinity, Dublin, against the declaration of the Archbishop of Dublin, that the tithes of the rents of the mill in the Brigge-street, Dublin, belong to William de Burgo, as rector of St. Audoen's.
Dated at Avignon, vii. Kal. Jul., 3° Benedict XII.   (25 June, 1337).

229. (206.) Memorandum that the Escheator has returned nothing for the rents and issues of the Priory of Holy Trinity, Dublin, in the King's hands by the deposition of Roger Goioun, the late Prior, from the 6° July to the 3rd October, 11 Edward III., because the Prior who now is and his brethren, having no respect for the Royal seisin, converted the same to their own use.—Circa 1337.

230. (205 bis.) The Prior and Convent of Holy Trinity Church, Dublin, reciting that they had always held their lands in free alms, and that the King or his ancestors had never caused them to answer in the Exchequer for the temporalities, petition the Council for relief from being required to account for the temporalities taken into the hands of Edward II. on the resignation of Hugh de Suttoun, late Prior, and into the hands of the King on the deprivation of Roger Goioun, the late Prior.—Circa 1337.   (French).

231. (207.) Inquisition taken before John Gernon and John de Grauntceste, commissioners of the King at Dublin, on the feast of St. Laurence O'Tothill, 12 Edward III., by Wolfrum de Berneval, John Cristofer, Thos. Wodelok, John Balygodman, Richard Derpatrick, Michael Moungomery, Nicholas Abbot, John de Newcastle, Thomas Waleys, John Fox of Bree, John fitz Michael of Killogh, David fitz Walter, John Marchal of Rathcoull, Philip Renevil, and William King, finds that the Prior and Convent of Holy Trinity from time immemorial held in free alms, and elected their Priors without licence from the King, nor was there any restitution of their temporalities, until Walter de la Pulle, escheator of Edward II., on the resignation of Hugh le Joevene, late prior, took them into the King's hands, 19° Edward II., but restored them subject to account if found to belong to the King; John Morrion acted similarly on the death of Robert de Gloucester; Edward Morteyn and Thomas Wogan acted similarly on the deposition of Roger Goioun, 11 Edward III.; and that until those cases the King had not possession of the temporalities when the office of Prior was vacant.—14 Nov., 1338.

232. (208.) Master Richard de St. Leodgario, archdeacon of Dublin, and Holy Trinity Church, having had a suit in the church of St. Patrick, Dublin, with reference to a right of Visitation claimed by the Archdeacon in the churches of St. Michael, St. John, and St. Nichan, Dublin, Balyscadan, Glasnevyn, Clonken, and Tylangh, and to receive proxies therefor; the parties having referred the matter to Alexander, archbishop of Dublin, he established the right of the Archdeacon to proxies as follows, viz., Church of St. Michael, 32d., Church of St. John, 2s., Church of St. Michan, 2s., Church of Balyscadan, 5s., Church of Glasnevyn, 20d., Church of Clonken with its Chapels, 5s., the Church of Tylaugh, 30d. Either party refusing to abide by the award to pay 100s., by way of alms, to the Archbishop and his successors, and £10 to the other party.

Dated at Swords, 8 May, 1339.

233. Holy Trinity Church grant to John de Grauntsete, the lime pit near Ormantown Green, formerly belonging to Edward Colet, a curtilage formerly belonging to Henry Fychet, and another curtilage between St. Michan's Churchyard and those which now belong to John, but formerly belonged to Henry Fychet and Robert do Bree : Rents 2s., 2s., and 6d. respectively.

Dated 10 Jan., 1342.

234. (210.) Simon de Lodegat, prior of Holy Trinity Church, Dublin, and the convent thereof, having granted to William Porter a messuage in Ormantown, lying between the land formerly belonging to Henry Fychet and that of Nicholas Norman, and between St. Michan's churchyard and the land of Nicholas, from a portion of which they have been deforced by Ralph de Okam ; William Porter undertakes not to implead them in respect thereto.

Dated at Dublin on the feast of St. Valentine the martyr (14 Feb.), 1345.

235. (209.) Roll of accounts containing the account of brother John Comyn, seneschal, from Monday the morrow of the feast of SS. Peter and Paul, 1343, to the vigil of the following Epiphany. The receipts include rents, tithes, &c. Payments include wages of carpenters (2d. a day), and smiths for repair of ploughs, carts, &c., and of ploughmen (1d. a day); purchase of iron, nails, saddles, traces, &c. ; shoeing the prior's palfrey, and the plough and cart horses ; timber, nails, wattles, straw, for building a granary and adjoining house, and thatching stacks of corn, and wages of men employed ; repairing the well and providing a bucket and chain ; buying spades, dishes, plates, pitchforks, earthenware ; weeding, reaping, binding, and stacking the corn of the manor ; collecting and watching tithes; payments to the Archbishop, Nich. Lombard, clerk, tester of measures, master Hervey Bagot, for proxies of Kilcolyn, the Chancery clerks for writs, the private clerk of the lord justiciary for a bill to the Chancery clerks, Stephen de Gascoyne for wine, Wm. Petyt, John Gernoun, and Hugh Broun, narrators, Henry Abbot, merchant, for cloth.

Account of issues of the Autumn grain of the Haggard of Gorman to the feast of All Saints, 17° Edw. III. (1343), amounting to 104 crannocs of wheat (at 7 heaped pecks for one crannoc). This is accurately accounted for by quantities given to brother Stephen the cellarer, used for seed, used for bread in the kitchen at Gorman, and given to the different servants. The produce of oats, &c., is similarly accounted for.

Account of John Chamberleyn, bailiff of Clonkeyn, for one year, beginning feast of S. Peter ad Vincula, 1344. Receipts include pleas of court, wool, wheat, oxen, and hides sold, also clay to make earthen ware. Payments include wood and iron for ploughs ; hemp, traces, wheels, clouts, and nails, for carts ; various building materials for the house ; wages to bailiff for a year (6s. 8d.), carter and ploughmen (5s.), plough drivers (4s.) (they also received quantities of corn, &c). ; two men watching for two nights on the mountain top for fear of the Irish, 4d. The account for harvesting gives the numbers of men employed on each day, on one as many as 88 (at 1d.) ; costs of bringing in tithes ; daily account of amount of corn used for baking or brewing, with cost of herrings (16d. for 200), chickens, candles, beef, mutton, wine, geese, salt.

Account of the issues of the Haggard of Clonken, Autumn, 18° Ed. III. (1344). 211 crannocs of wheat, besides barley, oats, beans, and peas, are accounted for minutely as in the account of the Haggard of Gorman above.

Expenses of brother John Comyn, seneschal, from the Nativity, 1344. For fur for the prior's cape, and for his esquires ; fur, robes, gloves, dishes and pewter plates, tunics, and a table for the prior ; various small payments to messengers and servants, to Roger de Palesdon, kinsman of the prior ; expenses of the Seneschal and other officers on business journeys, in detail ; sent to Archbishop for Easter, a carcase of beef (9s.), two muttons (2s. 8d.), two capons, besides pigeons and kids ; gratuities to Archbishop's servants ; small expenses, include hammer for breaking stones, lock and key, straw chairs, &c. for prior's chamber ; bolts and hooks for glass windows at Glasnevin ; brother John Savage for carving and painting 18 images for the pyx (17s.) Special articles for prior's table include stockfish, capons (2d. each), hens, bread, wine, pepper, salmon, &c. Account of wine supplied to refectory on feast days. Payments of different sums due.

Account of brother Thomas de Beuley, seneschal and treasurer of the Cathedral Church of Holy Trinity, Dublin, of all receipts and expenses from Wednesday before the feast of the Nativity of St. John the Baptist, 1346, to the feast of All Saints following. The receipts include money received from the prior, from Sir Wm. Watur, chaplain, for the tithes of Kilcolyn ; from John Dolphin, sub-prior, for tithes of Kildenball ; from the Archbishop, and from Robert de Hoghton, in repayment of loans, besides smaller sums from the bailiff of Clonken, Nicholas Chamburleyn, bailiff of Glasnevyn, Philip, chaplain of Rathogell, Sir John Dendredeby, the prior of Instyok, and others. The payments include disbursements to messengers despatched for various purposes, chiefly to collect money due and to procure writs, for example, to obtain the above payment from Wm. Watur at Kilcolyn, a brother rode down attended by a horseboy, and his expenses for three days amount to 9 pence. There are presents of wine sent by command of the prior ; the expenses of the prior and suits to the parliament at Kilkenny, 22s. 8d. There are also items for paint sent to the Archbishop at Balymor and Tanelach, for wine sent to him, or provided on occasions of his visits to the church. Rose water and sugar were provided for prior Simon de Ludegate during his illness, and the materials for his coffin amount to 4s. Breakfasts and dinners for the new prior form some items, followed by a long list of meals to the prior's guests, who are usually entertained in the sacristy, with geese (3d. each), larks, baked rabbit, pigeons and fowl, roast meat, bread, wine, white wine (6d. a gallon), and ale. The guests include master John Petyt, Sir Adam de Kingeston, master Thomas of Kylemore, John of Evesham, Edm. de Byrford, Sir John Dendredby, the dean of S. Patrick's, master Wm. de Notyngham, master Simon Lichesfield, master John Dolfyn, John Haket, Wm. Haket, Thomas de Bolton, Wm. de Barton, clerk, a monk of Malverne, John Passelewe, brother Thomas de Beuley, Robert de Hoghton, Robert de Moenes, Roger de Preston, Nich. de Suytarby, John Atte Gate, the prior of S. Wlstan's, John Rous, Wm. Starre, and Thomas Pypard.

Corn is bought by the cellarer at 16d. and 13d. a peck. On one occasion ale is bought for the refectory for one whole day (on account of the default of the cellarer) costing 16d. On the day of the exaltation of the Holy Cross wine is bought for the Refectory (5d.) Among miscellaneous payments are parchment for rentals, &c., repair of prior's saddle, needles and thread for mending vestments and the banners of church, ropes, salt for salting salmon, pair of shoes for prior (5d.), stockings, shoes for Andrew keeping the tithes at Karrykbranan and another (8d. and 3d.), pitching carts, reaping at Glasnevin, small pigs (3 for 8½d.), ducks (6 for 7d.); expenses of brother Robert de Saint Neots, of John Chamburleyn, bailiff of Clonken, Hugh Bolyngos, bailiff of Gorman, and Nicholas Chamburleyn, bailiff of Glasnevyn. Various old debts of the late prior are paid, as to Richard le Rede fisherman of Oxemanton; brother William Starrs, kitchener, to aid him in his office, 4s. 8d.; for 2 bends of iron, 8s. 6d.; 2 ploughshares, 12d.

Portion of the roll is occupied by an incomplete English poem (perhaps a morality play) of about 120 quatrains written in form of dialogue, the characters being Rex, primus miles, secundus miles, regina, episcopus, and nuncio.

The following quatrain is an example:—

th" art lord of lim and life
and King w' onten onde,
stif and strong and starne in strife
In londe qwher th" waude.

A separate membrane contains a continuation of a similar account of Thomas de Houley whilst he was seneschal until the Feast of St. Mark the Evangelist, 13 Ed. III., of wine, &c., for priors table, including some additional articles as figs, plovers, mustard, pyes, oysters, white fish, almonds, ginger, olive oil (a quart 6d.), turbot, gurnard, &c.

Expenses of husbandry of Gorman, repair of buildings, ploughs, &c.; oxen bought for ploughs, 6s. to 8s.; horses at from 6s. 8d. to 10s., a bull, 32s. 6d.—Circa 1339 to 1346.

236. (211.) Gilbert, late prior of Holy Trinity Church, Dublin, and the Convent thereof, having granted to John de Grauntsete the oblations to be placed before the image of the B.V.M., on Dublin Bridge for ten years from the 20th August, 1341, in consideration of certain meritorious works to be performed before the said image, Robert de Hereforde, the present prior, gives licence to him to build a chapel in honour of the Holy Trinity in St. Michan's Churchyard, in Oxmantown, on the north side of the church, in lieu of the works to be performed on Dublin Bridge.

Dated at Dublin, Friday after the feast of the Assumption B.V.M. (17 Aug.), 1347.

237. (212 bis.) Edward III., by writ, at Westminster, 4 April, 22° year, directs the Exchequer to restore to Holy Trinity Church, its temporalities, and not to take them in any future vacancy of the office of Prior, but permit them to be held as freely as previous to the time when Walter de la Pulle, escheator of Ireland, took them into the King's hands.

Dated at Westminster, 10 April, 22 Edward III. (1348).

238. (203.) Copies of the following deeds:—

(a.) Roger Goioun, prior of Holy Trinity Church and the Convent thereof confirm to Nicholas Taaff, land of the Cross of Holy Trinity, Dublin, in Leshkaathol, as granted in the deed below.

Dated at Dublin, on Sunday, feast of the Translation of St. Thomas the Martyr, 10 Edward III. (7 July, 1336).

(b.) The Prior and Convent of Holy Trinity, Dublin, grant to Richard White, the land of the Cross of Holy Trinity, Dublin, in Lochkaathol. Rent 20s., the tithes being reserved.

Witnesses.—Thomas, bishop of Down, H. de Lacy, earl of Ulster, W., prior of St. Patrick's, Down, Robert de Maundevill, Robert Talebot, Henry the Welshman, Ralph Peltelen, Thomas fitzBishop, William Savemall, William de Fokou, Tristan de Petrapont, Richard de Petrapont, Nicholas de Dunmalea.—Circa 1224.

(c.) Holy Trinity Church, Dublin, appoints Nicholas Taaff to collect the tithes of the church of the New Town of Rath in Lechoasl ; to build the said church at his discretion, and to collect the rents of the tenants who farm the land of the Cross of Holy Trinity, Dublin.

Dated as (a) supra (7 July, 1336).

(d.) Like appointment of Roger de Hynton and Thomas Valle to collect the rent of the land of the Cross of Holy Trinity, in Lechoathel, held by Richard White.

Dated at Dublin, 10 June, 22 Edward III., 1348.

239 (213.) Will of William Foyll states that the goods of himself, his wife and children in goods, drapery, shop, salt, cellar on the quay, and debts amount to £100 ; leaves his body to be buried in the church of the Friars Preachers, and bequests to the principal altar of St. Werburgh's parish church, and the high altar of St. Audoen's church for forgotten tithes, for his burial, and to the chaplain of St. Werburgh's, the building of St. Patrick's church, the works of Holy Trinity church, the Friars Preachers, Dublin, Friars Minors, Augustinians, and Carmelites, the poor of the house of St. John without the new gate, Dublin, the church of All Saints, Robert, John, Thomas, and William Foyll, his sons, Alice Foyll his maid, his sister's son Thomas, his daughter Helena, to prove his will and to the clerk of the court ; constitutes John Mercer, chaplain, Thomas Hamound, chaplain of St. Werburgh's, his sons Robert and John and his wife Helena, executors ; leaves to his wife houses and land in Castle-street for life, with a garden in Teyngmouth-street, with reversion thereof to his right heirs ; to Robert Foyll 10s. rent from Oxmantown, and 18d. rent from Nicholas Lymberner's dwelling there ; his arms and clothes to his sons, and his household furniture and goods to his wife and sons— 22 Oct., 1348.

240 (214.) William Clanyle, clerk of Salisbury diocese, notary public, certifies that John de St. Paul, confirmed Archbishop of Dublin, appoints Stephen prior of Holy Trinity church, Dublin, vicar-general over Dublin city, diocese, and province.

Witnesses—John Caylly and John de St. Neot, Peter Grenst and William Atte Water.

Dated at London at his dwelling-house, 21 Dec., 1349.

241 (215.) Maurice fitz Thomas, earl of Kildare, confirms to Stephen de Derby, prior of the Holy Trinity church, Dublin, and the convent thereof, the grant of his father Thomas fitz John, earl of Kildare, to Robert Gloucestyr, then prior, and the convent, of the advowson of Kildolyn church, both rectory- and vicarage, the prior and convent

F

binding themselves, should they withdraw from sustaining the canon therein mentioned for one year, in 40s. to the earl and his heirs, and, should they withdraw from supporting the chantry therein mentioned, in 40s. a month.

Dated 10 May, 27° Edward III. (1353) (a fragment).

242 (216 ter.) Maurice fitz Thomas, earl of Kildare, releases to Stephen de Derby, prior of Holy Trinity, Dublin, and the convent thereof, the advowson of Kylcolyn church, both rectory and vicarage.

Witnesses—Adam Lougetoo, mayor of Dublin, John Callan and Peter Wodare, bailiffs, Geoffrey Cromp, John Serjeant, sen., Robert de Moenes, Richard Colman, clerk.

Dated at Dublin, 8 June, 27 Edward III. (1353).

243 (217.) Pope Innocent VI. directs the precentor of St. Patrick's church, Dublin, as in No. 167 supra.

Dated at Avignon, viii Kal., Feb. 5° Innocent VI. (25 Jan., 1357).

244 (218.) Account of William Topper, collarer of the cathedral church of the Holy Trinity, Dublin, of money received for buying corn and oats, A.D. 1368. He accounts for receipts from the treasurer, Robert Haket, for tithes of Dalitibyrt, for tithes of Kylleny and from Master Peter; and for payments for corn at 6s., 6s. 8d., 7s., and 5s. 4d. the crannock, and oats at 3s. 4d. the crannock.—1368.

Calendared from the "Novum Registrum."

245 (219.) John Burys and Juliana his wife release to Flynn Coterell, a curtilage in Scbepe-street, parish of St. Michael.

Witnesses.—John Passavaunt, mayor of Dublin, Roger Bekeford and John Foyll, bailiffs, and Robert Halys, clerk, John Graunsester, Thomas White, clerk, Richard White, Hugh Possewyk, Richard Hauyn, John Barbour.

Dated Thursday after the feast of the Assumption B.V.M., 44 Edward III. (22 Aug., 1370.)

246. Milo, archbishop of Armagh, acknowledges that the churches of Dromsallan and Philippestown Nugent, with their chapels, in Armagh diocese, are the property of Holy Trinity church.

Witnesses.—Odo, dean of Armagh, Master John Barunn, archdeacon of Ferns, Master Henry Rathfoygh, rector of Kylwelach, in Meath diocese.

Dated at the chapel of the manor of Tarfechine, 7 Sep., 1372.

247. John Graunsete, of Dublin, leases to Holy Trinity church, a holding in High-street, Dublin, between that of Richd. Hygrowe, formerly mayor, on the east, that of Robert Callan on the west, and extending from High-street to Rochel-street, for 98 years: Rent, a rose.

Witnesses.—Nichs. Serjaunt, then mayor of Dublin, Robt. Perys and Robt. Stakpolle, bailiffs, Peter Woder, Peter Morryle, Nichs. Mones, Edmund Boerl, Thos. Manreward.

Dated Monday feast of St. Edmund the Martyr. (20 Nov., 1374.)

248 (220.) Pope Gregory XI. to the Chapter of the Church of Dublin, stating that in the time of Thomas, late archbishop of Dublin, it was decreed that the appointment of his successor should be reserved to the Apostolic See, and that after the decease of the said Thomas he had selected Robert elect of Dublin, then archdeacon of Winchester, to be archbishop of Dublin; directs them to receive Robert with all obedience.

Dated at Avignon iv. Id. Oct., (12 Oct.), 1375, 5° Gregory XI.

249 (221.) Grantor in No. 217 *supra*, appoints William Padeacye to put the grantees in possession of the premises there.

Dated at Dublin Friday after the Nativity of St. John the Baptist, 2 Richard II. (25 June, 1378.)

250 (222.) Stephen Derby, prior of Holy Trinity church, Dublin, Adam Payne, sub-prior thereof, Nicholas Bodenhan, vicar of the Friars Hermit, order of St. Augustine in Ireland, and Nicholas Serjeant, executors of the will of Thomas son of Thomas Smothe of Dublin, John Fitzwilliam and Christiana Pembrok his wife, co-executrix of the same will, grant to Adam Clerk, of Bewmarrys, and Richard his son, a messuage on the quay, in the parish of St. Michael, Dublin, granted to testator by Richard Houth, chaplain, and William Wells, and lying between the messuage of Holy Trinity church on the east, and that of Adam Boydou, formerly belonging to John Bath, on the west, to be held for ever after the death of Christiana. This conveyance is made irrevocable according to the laws and customs of the city of Dublin.

Dated at Dublin 9 March, 2 Richard II. (1879).

251 (223.) Will of John Foyll made on Monday after the Feast of the Purification of the B.V.M., 1379, enumerates salt, iron, cow-hides, corn, meal, house utensils of silver and brass, armoury, money, £40, horses, rabbit-skins, tallow, pepper, timber, and a two-horse carriage. He owes debts to Bacine Foyll, Alice Mychell, and Bet Nogan for salt. He bequeaths his body to be buried in St. Warbargh's church, to Walter Foyll his holdings in tail male, remainder to Stephen and Thomas Foyll respectively, and failing issue to be sold for pious uses; he leaves bequests to Walter, Stephen, and Thomas Foyll, Richard his chaplain, Stephen Spark's for forgotten tithes, Thomas Ramore, John Tym, the four orders of mendicant friars, the poor of the house of St. John without the new gate, the poor in the King's castle, Thomas del Vama, St. Patrick's church, the church of St. Michael del Poll, and the church of Balymadon. He appoints Johana his wife and Walter Foyll executors, John fitz Lucas, Richard Harburgh, William Fitzwilliam, and Richard his chaplain, supervisors, he leaves £40 for wax and 2s. to prove his will, and £10 for his soul to the monastery of All Saints, and to his wife Johana, for life, the holding where Agnes North dwelt, and a garden near his house in the parish of St. Nicholas, remainder to Walter, Stephen, and Thomas Foyll as above.

Probate granted 10 May, 1380.

252 (224.) The Prelates, Lords, and Commons of Ireland summoned to a Parliament in Dublin on the quindene of Holy Trinity, 5 Richard II., being informed that the Viceroy could not attend owing to illness, protest against holding a parliament except in the presence of the principal Governor of Ireland, as no parliament had been held without such Governor from time immemorial, and that they could not accept a parliament in future contrary to this form; nevertheless, considering the great perils to themselves and the land, they will that the present assembly be regarded as a parliament, saving to them their free usages, and pray that their protest shall be enrolled in chancery and exemplified.

Witness—Roger son and heir of Edmond de Mortimer, late earl of March and Ulster, Lieutenant of Ireland.

Dublin, 22 June, 6 Richard II. (*French.*)

253 (225.) Inquisition taken before William Fitzwilliam, escheator of Ireland, at Dublin, Saturday after the Assumption B.V.M., 6 Richard II., by Thomas Botiller, John Fynglas, Laurence Wodclok, John Tyrell of Pocreston, Richard Crays of Coulmyn, Nicholas Swyterby, Walter de la Feld, Nicholas Coalok, John Walsh of Thorgelaston, Gerald Tyrell, Richard son of Richard Crnys, Henry son of Adam Walsh, Richard Mylys, Roger Arthur, William Serjaunt of Huntoston, William White of Borondeston, Robert Cadell of Sperkleyeston, and Edmond Hackutt, finds similarly to No. 230 *supra.*

Dated 16 August, 1383.

254 (226.) Robert, archbishop of Dublin, with the consent of the chapters of St. Patrick's and Holy Trinity church, ordains that ten marks shall be paid by Holy Trinity church for proxies at the annual visitation.

Witnesses.—Thomas Wafre, clerk of Dublin, notary public, by whom the deed was written, John Sandall, precentor, John Karlell, chancellor of St. Patrick's, Master William Chambers, archdeacon of Dublin, John Elys, archdeacon of Glendalough, Thomas Bache, Robert Suttoun, Robert Lython, Thomas Tanner and Stephen Sparks, canons of St. Patrick's.

Dated 7 February, 1390.

255 (227.) The Mayor and community of Dublin grant to Thomas Mawereward, of Dublin, a messuage without the gate of St. Patrick's, extending on the east from the corner of the stone wall, without the said gate, beside the King's highway, as far as the arches of the old schools there, and from the said highway beyond the watercourse of the Mill del Poll up to the land of the said schools. Rent, 12d.

Witnesses.—Thomas Cusak, mayor of Dublin, Geoffrey Gallane and Richard Bertrame, bailiffs, Hugh Possewyk, clerk, Robert Burnell, Edmond Berle, John Passavaunt, Roger Beksford.

Dated at Dublin, Friday, 4th day after the Nativity, 14 Richard II. (29 December, 1390).

256 (228.) Sir Thomas de Clyfford, knight, escheator of Ireland, undertakes not to disturb Holy Trinity church with reference to the premises in the following deeds.

Dated Thursday before Easter, 14 Richard II. (23 Mar., 1391).

(a.) John Grannsete of Dublin leases to Holy Trinity church, a messuage in High-street, Dublin, between the holding of Richard Hegrowe, formerly mayor of Dublin, on the east, and that of Robert Callans of Dublin on the west, from High-street to Rochell-street, for 98 years. Rent of one rose.

Dated at Dublin, Monday, feast of St. Edmund king and martyr, 48 Edward III. (20 Nov., 1374).

(b.) Thomas Waffre, clerk, Richard Doget, Thomas Rathmore, William Thombe, chaplains, William Greaut, Nicholas Tauffu, and Hugh Wenables, lease to Holy Trinity church, seven shops in Holy Trinity-lane, St. Michael's parish, Dublin, formerly belonging to Nicholas Meones, for 98 years. Rent 1d.

Dated at Dublin, Wednesday, the morrow of St. Matthew the Apostle (22 Sep., 1382).

257 (230.) Richard II. grants to Holy Trinity church a custodiam of the premises in No. 256 *supra* (a and b).

Witness.—James le Botiler, earl of Ormond, justiciary of Ireland. Dated at Dublin, 5 Jun., 16 Richard II. (1393).

258. (230.) Richard II. grants licence to Holy Trinity church to acquire, notwithstanding the Statute of Mortmain, lands, &c., to the value of 100 marks a year; such as are held of the King to be held in frankalmoign, and such as are held of the chief lords of the fee to be held by the services due thereout.

Dated at Dublin, 20 Nov., 18 Ric. II. (1394).

259. Richard II. grants licence to Thos. Waffre, clerk, Wm. Thoume, chaplain, Wm. Gronot and Nicholas Taaf, to alienate to Holy Trinity Church, seven shops in Trinity lane, parish of St. Michael, Dublin, held in free burgage by the service of landgable; and to Thos. Comyn, of Ballygriffin, to alienate to the said Church, Ballygriffin and the advowson of its Church, held in capite.

The premises were found by inquisition before John Aldelyme, eschator of Ireland, to be of the yearly value of £7 13s. 4d.; and are to be held in frankalmoign, as of the yearly value of £20, portion of the 100 marks referred to in No. 258 supra.

Witness.—Roger de Mortimer, earl of March and Ulster, Lieutenant of Ireland.

Dated at Dublin, 8 July, 19 Ric. II. (1395).

260. Thomas Comyn, lord of Daligriffyn, grants to Holy Trinity Church, land called Cloghanagh, in Baligriffyn, lying opposite the lands of Daligriffyn Church, between the road from Baligriffyn to St. Dulck's on the west, the small meadow on the north, and the Glynd pasture on the south, together with the advowson of Baligriffyn Church.

Witnesses.—Sir Richd. Talbot and Sir John Cruce, knts., Robert White of Kyllestyr, John Talbot of Mayne.

Dated 8 July, 1395.

261. Thos. Comyn, lord of Ballygryffyn, is bound in 200 marks to Holy Trinity Church. Should the Church peaceably enjoy the premises in No. 260 supra, this bond to be void.

Dated at Dublin, 8 July, 19 Ric. II. (1395).

262. Similar to No. 261 supra.

Dated 10 July, 1395.

263. Release in confirmation of No. 260 supra.

Dated 20 July, 19 Ric. II. (1395).

264. (231.) The Prior and Convent of Holy Trinity and the Dean and Chapter of St. Patrick's, Dublin, appoint Robert, prior of Holy Trinity, and Robert Suttonn, canon of St. Patrick's, administrators of the See of Dublin, vacant by the death of Archbishop Richard.

Dated xvii. Kal. Aug. (16 July), 1397.

265. (233.) Henry IV. prohibits the Archbishop of Dublin and his commissaries from hearing the suit between John White, chaplain, and James de Rodenesso, the prior, and the convent of Holy Trinity church, Dublin, concerning the advowson of St. Sampson's of Balygriffyn, granted Holy Trinity church by Thomas Comyn, William Norragh being then chaplain, after whose death John White being presented thereto by Maria, wife of said Thomas Comyn, claimed same in the Court of Christianity.

Witness—Thomas de Lancoster, seneschal of England and Lieutenant of Ireland.

Dated at Kenlys, 17 May, 4 Hen. IV. (1403).

266 (232.) Thomas, archbishop of Dublin, prays the King to grant him a writ of consultation to proceed in the matter notwithstanding the writ of prohibition calendared No. 265 *supra.* The petition of John White, chaplain, praying to be admitted to Balygriffyn follows.—*Circa* 1403.

267 (234.) James, prior of the church of Holy Trinity, Dublin, reciting that two writs of consultation, one purchased in England, the other in Ireland, were issued to the Archbishop of Dublin, setting aside the writ of prohibition, No. 265 *supra,* petitions Lord Thomas de Lancastre, son of the King, seneschal of England and Lieutenant of Ireland, to recall the writs of consultation, or to remove the proceedings into Chancery or before the King's Council.—*Circa* 1403 (*French*).

268 (235.) Cecilia Hegreue grants to Holy Trinity church, the reversioners, her life estate in premises in St. Patrick-street, Rupell-street, St. Francis-street, Cook-street, High-street, Scarlet-lane, Ram-lane, beside the Polgate, and in Oxmantown.
Dated at Dublin, 10 Sept., 1404.

269 (236.) Holy Trinity church grants to Cecilia Hegreue, during her life, a rent of 20 marks, chargeable on its possessions in Dublin.—*Circa* 1404.
A copy, to which is added a copy of No. 268 supra.

270 (237.) Pope Innocent VII. confirms to Holy Trinity church, Dublin, all its liberties, privileges, and immunities.
Dated at St. Peter's, Rome, v. Non. Jul., 2° Innocent VII. (3 Jul., 1406).

271. Maria Burnell, widow of Thos. fitzWm. Comyn, knt., grants to Holy Trinity church, the premises in No. 260 *supra.*
Witnesses—John Drake, then mayor of Dublin, Walter Tyrrell and Robt. Gallon, then bailiffs, Thos. Cusak, Nichs. Woder, and Thos. Schortals, clerk of the city.
Dated 30 Aug., 1406.

272. Thomas Everdon and Thomas Waffre, canons, Vicars-General, in St. Patrick's church, adjudge Sir John White to pay 20s. for taking possession, on the death of Sir Wm. Norragh, the late rector, of Balygryffyn church, the right of Holy Trinity church.
Witnesses—Sir Robert Croll, prebendary of Swords, Thomas Cusak, of Dublin, Richard Carran, archdeacon of Dublin, William Pyrrou, Nicholas Wafre, and Thomas Peyntour.
Dated 30 Aug., 1406.

273 *bis.* Similar to No. 272 *supra.*
Dated 7 Oct., 1406.

274 (238.) Richard, son of Walter Passavaunt, releases to Holy Trinity Church, his claim to the Ramme in High-street, Dublin, lying between the holdings formerly belonging to Peter Woder and John de Grauntsete, citizens of Dublin, and extending from High-street to Rupell-street.
Dated at Dublin, 12 Nov. 10° Hen. IV. (1408).

275. Exchequer decree setting out that it appearing by the Exchequer accounts that 20s. was received by Thomas Petyt, deputy of John Aldelyn, late escheator of Meath, Louth, Dublin, and Kildare, from land belonging to Wm. Norragh, rector of Balygryffyn, taken into the

King's hands, by Sir Thomas de Clyfford, escheator of Ireland, Holy Trinity Church, as tenant thereof, was sued for the arrears.   A jury consisting of Simon Coslok, John Walsh of Surcoteston and others, summoned by Walter Tyrrell, Sheriff of Dublin County, having found that the premises had never been seised into the King's hands, but belonged to the said church, as rector of Balygryffyn, from time immemorial, the Court exonerated it from the arrears.

Enrolled in the Memorandum Rolls of the Exchequer, Michaelmas term, 6° Hen. V. (1418.)

276 (239.) Richard, archbishop of Dublin, reduces the proxies payable by Holy Trinity Church to 5 marks (see No. 254 *supra*).

Witnesses.—John Bryin, notary public, Master John Volsyn, Thomas Walsche, bachelors of law, William Podings, chaplain, and John Charnells, esquire.

Dated at Dublin, 27 Feb., 1421.

277 (240.) Richard, archbishop of Dublin, reciting that in solemn processions the Prior of Holy Trinity and the Dean of St. Patrick's together took the principal place after the Archbishop, then came the sub-prior of Holy Trinity and the precentor of St. Patrick's together, and after them the Canons of the Churches two by two, directs the Prior and Canons of Holy Trinity to wear cloaks with gray fur outside and monyver inside in solemn processions.

Dated at the Church of Holy Trinity, Dublin, 1 March, 1421.

(*This document is very much damaged*).

278 (242.) Nicholas Stauntoun, prior of Holy Trinity Church, grants to John Drake, late mayor of Dublin, that two Canons in every Mass they celebrate daily shall say a devout collect for him, his parents, and for the souls of John Buklane and Isabella his wife, the former wife of the said John Drake, and for all the souls of the faithful departed, and celebrate his anniversary on the Sunday after Easter, in which is chanted "*Quasimodo geniti.*"

Dated 5 April, 10 Henry V. (1422).

279 (241.) Richard, archbishop of Dublin, reduces to 10s. 8d. a rent of [   ] payable by John Barron, for land in Jurdaneston, parish of Glasnethan.

Dated 25 Apl., *circa* 1423.

280 (243.) William de Tynbegh, treasurer of Ireland, directs Richard, archbishop of Dublin, chancellor of Ireland, to grant to Richard Vale a custodiam of land lately belonging to Thomas Leger, clerk, in Eliestonrede, on the security of Henry Stanyhurst and James Delahyde, clerks, of Meath.

Dated, 12 March, 2 Henry VI. (1424).

281 (244.) William, son and heir of Richard Chaumberleyn, formerly of Dublin, grants to Robert Chamer of Dublin, lands of the said Richard, in Shepe street, suburbs of Dublin, lying between Shepe street on the west and the lands of All Saints and John Passavant on the east, and between the land of the said John on the north and the street near the cemetery of the Carmelite Friars on the south.

Dated 11 April, 2 Henry VI. (1424).

282 (245.) Pope Martin V., at the request of the Brethren and Sisters de poenitentia of the Franciscan order, grants an inspeximus of a Bull

of Pope Nicholas IV., dated at Rieti, xv. Kal. Sep., 2nd year of his Pontificate, with reference to the rules and regulations to be observed by the said order.

Dated at Rome, v Non. Maii, 8° Martin V. (3 May, 1424).

283 (246.) Richard, archbishop of Dublin, reduces the proxies payable by Holy Trinity Church to 2½ marks. (See Nos. 254 and 276 supra).

Witnesses.—John Bryis and Thomas Peyntour, notaries public, Nicholas Moynagh, official of Dublin and canon of St. Patrick's Church, Thomas Walsche, bachelor-of-laws, John York, chaplain, John Cuske, and Robert Cuske, esqrs.

Dated at Dublin, 2 May, 1426.

284 (247.) Nicholas Staunton, prior of Holy Trinity Church, Dublin, and the convent thereof, lease to Robert de Island of Dublin, Juliana Blake, his wife, John de Irland, and Iamay Philpot, his wife, land in Ponchestown, co. Kildare, for [   ] years. Rent 1d. for 6 years, and 40s. after ; should the lessees die without heirs, or the rent be in arrear for three months, the premises to revert to the Prior and Convent ; lessees are bound to build within six years and keep in repair, 6 tenements thereon.

Dated 13 June, 4 Henry VI. (1426.)

285 (248.) William fitz Thomas, prior of the Hospital of St. John of Jerusalem in Ireland and the brethren thereof, confirm the grant of Roger Outlaghe, late prior, and the brethren thereof, to Holy Trinity Church, of 10 pounds of wax at the feast of Holy Trinity yearly. The said wax or 40d. therefor, to be leviable off Kilmaynan.

Dated 25 July, 1428.

286 (249.) Pope Eugenius IV., reciting that the tithes of fish, taken by the Parishioners of St. Michan's parish, belonged to Holy Trinity Church until the Monastery of the B. V. M. near Dublin claimed them by summons before James Coytyuse, prior of St. John the Baptist without the New Gate, Dublin, and afterwards before the Priors of St. Lawrence and Ss. John of Drogheda, and John Elyote, rector of Clonmore church, dioceses of Meath and Armagh, to whom respectively Richard, abbot of the Monastery of St. Thomas the Martyr, Dublin, conservator, had committed his powers, that Holy Trinity Church objected that they were not qualified to hear the case according to the constitutions of Pope Boniface VIII. and appealed ; directs the Bishop and Archdeacon of Kildare and the Prior of All Hallows, Dublin, to hear the appeal.

Dated at Florence, iii. Id. Nov., 5° Eugenius IV. (11 Nov. 1435).

287 (352.) Pope Eugenius IV. directs the priors of St. John, All Saints without the walls, and St. Wulstans, Dublin, to hear the complaint of the prior and chapter of Holy Trinity Church, Dublin, that the Abbot and Couvent of the Monastery of the B. V. M. without the walls, Dublin, and Robert, archdeacon of the same church, have molested them with reference to the tithes of fish taken in Anfliffi.

Dated at Bologna, xi. Kal. Jan., 7° Eugenius IV. (22 Dec., 1437).

288 (251.) Pope Eugenius IV. confirms the grant of Richard, archbishop of Dublin, No. 288, supra.

Dated at Bologna, iii. Non. Jan., 7° Eugenius IV. (3 January, 1438).

289 250.) Pope Eugenius IV. grants an indulgence of 4 years and 160 days to those who, being penitent and having confessed devoutly

visit the church of Holy Trinity, Dublin, annually on the Sunday on which is chanted "Lætare Jerusalem," and bestow alms towards its repair and preservation.

Dated at Ferrara, xii. Kal. Mar., 7° Engenius IV. (18 Feb., 1438).

290 (253.) Will of Robert, son of John Passavaunt, junior, clerk, made 6 May, 1439, diocese of Dublin, enumerates his goods, vizt :— a silver cup called "grobb" worth 40s., another worth 20s., another called piper, worth 20s., a coat of mail, worth 40s., a short sword, worth 6s. 8d., and other goods, and the debts due him by Robert Stafford, John Hauwood, Nicholas Dowgane, William Rede, Robert Stratown, John Houley, serjeant, James Owoyn on a brass pot in pledge, Christopher Russell, Nicholas Clerke, Arland Cabere, merchant, the tenants of Tamloge, and by Hugh Sadler for a horse, 10s.; also the debts due by him, vizt :—To Philip Bedlow, to Thomas Schorthals, Thomas Hankyn, Thomas Schorthals, junior, Thomas Bertenagh, William Champancyne, merchant, John Wayte, Juliana Passavaunt, Arland Usher, merchant, Robert Tankard, Moline Wyntyr, Rawlin Helyer, Agnes Holdfast, John Wyxaune, Magine Ryver, Robert Stafford, merchant, Christopher Russell, and to the receiver of Castleknoc. He bequeaths his body to be buried in the chapel of the B. V. M. of Holy Trinity Church, Dublin, and money for the burial, wax, bread, ale, spices and wine. He bequeaths to the four orders, to the priests for his obsequies, and tolling the bells in various churches, to Geoffrey Calffo, chaplain, for the repair of the chapel of St. John of Boale street; he leaves his cup called Grubbe to his mother, Johanna Clerke, for life, and afterwards to Holy Trinity Church, his cup called piper to John Clerke, chaplain, and another silver cup to his mother, for life, and afterwards to the high altar of the church of St. John for a chalice, his garden called Darndale to John Abbay, flecher, for life, all his lands to his mother, for life, except the house where Nicholas Clerke inhabits on the quay, and the house which Walter Morvyll, "sporier," inhabits in Skinners street, which are left to them during their lives, afterwards to Juliana Passavaunt, for life, and then to the church of Holy Trinity; executors—John Clerke, chaplain, and Johanna Clerke, his mother.

Proved 31 May, 1439.

291 (254.) Will of Robert Chambre, formerly mayor of Dublin, who leaves his body to be buried in the chapel of the B. V. M., in Holy Trinity Church, his property to Johanna, his wife, and his niece, Johanna, wife of John Brayne; and on their deaths without issue, to Holy Trinity Church. He appoints his wife, niece, and John Brayne, executors. An inventory of his goods was furnished by them on the 18th July, 1441.

Proved 29 Apr., 1441.

292 (257.) John Doune of Dublin, skinner, Johanna, his wife, and Marion White, formerly wife of Thomas Edwards, release to Holy Trinity Church, Dublin, a messuage formerly belonging to John White, and situate within the Polgot, Dublin, between the King's way leading to the Polgot on the west, the stone house called the townprison, occupied by Robert de Irland and held of the Mayor and Commons of Dublin on the east, the prison lane on the north, and the stone wall of the city on the south.

Dated 13 May, 19 Henry VI. (1441).

293 (255.) Henry VI. grants to Holy Trinity Church, Dublin, £20 annuity, for 20 years, out of his fee farm in Dublin from the mayor

and bailiffs thereof; a former grant of the 3 June, 20 Henry VI., being now cancelled.

Dated at Westminster, 16 June, 22 Henry VI. (1444.)

Enrolled in the Memorandum Rolls of the Exchequer, Michaelmas Term, 23 Henry VI.

Enrolled in Domysday, Michaelmas Term, 23 Henry VI.

294 (256.) Henry VI. grants licence to William Denys, prior of Holy Trinity Church, Dublin, and the convent thereof, and to Nicholas Hyll, dean of St. Patrick's, and the chapter thereof, to elect an Archbishop of Dublin, in the room of Richard, the late archbishop.

Witness—Richard, Duke of York, Lieutenant of Ireland.

Dated at Drogheda, 22 August, 27 Henry VI. (1449).

295. The Mayor and Bailiffs of Dublin city certify that Smoys court beside Donaghbrok is within the franchises of Dublin city.

Dated 22 Mar., 28 Hen. VI. (1450) (*English*).

296 (258.) Will of Thomas, son of John Cusake, sets out his goods vizt.:—Two chequer boards, worth 10s., a sword, worth 6s. 8d., two mantles with one cape, 8s. 4d., and debts due him by John Grosse, Margery Roche, and Mauris Ocks; leaves his body to be buried in Holy Trinity Church, to which he leaves all his lands and tenements in the city of Dublin; he leaves to Thomas Bath, escheator of Ireland, his lands in the county of Meath, money for wax, and for his obsequies, a chequer board of ivory with the men to the Prior of Holy Trinity Church, and another of cypress with the men to the sub-prior, his sword to Richard Browne, a house in High street, parish of St. Michael, Dublin, inhabited by William B[ourke] "Obcarman," to Richard and Johanna Wyse, his wife, during their lives, reversion to Holy Trinity Church, the remainder of his goods to William Lynton, sub-prior of Holy Trinity Church, and Thomas Bath, his executors, for the good of his soul.

Dated 20 Jan., 1451.

297 (259.) Edward IV., considering the injuries by Irish rebels to the property of Holy Trinity Church, Dublin, and the destruction of the two chief windows, commonly called Gabilles, which cannot be restored without the aid of christians and the oblations of pilgrims, with the assent of Sir Roland fits Eustace, knight, lord of Portlester, deputy of George, duke of Clarence, lord lieutenant of Ireland, takes into his protection all who shall come to the said church, as well English rebels as Irish enemies in time of war or peace for the sake of pilgrimage or presenting alms, and return thence to their own affairs; every safe conduct to last for 8 days and to apply to the goods of the persons making the pilgrimage; and the granting safe conducts to cease after 3 years.

Dated at Dublin, 26 Oct., 2 Edward IV. (1462).

298 (260.) In the church of Holy Trinity, Dublin, on the 17 September, 1463, before John Bowland, notary public, William Lynton, prior of the church, Robert Warren, official of Dublin, Thomas Warren, canon of St. Patrick's and commissary general of the Dean, Sir Robert Dowdall, chief justice of the King's Common Bench in Ireland, William Suttoun, baron of the Exchequer, Richard Harford, chaplain, and John Hygley, of Dublin; John Walyngton, vicar of Donabate, Dublin diocese, deposes that Johanna Seynt Leger, formerly wife of Thomas Suetterby, gentleman, constituted him executor, and left him all her

lands except Blakiston, left to Holy Trinity church, Mapartiston, to the church of Athirde, and one half of Cuakiston to the church of Tavelaght, if that half could be legally bequeathed, otherwise the town of Mapartiston to be divided between the churches of Athirde and Tavelaght.

John Power, chaplain, deposes to the like effect, but added that a house in Athirde was left to a woman called Marion, and another to Elena Leger, whether for their lives or not he does not recollect.

Margery Prestoun, gentlewoman, deposes she was present when Johanna left everything to Thomas Suetterby.

17 Sep., 1463.

299 (261.) In the chapel of the B. V. M., St. Patrick's church, Dublin, John Rathe, chaplain, and John Roche, citizen of Dublin, depose that two years ago they heard James Palmer alias Tiler, declare that, 30 years before, Alicia Lawless, his wife, bequeathed to Holy Trinity Church, Dublin, her lands in Rathmore, diocese of Dublin, and directed deeds thereof to be delivered immediately to the Prior by her husband, as the said Alicia declared that Matthew Crumpe, her first husband, left them to the church after her death. The said James detained them, but the Prior of Holy Trinity Church and Thomas Boneville being brought to him he delivered them up in the presence of deponents.

Witnesses—John Bowland, notary public, James Selyman, John Swetman, William Bonvill.

Dated 5 July, 1467.

300 (262.) Peter White, abbot of the Monastery of the B. V. M., Navan, diocese of Meath, and the Convent thereof, authorise Nicholas Crum, one of the canons, to absent himself on a pilgrimage to Rome and schools for study, for 10 years.

Dated 3 April, 1468.

301 (264.) William Donogh, John Whitaker, and Matthew Fowler, executors of the will of Walter Donogh, late citizen of Dublin, acknowledge receipt from William Lynton, prior of Holy Trinity Church, of £14 13s. 4d. on account of £84 due under the bond of the Prior and Convent, dated 15 May, 8 Edward IV.

Dated 14 May, 10 Edward IV. (1470).

302 (263.) John Alleyn, dean of St. Patrick's and the chapter thereof, having bound themselves on the 18th Mar., 12 Ed., IV. to the prior and convent of Holy Trinity in 100 marks, they agree that this bond shall be void should the prior and convent suffer no loss in respect of a deed, dated 20 Feb., 11 Ed. IV., whereby Richard Eustace, treasurer of St. Patrick's, and late prebend of the further portion of Luak (on behalf of the said dean and with the assent of Wm. Lynton, prior of Holy Trinity, and the said dean, custodians of Dublin diocese, the See being vacant), leases to Simon Fitz Rery, merchant of Dublin, Robert Fitz Rery, "narrator," and Patrick Fitz Leones, merchant of Dublin, the profits of the prebend of further Luak and the glebe thereof, at a rent of 40 marks until they shall be repaid a sum of £80.

Dated 23 Mar., 12° Ed. IV. (1472). (*Partly in English.*)

303 (264°.) Like receipt as in No. 301 *supra*, for £8.

Dated 8 May, 13 Edward IV. (1473).

304 (265.) In the Western Gate of the precincts of St. Patrick's, Dublin, David Wynchester and Thomas Fyche, canons of Holy Trinity,

Dublin, and Nicholas Beket, of St. John of Jerusalem, farmer of their manor of Clontarf near Dublin, agree, with reference to the tithes of salmon taken at Polbeg in the river Aniliffy, (Walter Whithir, James White, John Ullester, and Denis Gaffney, takers of salmon there, being cited at the instance of the Prior of St. John, having appeared personally), in accordance with the testimony of Sir Robert Dowdall, chief justice of the King's Common Bench in Ireland, who had held the farm of the manor of Clontarf for various years from the Hospital aforesaid, that he never received tithes of the salmon taken at Polbeg, but that the Prior and Convent of Holy Trinity had always enjoyed them peacefully.

Witnesses—John Bowlond, notary public, Philip Bermyngham, esq., Richard Nangle, clerk, Robert de Lyn, clerk, John Dous, John Severn, William Reagh, Patrick Tole, Christopher fitz Eustace, and Master Thomas Northerne, notary public.

Dated 23 May, 1473.

305 (260.) William Corr, vicar of the church of the B. V. M. of Athirde, and Walter Verdon, chaplain thereof, confirm to William Lynton, prior of Holy Trinity, Dublin, and the Convent thereof, the lands granted to them by John de Seyutlegger in Blakiston, co. Louth, and in the parish of Kildymok.

Dated 26 April, 14 Edward IV. (1474).

Attached is a release dated 29 April, 14 Edward IV. (1474).

306 (307.) Edward IV. reciting that the Chapters of St. Patrick's and Holy Trinity, Dublin, having appeared, at a Parliament held in Dublin, on Friday after the feast of St. Margaret the Virgin last past, before William, bishop of Meath, deputy of George, Duke of Clarence, by John Leche, chancellor of St. Patrick's and Thomas Fyche, canon of Holy Trinity, who granted £23 6s. 8d., for the wages of 100 archers and 40 horsemen, and selected Richard Skirrett, canon of Holy Trinity, and Robert White, chaplain of St. Audoen's, as collectors, with the assent of David Wynchester, sub-prior of Holy Trinity, and James Hacket, canon of St. Patrick's; commands the said collectors to levy and deliver the same to Walter, abbot of the B.V.M., Dublin, Robert, lord Houth, and Robert Holywood, esq., receivers duly appointed; one half to be delivered before the feast of the Nativity of the B.V.M. next ensuing, and the other half before the feast of St. Martin, Bishop, then next ensuing.

Dated at Dublin, 4 Aug., 15 Edward IV. (1475).

307 (208.) Thomas, prior of Holy Trinity Church, Dublin, and the Convent thereof, grant to Philip Bermyngham, chief justice of the King's Bench, the custody during minority of Alexander Balfe, son and heir of William Balfe together with his marriage, as William held land in Kynsaly, Co. Dublin, of the late Prior of Holy Trinity by homage.

Dated at Dublin, 20 Feb., 16 Edward IV. (1477).

308 (269.) William Sutton, baron of the Exchequer, grants to Thomas Harold, prior, and the Convent of Holy Trinity Church, all his goods (except two silver cups) reserving his life use, and deposes that should his son Nicholas claim any right to the aforesaid goods by reason of any grant, he has made no other grant.

Present—John Bowlond, notary public, master Richard Fyche, official of Dublin, Robert Water, chaplain, John Strete, lawyer, Thomas Petite, clerk, and John Brakdall, literate.

Dated 4 May, 1477.

309 (271.) Robert Noryce of Dublin, esq., and Jonets Chamber, his wife, cousin and heiress of Robert Chamber late mayor of Dublin, grant to Thomas, prior of Holy Trinity church, Dublin, and the convent thereof, their possessions in Dublin city and suburbs, Lucan and Waspaylcston, co. Dublin, and in Thurstaldermot, co. Kildare, which premises came to grantor's wife, as daughter of Robert Chamber, senior, brother of the said Robert Chamber, junior.

Witnesses—Sir Robert Donedall, Philip Byrmyngham, esq., John Bedlowe, esq., Thomas Fitz Symond, John Estcrret.

Dated at Dublin, 23 Aug., 17 Edward IV. (1477).

310 (271ᵃ.) Grantors in No. 309 *supra* appoint Simon Glasier of Dublin, yeoman, to deliver possession of the premises therein.

Dated Dublin, 23 Aug., 17 Edward IV. (1477).

311 (271ᵇ.) Grantees in No. 309 *supra* appoint Peter Protofote, yeoman, to receive possession of the premises therein.

Dated at Dublin, 23 Aug., 17 Edward IV. (1477).

312 (270.) Octavian del Palatio, priest of Florence, nuncio in Ireland and the adjacent isles, reciting that pope Sextus IV. had granted a plenary indulgence to the faithful visiting churches in Ireland, appointed by the papal nuncio, and there saying thrice the seven psalms with the lections, or the Lord's prayer and angelic salutation 60 times, and giving for the aid of the cross and holy faith, if archbishops, bishops, earls, or countesses 2 marks, if abbots, barons, or baronesses 1½ marks, if nobles or doctors 1 mark, and all others half a mark, provided they be penitent and have confessed; appoints the churches of Holy Trinity, St. Patrick's, Dublin, the B.V.M. of Drogheda, and St. Thomas, as such churches, for two months.

Dated at Dublin, 1 Oct., 7° Sextus IV. (1477).

313 (272.) Edward IV. reciting that the dean and chapter of the cathedral churches of Holy Trinity and St. Patrick's, Dublin, appeared by Walter fitz Simond, precentor of St. Patrick's, and Thomas Fyche, canon of Holy Trinity, at a Parliament in Trym, on Wednesday after the feast of All Saints last past, before Henry lord Grey, deputy of George duke of Clarence, and thence adjourned to Drogheda, granted to the deputy £23 6s. 8d., and selected Nicholas Loghun, canon, and Adam Gary, chaplain of St. Werburgh's, with the assent of Richard Eustace, treasurer of St. Patricks, to collect it; commands the collectors to levy and deliver the same to the hands of the deputy and Robert (sic).

Dated at Drogheda, 20 Nov., 18° Edward IV. (1478).

314 (276.) Johanna Power, widow of William Thondir, husbandman, deposes that her husband held at a yearly rent from Wm. Suttoun, then baron of the Exchequer, a messuage with a loft on the south side of St. Warburge's church, between the orchard of Thos. Foyll, citizen of Dublin, on the east, St. Warburges-street on the west, and the lands of St. Warburges church on the north and south; and that she had heard Wm. Suttoun will that his son Nicholas should have the same, but nobody else was present nor did she see seisin delivered to the said Nicholas.

Witnesses—John Sowland, not. pub., John Estrayt, lawyer, John Proutfot, Richard White, John Mulghan, Thomas Sprote, Peter Proutfot, Nicholas Walshe, John Raynolds, and Thomas Bardor.—25 Aug., 1478.

315 (275.) Thomas Eyre, yeoman, Patrick Gerot, citizen of Dublin, John Cradok and Christiana Nugent, his wife, depose that they heard Nicholas Suttoun, late baron of the Exchequer, express, on his death-bed, his sorrow for the great injury he had done to his father, William Suttoun, late baron of the Exchequer, by detaining his goods: and Christiana Nugent, his nurse, heard him declare that he wished resti-tution to be made for such goods, as well as for the house he dwelt in against his father's consent.

Witnesses— John Bowlond, not. pub., Peter Prountefote, Patrick White, and John Alexander.

17 Nov., 1478.

316 (274.) Wm. Sutton, late baron of the Exchequer in Ireland, grants to the Prior of Holy Trinity church, Dublin, his shops called News Rent on the key, Dublin, and his lands in Athboy, for ten years, at the accustomed rent, and after his death leaves them the promise in frankalmoign.

Witnesses — Sir Robt. Dowedalle, Thos. Bardore, clerk, John Elymndyr, Laurence Gafry, clerk, Peter Prowcford, John Laynagh, Robert Skyret, not. pub., and John Bowlond, not. pub.

19 January, 1479.

317 (274ʹ.) Wm. Sutton, late baron of the Exchequer in Ireland, declares that he had granted to Thos. Abell of Athboy, chaplain, his shops called the New Rent on the key, Dublin, in trust, to dispose of them as the said Wm. should direct; and that it is his will that the said Thomas should grant them to the Prior and Convent of Holy Trinity in frankalmoign.

Witnesses as in No. 316 supra, except John Bowlond, not. pub.

10 Jan. 1479.

318 (277.) Inquisition taken at Clony on Monday after the feast of SS. Philip and James, 19 Edward IV., before Nicholas Rovoe, clerk, seneschal of the court of Thomas Plunket for the manor of Gonnok, by John Gryffyn, Thomas Lamkyn, Philip Mellyn, James Welsh, William White, Thomas White, James Broun, Richard Cristyn, John Thondyr, John Walsh, Patrick Russell, and Thomas Roch, jurors, finds that John Haklet died seised of Portan and Clony, held of the manor of Gonnok by service of 21s. and suit of court, that Margaret Haklet, daughter and heiress of the said John, is 30 years of age and upwards, and has married Thomas Sprot.

Dated 3 May, 1479.

319 (279 bis.) Thomas Bennet, son and heir of John Bennet, late mayor of Dublin, for the souls of himself, Elizabeth Bellew, his wife, his father, Johanna Sueterby, his mother, and his friends, grants to Thomas, prior of Holy Trinity Church, Dublin, and the convent thereof, Bally-more, county Kildare, held of the archbishop of Dublin as of his manor of Ballymore in capite, to sustain 4 choristers to be instructed and to assist at certain specified divine services; grantor to have some further religious privileges.

Witnesses—John Fyane then mayor of Dublin, Wm. Grampey and Thos. Myler, bailiffs, Phil. Bermyngham, chief justice, King's Bench, and Sir Robert Douedall, chief justice, Common Pleas.

One dated at Ballymore and the other at Chapter House, Holy Trinity church, 15 April, 20 Edward IV. (1480).

320 (260ᵃ.) Grantees in No. 510 *supra* appoint Nicholas Clerke. gentleman, to receive seisin of the premises therein.
Dated at Ballymore, 15 April, 20 Edward IV. (1480).

321 (280.) Grantor in No. 310 *supra* appoints Richard Roche, yeoman, to deliver seisin of the premises therein.
Dated at Ballymore, 15 April, 20 Edward IV. (1480).

322. Thomas Launday, chaplain, grants to Holy Trinity church, one-half the New Rent, on the key of Dublin, granted to him by Thos. Abell, of Athboy, chaplain.
Dated 23 April, 20 Ed. IV. (1480).

323. Thomas Launday, chaplain, grants to Holy Trinity church lands in Athboy, granted to him by Thos. Abell, of Athboy, chaplain.
Dated 26 April, 20 Ed. IV. (1480).

324 (281ᵃ *bis.*) Grantor in No. 323 *supra* appoints [Robert Scurlog], of Athboy, and Simon Glasyer, yeoman, to deliver seisin of the premises therein.
Dated 26 April, 20 Edward IV. (1480).

325 (281.) Grantees in No. 323 *supra* appoint Peter Prontefote, yeoman, to receive seisin of the premises therein.
Dated 26 April, 20 Edward IV. (1480).

326 (276.) Exemplification of proceedings in chancery by the Prior and convent of Holy Trinity church with reference to one-half of the shops called the New Rent, on the key, Dublin, and the shops called the New Work in Athboy. The Bill sets out that Sir Thomas Abell, chaplain, was seised of the premises to the use of Wm. Sutton, one of the Barons of the Exchequer, and assigned them to Sir Thomas Launday, chaplain, for Holy Trinity church; and that Patrick Burnell, gent., husband of Anne Cusake, formerly wife to Nicholas son of Wm. Sutton, and Walter, abbot of the B. V. M., near Dublin, claim them under a release from Sir Thos. Abell to Nichs. Sutton, who left them to Anne for life, remainder to the said Abbot. Robert Scurlok, of Athboy, named as witness to the release, deposed that no release had been made to anybody except Sir T. Launday, but that Nicholas Tege, of Athboy, had informed him that the premises had been given by Wm. Sutton to his son Nicholas. Sir Thos. Abell deposed before Comrs. John Danstan, justice of the Pleas, Richard Nangle, clerk and custos of the Hanaper, Thos. Dardys, late provost, and Thos. Wattenhall, recorder of Athboy, that, having been seised of the premises to the use of Wm. Sutton, the reversion after the death of Alison Darby, wife of said Wm., belonged to him, but he never released them to Nichs. Sutton.
Dated 22 Sep., 1480.

327. (273.) John Fynglas, official of the Court of Dublin, exemplifies for the proctor of St. Warburge's, Dublin, the will of Nicholas Suttowne, clerk, who leaves his body to St. Warburge's Church to be buried, and a crucifix; the house where he lives, the New rent on the key, and a third part of his goods to his wife for jointure; he leaves legacies to the monastery of the monks of the B.V.M., the four orders of Friars, his five boys, the prison at the Castle and the lepers, for victuals, the poor of St. John without the walls, Dublin, Anne White, Walter Holme, John Waltir, the poor of Rechell-street, Simon Walshe, clerk, a priest to celebrate for him for three years the trental of St. Gregory, his father for his blessing, Justice Dowedall for restitution, Philip Bermyn-

lum to look after his wife, children and rents; to Walter Ryan, James Clerke, and to Adam Cory: should his heirs die without issue he bequeaths one half his lands in England and Ireland to St. Warburgo's Church for the support of a priest to pray for the souls of himself his wife, &c., and the other half to the abbot and monks of St. Mary near Dublin; he leaves 6s. 8d. to his rector for forgotten tithes, and constitutes John Suttown, his son, and Anne Cusack, his wife, executors, Walter Champflour, abbot of St. Mary's, to be supervisor and tutor over his children.

Dated 20th July, 1478, and probate granted 8th August, 1478.

The copy above was sealed by the official on the 9th January, 1479.

Hugh Blakton, archdeacon of Dublin, attached his official seal to the same copy on the 16th October, 1480, in presence of John Bowland, notary public, Richard Mulghan, canon of St. Patrick's, notary public, John Reynolds, literate, and Thomas Sparks.

328. (282.) Simon Walshe, of Dublin, skinner, releases to John Estrete, senior, gentleman, all right of action against him.

Dated 15 May, 21 Edward IV. (1481).

329. (283). Account of arrears of rent and port corn due by John Bedlowe, late mayor of Dublin, to the Prior and Convent of Holy Trinity from M. term 11th to M. term 21st Edward IV.

Dated Michaelmas term, 1481.

Calendared from "Novum Registrum."

330. (284.) Donald O'Fallan, deputy of the Friars minors, permits Richard Skyrret, canon, to appoint a confessor to enable him to get the benefit of the Indulgence granted by Pope Sextus IV. to Crusaders.

Dated 1482.

331. (286.) Exemplification of an Act passed at a Parliament in Dublin on Friday after the feast of St. Luke the Evangelist last past, before Gerald earl of Kildare, deputy of Richard of Shrewsbury, duke of York, and thence prorogued to Monday after the Feast of the Purification of the B.V.M., reciting that the Prior and Convent of Holy Trinity Church, Dublin, possessed a box of wrought silver to hold the Sacrament, weighing 38 ounces, and worth £12 : 12 :—; that Henry Alton of Athirde, gentleman, about Pentecost 6° Edward IV. took it away and damaged them to the amount of £20; and ordaining that Henry should come to Dublin Castle on Monday after the feast of St. Patrick the bishop, next, and remain under guard of the constable thereof until he has satisfied the prior and convent, otherwise they may enter upon and hold his lands until satisfied. (*French.*)

Dated at Dublin 12 Mar., 22 Edward IV. (1482).

332. (285.) John Walshe, late of Stalorgane, co. Dublin, gentleman, having on the 26 March, 22 Edward IV., become bound to Holy Trinity Church, Dublin, in 100 marks, it is agreed that the bond shall be void should John Walsh keep the peace, or make restitution for any injury he shall commit. (*English.*)

Dated 27 March, 22 Edward IV. (1482).

333. (285a.) Edmond Harrold of Kylmahyok, Nicholas Walsh of Dondrom, Theobald Walsh of Balybother, John Laweles of Shenckyll, Morice Walsh of Oylgoban, James Godsman of Ballylaghnan, and Charles Walsh of Shanngnagh, gentlemen, having on the 26 March, 22

Edward IV., become bound to Holy Trinity Church, the prior agrees that these bonds shall be void, should John Walsh, brother of the said Nicholas and Theobald, abide by his agreement in No. 332 *supra*.

Dated 27 Mar., 22 Ed. IV. (1482). (*English*)

334 (287.) Exemplification of an act, passed at the parliament referred to in No. 331 *supra*, ordaining that the Prior and Convent of Holy Trinity Church, Dublin, may hold all their grants notwithstanding the statute of mortmain, and that anybody may grant possessions to them without licence, 6s. 8d. being paid into the Hanaper ; without prejudice to Patrick Barnell, and Anne his wife, Walter, abbot of the monastery of St. Mary, Dublin, and the convent thereof, Thomas Sharpe, the proctors of St. Warburge's Church, the mayor, bailiffs, and commons of Dublin, John, archbishop of Dublin, John, abbot of the house of St. Thomas the martyr near Dublin, Sir Roland Eustace, lord of Portlester, the prior of Kylmaynan, Sir James Fleunyng, baron of Slane, Sir Robert St. Lawrence, lord of Howth, or to the heirs of Nicholas White, esq., late of Kiloster. (*French*).

Dated at Dublin, 13 June, 22 Edward IV. (1483).

Enrolled in the Exchequer, Trinity Term, 2 Richard III.

335. Henry Alton and Henry Babe of Athyrde grant to Holy Trinity Church, lands in Athirde, viz. :—one garden lying between the street called " Horslaue " on the west, the land of John Walshe alias Hobbok on the east, that of Walter Vordon, chaplain, on the north, and that of Wm. Moriell on the south ; another garden lying without the west gate of the town, between the way to the great water on the east, the land of Henry Mann on the west, the highway to the common pasture of the town on the north, and the land of Wm. Nicholl on the south ; the meadow park called Maynart's Anhe lying without the said gate, between the highway on the north, the great water on the south, the common pasture aforesaid on the east, and the land of Wm. John on the west ; and the four acres called the Cullyrfuld, lying on the north side of the town, between the park of Henry Alton towards Bowis More on the south, the highway to Rodlistan on the north, and the land of Walter Verdon, chaplain, on the east and west.

Witnesses—Wm. Hazard of Athirde, chaplain, Thos. Hazard of Athirde, Peter Taaff of Athirde, gent., Nicha. Taaff, yeoman, Walter Kynton of Athirde, Thos. Petyte of Dublin, clerk, Walter Dewnysh, yeoman of the Prior of Holy Trinity, and Wm. Kelly of Athirde, yeoman.

Dated 2 July, 1 Ed. V. 1483.

336 (288.) John Weste, mayor of Dublin, Reynold Talbot and [John] Geydon, bailiffs thereof, being required by the prior and convent of Holy Trinity to certify how lands may be acquired by testament in Dublin City, and whether the testament of Nicholas Sutton is inrolled in the Tholsel, certify that every citizen may devise lands and rent within the bounds of the city, except to houses of religion, and such as cannot aid the city in time of need ; that every such testament should be certified, under seal of the spiritual Court, to the mayor and bailiffs within the day and year after Testator's death ; proclamation thereof should be made on three market days within that period at the High Cross of Dublin ; twelve citizens before the Mayor and bailiffs should find that Testator had good title, such finding to be enrolled in the records of the city ; every testament not complying with these conditions to be deemed void ; and that Nicholas Sutton's will has not been enrolled in the records of the city. (*English*).

Dated [   ] Oct., 1 Ric. III. (1483).

337. Henry Alton and Henry Dabe of Athirda, grant to Holy Trinity Church, land called the " three stangs of arable land " near the " Crowe Bushe " on the eastern side of the town, and lying between the common pasture of the town on the south, the lands of grantors on the north, the lands of Patrick Mann on the west, and that of Walter Verdon chaplain on the east.
Dated 23rd Nov., 1 Ric. III. (1483).

338 (289). Johanna Suetorby of Dublin, widow, daughter and heiress of Reginald Suoterby, grants to Thomas, prior of Holy Trinity Church, Dublin, and the convent thereof, Ballymore, co. Dublin.
Dated 4th May, 1 Richard III. (1484).

339 (289ᵃ). Grantor in No. 338 *supra* appoints William Englysh of Dublin, clerk, to deliver seisin of the premises therein.
Dated 4th May, 1 Richard III. (1484).

340 (289ᵇ). Grantees in No. 338 *supra* appoint Walter Dewnyshe of Dublin, yeoman, to receive seisin of the premises therein.
Dated 4th May, 1 Richard III. (1484).

341 (290.) Inquisition taken at Ballymore on Monday after the feast of St. Brendan, 1 Richard III., before William Englysh, seneschal of the archbishop of Dublin, for the manor of Ballymore, by Thomas Gammage, William Ballard, John White, Richard Gammage, John Gailally, John FitzRobert, Patrick Haket, Laurence Barry, James Flemyng, John Flemyng, Henry Corcran, and Thaddeus O'Bulgy, finds that John Bennett, on his death, held of the archbishop's said manor, lands in Afanyncshaine, with other small plots ; that, Isabella Coleman held on her death, lands in Glosknoko, with sundry small plots ; and that Thomas Suerterby held a stony tenement, formerly belonging to Thomas Purcell and other lands. A like inquisition taken there on Monday after the feast of St. Barnabas, apostle, in the same year, by James Dowdyn, Richard Camford, Patrick Brangan, Thadeus O'Bulgyn, John Galbarry, Richard Gammage, Walter Gammage, John Whyte, Lawrence Berry, William Ballard, John Flemyng, and John FitzRobert, finds that Anastace Rede held on her death, land in Ballymore.
Dated 14 June, 1484.
Memorandum at foot.—These lands were given by Thomas, son and heir of John Bennet, unto Holy Trinity church, Dublin, to establish four choristers.

342. Copies of (a) a Rental of the lands in the lordship of Ballimore belonging to Holy Trinity Church, made by Richard Skyrret, prior, and Thomas Fyche, sub-prior, which gives the lands in the possession of John Denet, Isabella Colmar, and Thomas Suetterby, and the rent due thereout to the Archbishop of Dublin.

(b.) An Inquisition taken at Ballimore on Monday after the feast of St. Brandan, the abbot, 1 Ric. III., by Thomas Gamage, Wm. Ballard, John White, Richd. Gamage, John Gallally, John FitzRobert, Patrick Hakket, Laurence Berry, Jas. Flemyn, John Flemyn, Henry Corcrane, and Thaddeus O'Bulgyn, finds the denominations, acreage, and chief rents of the lands of Holy Trinity Church in Balimora.

(c.) An Inquisition by James Dowdyng, Wm. Ballard, John White, Laurence Barry, Thaddeus O'Bulghyn, Richd. Camford, John Flemyn, John FitzRobert, Walter Gamage, John Galbarry, Patrick Brangan, Henry Corcran, and Richard Gamage, finds that Anastace Rede died seized of seven messuages and 133 acres.
Dated 14 June, 1484. See No. 341.

343. Nicholas Whyte and Simon Dove, chaplains, grant to Holy Trinity church, a messuage in Fishamble street, Dublin, granted to them by Nicholas Bourke, and lying between the land of Thomas Seys on the west, that of John Dyrraunt on the east, Fishamble street on the south, and the old city wall on the north.
Dated 20 April, 2 Ric. III. (1485).

344. (292ª.) Grantors in No. 343 *supra*, appoint Thomas Petyte, clerk, to deliver seisin of the premises therein.
Dated 20 April, 2 Richard III. (1485).

345. (292.) Release of premises in No. 343 *supra*.
Dated 24 April, 2 Richard III. (1485).

346. (293.) Thomas, prior of Holy Trinity church, Dublin, and the convent thereof, grant to John Estrete, gentleman, a messuage in Skinner street, Dublin, wherein John Barry the weaver dwells, a garden in rere, and another garden opposite the churchyard of the Augustinian friars in the suburbs of Dublin, lately the property of Thomas Foill of Dublin, fisher.
Signed by prior Harrold, sub-prior Wynchester, William Kerdy, T. Fyche, R. Calf, R. Skyrret, John Hygley, N. Loghan, John Hassard, P. Whyte, and John Monteyn.
Dated 14 July, 3 Richard III. (1485.)

347. (293ª.) Grantors in No. 346 *supra*, appoint William Cashell to deliver seisin of the premises therein.
Dated 14 July, 3 Richard III. (1485.)

348. John Estrete of Dublin grants to John Waryng, parson of Molahidderd, and Sir Thomas Launday, chaplain, premises in the Fishamblys, wherein Philip Flemyng the fisher lives; a messuage and tan-house with a bawn and haggard place without the Pole gate in St. Bride's parish where John Browne dwells, and an orchard called Paradise adjoining; a messuage in Skinner's row wherein John Barry the weaver dwells, a garden in the street behind, and a garden before the Freyr Austins, which formerly belonged to Thomas Foyl the fisher; a garden near dame Jenet Suoterbie's house in St. Patrick st., wherein John Baker now dwells; a messuage and land formerly called Kevyngys-land in the town of Crumalyn; a messuage place, divers cottage places, land, and meadow called the Glynd in Midnyghtis town, near Colp, co. Meath; a messuage, land and meadow in Helroddan, lordship of Galtrym, co. Meath; a messuage, wood and pasture in Bryneston, lordship of Myclare. In trust to convey to the prior and convent of Holy Trinity church, for a canon to celebrate mass of the Holy Ghost for ever, premises of the yearly value of four marks, the messuage and gardens that were Foyl's to be parcel thereof, except the messuage and orchard in St. Bride's parish; and on Estrete's death to convey the residue to his son George in tail male, remainders to his own heirs and Holy Trinity church.   (*English*).
Dated 26 Jul, 3º Ric. III., 1485.

349 (291.) John Estrete, gentleman, sergeant-at-law, surrenders to the Prior and convent of Holy Trinity church, Dublin, 40s. yearly granted him by them, and grants them, for his life, half of the New rent which formerly belonged to William Suttone, for a mass in the chapel of St. Lawrence O'Toyle, in the south aisle next the high choir, and appoints master John Waryng and Thomas Launday trustees, to convey to them

after his death, land in Ireland worth 4 marks; they bind themselves to celebrate the mass daily, and every Thursday to cause the choir to sing a mass for the said John, and his benefactors, Gerald earl of Kildare, Sir Roland fitz Eustace, knight, lord of Portlester, treasurer of Ireland, Thomas Donedall, esq., Richard Stanyhurst, John Flemyng, Jenetta Estrete his mother, George Estrete, William Cawhell, Margaret Blake, and for the souls of John Estrete senior, John Estrete junior, Christopher and Patrick his brothers, Sir John Chaler and William Eliott; and to keep grantor's obit in Whitsun week.   (*English*).

Dated 8 Oct., 1486, 1 Henry VII.

350 (295.) Thomas, prior of Holy Trinity church, Dublin, and the convent, appoint Walter Devenysh, yeoman, to receive from Gerald, earl of Kildare, Sir Roland Fitz Eustace, lord of Portlester, and treasurer of Ireland, Walter de Lahyde, lord of Moyclare, John Estrete, gentleman, sergeant-at-law, master John Waryng, archdeacon of Dublin, late rector of Malahidered, and Thomas Launday, chaplain, seisin of land in Ballirodan, Fynnakismeile, land between Athtuly and Cammoky's Greym, all situate in Ballirodan, in the lordship of Galtrym, land in Aghknuk, in Brynestown, near Ballirodan, premises along the little Moreway, land in the Glynfeld, land between that lately belonging to Richard Staunton, and that lately belonging to Roger Bag, the Glynd in Midnyghterston, near Colp, county Meath, lately belonging to Robert Sewell, premises in the Fyshamlys-street, Dublin, where Philip Flemyng fisher now dwells.

Dated 26 July, 3 Henry VII. (1488).

351 (295ᵃ.) Gerald, earl of Kildare, and others, as in No. 350 supra, appoint John Walshe, yeoman, to deliver seisin of the premises therein.

Dated 26 July, 3 Henry VII. (1488).

352. (293ᵇ). John Waryng, archdeacon of Dublin, late rector of Molahidered, and Thomas Launday of Dublin, chaplain, grant to John Estrete of Dublin, gentleman, premises with an orchard called the Paradise situate outside the Polegate and lying between the land of John Benet on the east, the land of St. Brigid on the west, the street in front leading to the Pole mill on the north, and the street leading from the Polegate to St. Brigid's church on the south and rere, also Keryngislands, in Cromlyn; to hold to John Estrete during his life, remainder to his son George in tail male, and failing issue, remainder to Catherine Estrete for life, remainder to the heirs of John Estrete, remainder to the Prior and convent of Holy Trinity church, Dublin, for the purpose in No. 349 supra.

Dated at Dublin 31 July, 3 Henry VII. (1488).

353 (294.) Thomas Fyche, David Wynchester, sub-prior, Robert Calfe, Richard Skyrret, John Higley, John Haward, Patrick Whyte, and John Montayn, canons of Holy Trinity church, Dublin, inform Walter, archbishop of Dublin, that they have elected David Wynchester to be prior in the room of Thomas Harrold, late prior.

Witness, Thomas Browne, clerk, of Dublin, notary public.

Dated 5 March, 1488 (1489).

354. Thos. Rowe, of Athirde, and John Kerny, of Dundalk, chaplains, executors of Wm. Cambel of Dublin, clerk, grant to Holy Trinity church, a meadow in the franchise of Dundalk, lying between the land of Christopher Dovedall, late of Dundalk, gent., on the north and east, the Blackwatyr on the south, and the land of Walter Galtrym on the west; land in the Smale way field between the Smaleway on the

north, the highway on the south, the land of Wm. Dovedall, of Dundalk, on the west, and that of Patrick Alger, of Dundalk, on the east; land in the Stanguys field touching the lands of Laurence Saryne, of Dundalk, John Baggrott, gent.,   Heyward, Wm. Dovedall, of Dundalk, Thos. Feld, John Lowyes, and Walter Gultryn, of Dundalk.

Dated 14 May, 4 Hen. VII. (1460).

355 (296.) John Casahell, of Dundalk, merchant, son and heir of John Casahell, senior, late of Dundalk, releases to David, prior of Holy Trinity church, Dublin, and the convent thereof, the lands in No. 334 *supra.*

Dated 31 Jan., 6 Henry VII. (1491).

356 (297). William Donnogh releases to David, prior of Holy Trinity church, Dublin, and the convent thereof, all right of action for any account between them.

Dated 20 May, 6 Henry VII. (1491).

357. (298.) David Wynchestyr, prior of Holy Trinity church, Dublin, and the convent thereof, establish a music master to teach four boys, and four boys who shall attend daily mass of the B.V.M. and the mass and antiphons of Jesus every Friday in Lent, and at all other times when required; the oblations offered to the relic of the Holy Staff of Jesus within the said church, the rent of the messuage wherein William Cantrell now dwells in High street, Dublin, in the parish of St. Michael, commonly called Holm's Innys, rent of Roganestown in Swerds, and a yearly rent of 20s., which Henry Alton granted to them from his lordship in Athirde, co. Louth, to be allocated to pay the Master and to clothe the boys.

Signed by Prior Wynchester, sub prior Skyrret, T. Fyohe, R. Oulf, John Hygley, John Hassard, P. Whyte, J. Beon, John Kendyll, and William Hassard.

Dated 28 Aug., 1493.

358 (299). Walter, archbishop of Dublin, approves of No. 357 *supra.*

Dated at the Castle, Dublin, 10 Sep., 1493.

359 (300). Geoffrey Fyohe, official of Dublin, at the suit of Thomas Fyohe, proctor of David, prior of Holy Trinity church, Dublin, and the convent thereof, against Dalvaticus O'Tole, tenant and farmer of Thomas Sale, gent., son and heir of Geoffrey Sale, late lord of Chamerstown, in the parish of Fynglas, for the sacrilegious detention of half a pound of wax yearly for over 16 years; fines Dalvatious 6s. 8d., and sentences Thomas Sale to render the wax punctually for the future under penalty of excommunication.

Witnesses—Sir Nich. Boys, canon of St. Patrick's, Thomas Broun, Thomas Young, John Staunton, Robert Lyn, notaries public, Paul Telyng, clerk, Patrick Whyte, apparitor.

Dated 19th October, 1493.

360 (301.) Geoffrey Fyohe, principal official of the metropolitical court of Dublin, having been requested by David Wynchester, prior of Holy Trinity, and the convent thereof, to decide their rights to tithes of salmon and other fish taken in the Anilyffy, within the franchise of Dublin, appoints, 10 November, 1494, Robert Skyrret, canon of St. Patrick's and prebendary of Typnyr, diocese of Dublin, to inquire. Citations issued to John Randyll, Walter Deveuesh, Nicholas Gorman, William Barbor, John Dowgan, James Eustace, John Kruone, Nakyn Kelly, Thomas Rede, Thomas Kelly, Nicholas Loghnan, John Barnard, and Thomas Levett. The inquiry held in St. Bridget's church, near Dublin, found that the Prior and convent of Christ Church were entitled to tithes of salmon, herrings, and other fish, taken in the Anilyffy from the seashore to the middle of the river, from Isold's fount on the west, to the Bar flots on the east, and from the monks' salmon fishery on the north, to the Stayn on the south.

Dated 20th Nov., 1494.

361 (803.) Walter, archbishop of Dublin, at a provincial council held in the church of Holy Trinity on the 5th of March, 1494, with the consent of the Bishops of Ossory, Leighlin, and Kildare, confirms the Act of Parliament referred to in No. 363 *infra*.

Witnesses.—Geoffry fich, principal official of the metropolitan court of Dublin, and prebendary of St. Andoen's, Dublin, William Stevenote prior of All Saints, Symon Walsh, prior of St. Thomas the Martyr, near Dublin, and John Wale, prior of the church of the hospital of St. John of Kylmaynane, John Swayne, sub-prior of Holmepatrick, Richard Mylyne, prebendary of Kylmatalwey, Nicholas Boys, prebendary of Castleknock, John Boys, prebendary of Malahyddert, and Dermot Baylie.

Dated 30th April, 1495.

362 (302.) Octavian, archbishop of Armagh, John, bishop of Meath, Tiberius, bishop of Down and Connor, George, bishop of Dromore, Donald, bishop of Derry, and Thomas and Cormac, bishops of Kilmore, at a provincial council held in St. Peter's church, Drogheda, on the 6th of July, 1495, at the request of David Wynchestro, prior, and the convent of Holy Trinity, confirm an act of the parliament of Friday after the nativity of St. John the Baptist, 9th Henry VII., inflicting a fine of £20 on all who molest pilgrims to the church of Holy Trinity, or those who have taken sanctuary therein, and command their clergy to excommunicate all who transgress this ordinance.

Dated 10th July, 1495.

363 (304.) Exemplification of a provision in the Act of Resumption, passed in a parliament held at Drogheda, before Sir Edward Ponynga, knight, Deputy of Ireland, on the day after the feast of St. Andrew the Apostle, 10th Henry VII., excepting from its effect, grants from the crown to the Prior and convent of Holy Trinity, Dublin, not exceeding 40 marks a year, which are to be suspended for five years only. (*Partly English.*)

Dated 15 Dec., 11 Henry VII. (1495.)

364 (306.) Insparimus of three enrolments on Exchequer Memorandum Roll, Easter term, 3 Edward IV.

(a) Laurence, archbishop of Dublin, grants to the canons of Holy Trinity of the order of St. Augustine, in frankalmoign, the church of Holy Trinity, with the churches of St. Michan, St. Michael, St. John the Evangelist, St. Brigid, and St. Paul, their gardens and houses without the wall, the mill near the bridge, the fishery and tithes of salmon and other fish on both sides of the Anilyffy, the lands of Rochen, Portrechrann, Rathchillin, and Cansale, the third parts of Clochuri and Cellalin, Lealuan, Callearn, Duncuanagh, Glasneoden, Magdama, Calldulich, Balemicamlaib, Cluaincocin, Talgach, Tulachepain, Cellingenolcain, Celtinen, Rathsalchao, Tillachnaescop, Drumhyng, Ballerochucan, half of Rathnahi, Tirudran, Ballerochran, and Ballomoailph.

Witnesses—Edanus the bishop, Malachy, bishop of Lobgud, Eugenius, bishop of Clanimirirt, Nehemiah, bishop of Caldarch, Thomas, abbot of Glendolacha, Radulfus, abbot of Bildulm, Adam, abbot of St. Mary's, Dulilia, Patrick, abbot of Millefont, Cristinna, abbot de Valle Salutis, Torquellus the archdeacon, Joseph, priest of St. Brigid's, Godmundus, priest of St. Mary's, Edanna, priest of St. Patrick's, Cenninus, priest of St. Michael's, Peter, priest of St. Michen's, Richard, priest of St. Columba's, Gillbert, priest of St. Martin's, Hugh de Lacy, constable of Dublin, Wildelmus de Miset, Robert de St. Michael, Adam de Pheipo, John [the bishop], Herding his brother, Adelmus, Rotger Ficin, and Wildelmus de Bruryng.

Dated 14th May, circa 1178.

(b.) Richard, archbishop of Dublin, confirms the ordinance of Pope Nicholas III. as to the rights of the cathedral churches of Holy Trinity and St. Patrick's. Every archbishop to be consecrated in Holy Trinity, which foundation is entitled to seniority. The crozier, mitre, and pontifical ring of every archbishop at his death to belong to Holy Trinity, and his body to be interred in Holy Trinity, unless he wills otherwise. When the see of Dublin is vacant the Prior and Convent of Holy Trinity are to have the same liberty in their rural churches as the Dean of St. Patrick's has in his prebendal churches.

Dated 2nd March, 1800.

(a.) King John confirms to Holy Trinity church its lands and possessions granted before and after the arrival of the English in Ireland, as confirmed by Laurence, Archbishop of Dublin, viz.—the place where the church is erected, Bealdulig, Roohan, and Portracbaru, granted by Cithuric, son of Alsolea, earl of Dublin; Minoreni, by Macdeardan Macdulm; Clonchen, by Donogh, son of Donald Grossus; Realgeallyn, by Enad, son of Donald, King of Leinster; Achatillagh nuneascoil and Gulaght by Signghro, son of Thorkil; Dmurmbing, by the son of Meirboillan; Alokeis, by Durriths; Kalgng', by Gillacriste Macumalyn; Dallaengan, by Dormlagh, son of Pole; Baliucharan, by Pole, son of Thorkil; Tirodran, by Brodar, son of Thorkil; Dallyrodilf, by Donal Eni Breain, King of Ireland; Thenchabreaian, by the Ostmen; Kembonum by purchase; Raithachran by Maelcallan Maurelardan; Gisnedoon by purchase; Drinchuamach, by Raillic, son of Gillagoygro; the land between Kealmuntamoch and Ballymore Abbot, by Downall, son of Halgo; Tudresan, by Iarraibyn, son of Eifarn; Rathkyllyn, by Dearmarth, son of Imarchadan, king of Leinster; one half of Tracualiy, by Marmaorundin; Balyhamind, Lcauleran, and Balleghogan, by earl Richard; the land which "divini" have converted to their use, by Torfyn son of Torgnir; the land opposite Trinity Church, by Galgedcall McGillabrida; the garden in St. Putrick's parish, by Gillacormda the wealthy; the land between St. Patrick's Church and the City wall, by the Ostmen; the mill near the bridge and the lands on both sides thereof, by Gillamurra; the church of St. Michan with the land on both sides thereof, by Isaak the priest; the church of St. Michael, by Bastobien Gormelaoh the son of Pole; the churches of SS. John and Paul, by Gillamychell son of Gillamurry; the land in St. Brigid's parish stretching to the City wall beyond the garden, by Cristine son of Raba; the church of St. Brigid and the lands belonging to Holy Trinity in the same parish, by earl Hasgall; his burgage, by Seger the aged; her land near St. Nicholas Church, by the daughter of Francis Gonu; land in the same street, by Hellas Salynger; land in St. Warburg's parish, by William de Essex; a fourth part of the land which Robert Lorymer holds, by Adam

Pidala ; land in St. Thomas's Parish which Rolkyftis holds, and Gigena, by William Brune ; land in Krokkerat., by Roger brother of Heyn' ; land in the parish of the Hospital of St. John by Walter the Chamberlain ; land in St. Martin's parish, by Simon de Sanlo ; one half his burgage, in St. Audoen's parish, by Hebertan Ginagana ; the Church of Rashullyn by Richard Grossus Edmond, for the soul of earl Richard ; a carucate of land at Kanaleana, by Thomas son of Albred ; land between St. John's Church and the house of Walter the goldsmith, by Giffy the priest ; land outside the gate of St. Michael's by Ganald ; land which Vala holds, by Adalam ; land beyond the cemetery of Holy Trinity from the corner of the court-yard to the corner of the land of bishop John, by earl Richard and the Burgesses of Dublin ; a boat in the Auliffy to fish for salmon, &c, &c, toll, &c.

Witnesses.—John Lachan, bishop of Lincoln, William de Lychefeld, bishop, William Marascall earl of Pembrok, I. de Dryware, Hugh de Nevyll, W de Samforde, Walter de Gumpilupo, R. fitz Philip.

Dated at Pembroke 6 Mar., 3 John, by the hand of H. de Wells archdeacon of Wells.

Inspeximus dated 10th May, 11 Henry VII. (1496).

Witness—John Topclyff, chief baron.

365 (307.) Thos. Pecok, chaplain, Denis Guffncy, Thomas Levet, Wm. Herbard, Edmond Walsh, Richd. Stanyhurst, Wm. Stevenot, prior of All Saints, Richd. Danyall, Nichs. Oromale, John Kyushoko, tailor, Thos. Bowes, chaplain, and Wm. Drckaper, husbandman, depose that the Prior and Convent of Holy Trinity were the true rectors of the Anilyffy from Isold's Fount to the Bar Fote, and that they were entitled to tithes of fish taken therein, and enjoyed the same, from time immemorial.

Witnesses.—Thos. Walsh and John Malghan, not. pub.

Dated 10 Nov., 1490.

366 (305.) Exemplification of proceedings in a suit between the prior and convent of Holy Trinicy, and the abbot and convent of the D.V.M., Dublin, with reference to the tithes of Crinach, Ballickeran, Tiodrane, and Andrew Harang's town, in the parish of Kilculin, reciting the Bull of Pope Honorius [III.] directing the bishop and archdeacon of Kildare, and the prior of Ounall, diocese of Kildare, to try the cause.

The matter is decided in favour of Holy Trinity, and Radulfus, abbot of the B.V.M., Dublin, is excommunicated for resisting the decision.

Witnesses—Geoffrey Fich, archdeacon of Glendalough, Robert Skirret and William Mayown, canous of St. Patrick's, Dermot Rayle, perpetual vicar of Swerdis, John Stanton and Tho. Walsh, notaries public.

Dated, 11th Feb., 1497.

367 (198.) Exemplification of No. 218 supra, before Geoffrey Fich, official of the court of Dublin, by Thomas Walsh, notary public.

Witnesses.—[   ] notary public, Stephen Rondnyl, Peter Wolff, clerks, Robt. Andrew, Patrick Whit, John Soutero, Wm. Dromine, and Thos. Hohhoenne.

Dated, St. Patrick's, Dublin, [   ] 1497.

368 (309.) Exemplification of an appeal wherein, at St. Peter's church, Drogheda, on the 13th April, 1497, Wm. Hassard, canon and proctor of Holy Trinity church, in a suit against the abbot and convent of the monastery of the B.V.M., Dublin, appealed from the interlocutory

judgment of James White, archdeacon of Armagh, one of the delegates to determine the suit.

Witnesses.—Masters Michael Goldyng, of Drummyng, diocese of Armagh, Wm. Folane, of Kylmone, diocese of Meath, rectors, Jas. Dokkets, Richd. Conn', John Erward and John Gruyr, chaplains, Philip Duff, John Barnard and Thos. Walsh, laymen, Wm. Chapman and Richd. Corkenu, apparitors. Witnesses to exemplification, Robt. Skyrret and Richd. Heyne, canons of Holy Trinity and St. Patrick's, Peter Wolf, Nicholas Wynchestor and John Heyne, literates.

Dated 13 July, 1497.

369 (308.) Henry VII. grants to Holy Trinity church, Dublin, authority to collect and destrain for three pounds arrears of the double subsidy granted to him, for five years, by the Parliament held at Drogheda, before Sir Edward Poynyngs, on Friday next after the feast of St. Andrew, in the 10th year of his reign.

Witness.—Walter St. Lourence, chief baron of the Exchequer.

Dated at Dublin, 28th April, 13th Henry VII. (1498.)

370 (313.) Pope Alexander VI. directs the Prior of Holmpatrike, diocese of Dublin, and the dean and archdeacon of Kildare, to bear the appeal, of the Prior and chapter of the church of Dublin of the order of St. Augustine, from James White, archdeacon of Armagh, apostolic delegate, in a suit between them and the Abbot and convent of the B. V. M., near Dublin, with reference to tithes of fish.

Dated at St. Peter's, Rome, iii. Kal. Aug., 7° Alexander VI. (30 July, 1499.)

371 (312.) Nicholas Conyll, dean of Kildare, on the authority of No. 370 supra, inhibits James White, archdeacon of Armagh, from proceeding with the case mentioned in No. 368 supra, and summons him and the parties, to the parish church of Saint David of Nass, diocese of Kildare, on the 12th day of May next.

Dated 27th April, 1500.

372 (310.) The Abbot and convent of the monastery of the B. V. M., Dublin, with consent of John Troy, abbot of Mellefont, bind themselves in £100, to submit their dispute with the Prior and convent of Christ Church, in reference to tithes of fish taken in the Anilyffy, to the arbitration of master John Wards, doctor, master Richard Heyn, principal official of Meath, Thomas Barmyngham and Robert Forster, citizens of Dublin.

Dated 14th July, 1500.

373 (311.) The arbitrators in No. 372 supra, declare that the Prior and convent of Holy Trinity are entitled to all the tithes of fish on both sides of the AniLeffl, except half of the tithes of fish landed on the north side of the Fyr pole which belongs to the Abbot and Convent of the B. V. M., and that marks should be erected to define the Fyr pole.

Witnesses.—Robt. Evers, prior of Kilmainham, Wm. Kerdyff, Richard Beth, Gerald Delyon, gent., Bartholomew Rossell, John More and Walter Fyane, merchants.

Dated 17 July, 1500.

374 (314.) Inquisition taken in the court of William Thoumbe, prior of the House of God, Molyngar, in his manor of the Byssopstret of Dunboyne, before Patrick Luttrell, seneschal of the court, on Monday after the feast of St. Columba, abbot, 16 Henry VII., by John Griffyn alias Genkyn Griffyn, Thomas Phaypow, Christopher Petyt, Thomas

Lankyn, senior, John Lankyn, junior, Nicholas Collyn, Philip Morm, James Fynnor, Stephen Whyt, Thomas Barnewall, John Hogan, and Ralph Downing ; finds that Johanna Lankyn was seized in fee of land called Jakhery's land, rent 15 pence, and granted it to Holy Trinity Church, Dublin, that the prior was in possession since the death of Johanna, and that Thomas Lawles of Clony claims it as her heir.

10 June, 1501.

375. John Graunger of Rathmore, diocese of Dublin, deposes that James Taler of Rathmore gave lands and goods to Holy Trinity Church for a corody, during his life, and directed him, his sub-tenant, to pay his rent to the said church ; that Johanna Wase brought a suit in the Exchequer against Holy Trinity for these lands, and that judgment was given for defendant, with 14s. costs, which were paid by defendant in consideration of her release of the promises.   Deponent further declares that he was not sworn in an inquisition concerning these lands taken before the seneschal of Rathmore lordship on behalf of Jenkyn *alias* John Rowe.

Witnesses.—Robert Seyrret, canon of St. Patrick's, Dublin, William Bath, gent., John Heyn and John Broun, literates, Moredagh Fydor, Jenkyn *alias* John Rowe, Patrick Myrryman and John Mulchan, clark, notary public.

Dated 22 June, 1502.

376. Richard Canton of Kylcolyn deposes that Kynnegh is in Dublin diocese, and that the residents attend in, and pay their oblations, &c., to Castlemartyn chapel.   Henry Kelly of Folyeston in Kylcolyn deposes similarly, and that residents were generally buried at Kylcolyn : both sworn 18th June, 1503.

19 June, 1503, Sir Edmund Vale, chaplain, deposes that residents in Kynnegh and Canonrath are parishioners of Kylcolyn and generally buried there ; that their children are baptized at Castlemartyn, and that they pay 3 pence to Kylcolyn church, and a third penny to Castlemartyn chapel ; that John archbishop of Dublin declared that the small tithes thereof belonged to Holy Trinity Church ; and that deponent, as commissary of the said archbishop, had approved of wills, and pronounced sentences of divorce, including that between Conghnor O'Kelly and Bevyn yny Malawley, concerning the residents there.

Sir Cornelius O'Connyll, archdeacon of Kildare, deposes similarly as to burials and baptisms.

Cormaah Scholler of Castlemartyn deposes that he saw Sir William Rothe chaplain, canon of Cartmayle in England, Sir Nicholas Hynnows and Sir Edmund Vale, chaplains, serving in Castlemartyn chapel wherein the residents of Kynnegh were wont to attend ; and similarly to Sir Edmund Vale as to burial and baptism.

Eugene *alias* Odo More of Castlenmartyn. husbandman, deposes similarly to Richard Canton and Sir Edmund Vale ; and that Sir John Davy, canon of Kildare, never urged the residents to attend the church of Agarvana.

Witnesses—Sir James Conyll, chaplain, Bartholomew Lang and John Broun, literates, John Heyn and David Hach, laymen, and Robert Skyrrett, clerk, of Meath, notary public.

Dated 19 June, 1503.

377. (315.) Robert Skyrrett, notary public, declares that John *alias* Jankyn Rowe of Rathmore, co. Kildare, in the great chamber of Richard Skirrett, prior of Holy Trinity, acknowledged a release, dated at

Dublin, 20 May, 18 Henry VII., from the said John, to Holy Trinity church, of land in Rathmore which formerly belonged to Richard Crompe.

Witnesses, Thomas Fyche, sub prior of Holy Trinity, Master Nicholas Cardyff, chancellor of St. Patrick's, Thomas Bathe, gent., servant of master Nicholas, Roger and John Browne, David Hach.

Dated 6 Aug. 1503.

378 (316.) Richard, prior of Christ Church, petitions Walter, archbishop of Dublin, lord chancellor of Ireland, for a subpœna against John *alias* Jenkyn Row, to answer for having intimidated the tenants of the premises in No. 377 *supra*. (*English*)—*Circa* 1503.

379. (318) Walter, archbishop of Dublin, confirms to Holy Trinity church, the churches of St. Michael the Archangel, St. John the Evangelist, within the city of Dublin, St. Michan's without, and their tithes; the place where St. Paul's church was founded, and the tithes and gardens thereof; the Polle and Wode mills and the water thereof, tithes excepted; its possessions in Dublin city and suburbs; tithes of fish taken in Anilyffy, the gift of Laurence, archbishop of Dublin, subject to the right of Mary's Abbey in the Fyrpole; the Grange of Grangegorman with the tithes; Selkok and its wood; Garget's meadows and their tithes; the town of Glasmevyng, with its church, tithes, and mill; the towns of Clonmell and Dromconragh with their tithes; the chapel and tithes of Kyllestyr, and 8s. chief rent to buy the Prior a pair of greaves; the church of Dalgryffyn with its glebe; the chapel and tithes of St. Dolach; £5 chief rent from the town and lordship of Kynnaly, and wardship, marriage and homage thereof; 5 marks and homage from Mableyston; the church of Balscadan with its tithes, profits and advowson; lands and possessions in Grange, New Town, Dermoteston, Tobyrton, Ballygaddy, and Stobildekyn, with their tithes; chief rents of 20s. on Tobirsowll, 13s. 4d. on Myleston, 13s. 4d. on Kylloghir from Christopher Goldyng and his heirs; Fraytor's land, and the wardship, marriage, and homage thereof; the "Church Landes"; a messuage in Myleston where an old mill was formerly; a messuage in the town of Balscadan called Mary's place; land in Rogmeston, in Swerdis lordship, the gift of Richard Caddell and Janet Fitzwyllium, his wife, daughter of Robert Fitzwylliam, and the feoffments of Thomas Laundey and Wm. Fowll, chaplains; land in the Rede More near the Ward; a messuage in Cowlok; a messuage in Lespopell; half the town of Stagob in Castleknok parish; in the marches of Dublin, the churches of St. Fyntan of Clonkene, St. Brigid of Stalorgan, St. Brigid of Tyllagh, the church of Kylleny, chapel of St. Brigid near Carrykmayn, with their tithes; the church of St. Begnet of Dalkey with its tithes, and a messuage on its western side; the town of Churcheston with the Grange of Clonkene, the towns of Kylleny, Ballyloghan, Ballybrenan, Ballymulghan, Ferncoste, Walter's lands, Ballitobbir, Tyrodaran, Dromyn and Ballyogan, with their tithes; also Smothescourt, Coolecott, Sculliet Hyllis, Kilmahyok and Ballyardor, with their tithes; the tithes of Ballyfynche; messuages in Lakan; a messuage in Eskyr; in county Kildare, Ballymor the gift of Thomas Bennett and Janet Suetirby; tenements in Rathmorn; the town of Poncheston near the Naas with its lands; the church of Kylcolyn, right of advowson to the rectory and vicarage, together with the annexed chapels, viz., the chapel of the B.V.M. of Castlemartyn, the chapel of St. Canice of Kynnegh, and tithes of land in Kynnegh near Adgarvan, tithes of Blakrath *alias* Cancnrath, in Kylcolyn parish, the chapels of St. Mary of Galmolaston,

St. David of Birdynchapell, and St. John the Baptist of Kylgone, together with their tithes, the gift of Thomas son of John, earl of Kildare ; a tenement and castle in Kyloolyn ; lands in the lordship of Kyloolyn, with their tithes, the gift of Thomas Walleys ; the church of Rathcole with its tithes ; tithes of Rathsallagh, Dublin diocese ; in Munster, the church of Kyldenall, with the chapels and right of advowson thereto belonging, in the diocese of Cashel ; the church of St. David near Athorler, in Arkslow Deanery ; land and a wood with their tithes in the diocese of Dublin ; the town and church of Dromsalan with its tithes ; the church of Philoppeston Nugent with its tithes in Armagh Diocese ; lands in Dundalk the gift of William Cashell ; 10s. on Dromkar the gift of the said William ; lands in Atkinlu the gift of Henry Alton ; three tenements in Carlingford the gift of John Leynagh ; in Meath, lands in Athboy, called the Newe rent, the gift of William Sutton ; a tenement in Drogheda near the Parish Church of the B.V.M. ; a tenement in Dunboyn, and lands in Dryneston, near Maynolar, the gift of John Estreta.

Witness—Thomas Walsh, clerk, notary public
Dated 17 Sep., 1504.

380 (319.) Depositions taken in the chapel of St. Lawrence, Holy Trinity Church, Dublin, 11 May, 1504, &c.

Richard Walsh, canon of Holy Trinity Church, deposes that, when clerk of St. Warburgh's, he went with the curates, Sir Henry Mulghan, to administer the last Sacraments to Richard Wydon, who declared to them, that, when, at the age of eleven, he was with his grandfather Robert Wydon and Alice Isauk his wife, both ill and his grandfather insensible, Walter Charellor, abbot of the monastery of the B.V.M., near Dublin, desired Robert to release his lands in the lordship of Sauntry to Alison Wydon their daughter for life with reversion to his monastery, but Alice refused to do so ; and that Sir Roger Roche, chaplain, then curate of Ballybaghill, denied he was seized of the lands of said Robert.

Sir Thomas Philpots deposes similarly.

Thomas Hobbok deposes similarly, and adds that Thomas Fyohe, sub-prior of Holy Trinity, and Sir Thomas Philpots were present.

Witnesses—Sir Thomas Fyohe, sub-prior, John Brown, literate, John Heyn, Walter Synott.

On the 8th November, 1504, William Hobbard deposed that he was parish clerk of Sauntry, where Robert Wydon lay insensible ; and that Alicia Wydon, his daughter, had certain deeds not sealed.

Witnesses—Sir Thomas Pecok, Richard Walsh, chaplains, master William Walsh, notary public, John Hay, literate, and John Mulghan, clerk, of Dublin, who at the request of Jonet Algan, widow of Richard Wydon, and Wm. his son, exemplified the same.

Dated 8 Nov., 1504.

381 (317.) Johanna Waryng, widow of Peter Barthilmew of Dublin, grants to Holy Trinity Church, lands in Dalkaye, county of Dublin.

Dated 18 Feb., 20 Henry VII., (1505).

382. (317*.) Grantor in No. 381 supra, appoints Thomas Bathe of Dublin, to deliver seisin of the premises therein.

Dated 18 Feb., 20 Henry VII. (1505).

383. (320 bis.) Walter, archbishop of Dublin, exemplifies Bulls Nos. 6 and 8 supra.

Witnesses—Geoffrey Fych, Henry Levet, canon, William Power, chancellor, Sir Christopher Planket, knight, lord of Rathmore, Walter

Wellisley, canon of Kildare, Richard Garrot, Dublin, and Thomas Walsh, notary public.

Dated at St. Patrick's, Dublin, 8 Nov., 1505.

384. Henry VII. reciting that John Burnell, of Balgryffyn, gentleman, granted to John Yong, chaplain, for a chantry in the chapel of St. Dulacha, the lands of Bothomer, Balmancaryk and Notilbed, worth £4 per annum, as appears by the Inquisition taken before John Fale, escheator of Dublin, and that John Yong had paid a fine to Gerald earl of Kildare; pardons the alienation, and confirms the grant.

Dated 22 Jan., 31 Henry VII. (1506).

[Indorso.] Enrolled in the Memorandum Rolls of the Exchequer, Easter, 21 Henry VII. (1506).

385. (321.) William Englysh, mayor, and William Talbot and Nicholas Roch, bailiffs of Dublin, exemplify a civic ordinance, 12° Henry VII., providing that pilgrims and refugees may have free access to Christ Church. (Partly English.)

Dated 10 Sep., 23 Henry VII. (1507).

386. Geoffray Fych, archdeacon of Glendalongh, commissary (by commission, 6 Mar., 1508), of Robert Fitzsimon, precentor of St. Patrick's and official of the metropolitan court of Dublin, to take the depositions in a suit between Holy Trinity church, and John Englysh, canon of St. Patrick's and custos of the lepers of St. Stephen near Dublin, about the limits of lands at Ballytyhirrle near Ballowyr, county Dublin, and the ownership thereof, returns that, in presence of John Mulghan, notary public, and John Englysh, John Hore of Sauntri deposed that the Prior of Christ Church is lord of the town of Ballityppir alias Ballitobbyr in the marches of Dublin, and that his carts brought the tithes thereof to the Grange of Clonken; that the lands had been set to Nicholas son of Adam Laghnan of Clonken for 3 years, and that, excepting this, the tenants of Clonken held the lands aforesaid with common of pasture; that those lands are bounded by Kylmahnil, Ballowr and the Grange of Clonken; that "the Moralawn" belonged to the church aforesaid, and contained Tyrrooght, near the pond of Ballowr, and Tyrcorryn between Ballitobbir and Clonken. Manrice O'Tole of Sauntri deposed similarly, and that Walter Hakkett held the lands. William Denys, William and Richard Garrott, Nicholas Fannyn and John Glan, of Clonken, deposed similarly, in the chapel of the B.V.M., Holy Trinity Church, on the 3 June.

Witnesses at Sauntri.—Thomas Fitzwillim, William Poswyke, Richard Loghnan and William Davy; and in Holy Trinity church— William Davy, Richard Loghnan, Thomas FitzWillim, and Thomas Walsh, clerk, notary public.

Dated 3 June, 1508.

387 (322.) The Prior and convent of Holy Trinity command the serjeant of Grange German lordship to pay 10s. 0d., portion of a subsidy assessed on their lands at a parliament in Dublin, on Friday after the Feast of St. Michael the Archangel.

Dated 21 Nov., 24 Henry VII. (1508).

388 (323.) Exemplification of an assize of novel disseisin at Drogheda, before John de Stanley, Justiciary of Ireland, on Friday after the Feast of the Purification of the B. V. M., 14° Richard II., wherein the

Prior and convent of Holy Trinity Church recovered against Philip, rector of the church of St. Stephen of Ballowre, land in Tobberstown *alias* Ballitobber near Ballowr.

Dated at Rathcoole, 17 Aug., 2 Henry VIII. (1510).

389 (324.) Richard Skyrret, prior of Holy Trinity Church, and Master Thomas Rochfort, dean of St. Patrick's, Dublin, appoint William Hassard, canon of Holy Trinity, and the said dean, proctors to obtain Royal licence to elect an archbishop of Dublin.

Dated 20 May, 1511.

390. Richard Skyrrett, prior of Holy Trinity, and Thomas Rochfort, dean of St. Patrick's, Dublin, request Nicholas Roch, mayor of Dublin, John Fitzsymon and Robert Fawconer, bailiffs thereof, to put the Prior and convent of Holy Trinity in possession of two houses near the High Cross of Dublin, in the Parish of St. Nicholas within the walls, bequeathed to them by John Bowrke for ever, for prayers for his soul, &c.

Dated 12 July, 1511.

391. Simon Duff, chaplain, and Geneta Fannyng of Dublin, widow, grant to Holy Trinity church, a messuage in Oxmantown, bounded by the lane leading to the monastery of B. V. M., near Dublin, on the north, the lands of the monks of the said monastery on the south and west, and by Kingeslane on the east.

Dated 20 Feb., 3 Henry VIII. (1512).

392. Grantors in No. 391 *supra*, appoint James Cogan, clerk, to deliver seisin of the premises therein.

Dated 20 Feb., 3 Henry VIII. (1512.)

393 (325.) Grantees in No. 391 *supra*, appoint John Huyn, to accept seisin of the premises therein.

Dated 20 Feb., 3 Henry VIII. (1512).

394 (326.) Henry VIII. directs the mayor and bailiffs of Dublin to pay the Prior and convent of Christ Church an annuity of £20, granted them by Henry VII., and the arrears thereof.

Dated at Dublin, 10 April, 3 Henry VIII. (1512).

Enrolled in the Memorandum Rolls of the Exchequer in Trinity Term, 4 Henry VIII.

395. (327.) Henry VIII. releases the Prior of Holy Trinity Church as spiritual custos of Dublin diocese, the see being vacant, from all claims, actions and accounts in respect of the same.

Dated at Dublin, 26 May, 4 Henry VIII. (1512).

396. (329.) Thomas Plunkete of Dunsoghly, gent. grants to Holy Trinity Church, lands in Moch Cabberaght, co. Dublin, to support a regular canon to pray for him and Jonet Fynglas, his wife, Phillppa Bremyngham and Helena Strangwyche, his wife, and their relations.

Dated at Dublin, 17 June, 4 Henry VIII. (1512).

397. (329ª.) Grantor in No. 396 *supra*, appoints John Searle to deliver seisin of the premises therein.

Dated 17 June, 4 Henry VIII. (1512).

398 (328.) William, archbishop of Dublin, at a provincial council held at Holy Trinity church, 21 September, 1512, confirms the rights of Holy Trinity church with reference to pilgrims and refugees.
Witness, Thomas Walsh, notary public.
Dated 21 Sep., 1512.

399. (331.) William Walsh, diocese of Kildare, and Thomas Walsh, diocese of Ferns, notaries public, declare that Thomas Fyuh sub-prior of Holy Trinity, and John Eustace of Castlemartyn near Kilcolyn Bridge, exhibited to them an indenture of 4 May, 1512, whereby Richard, prior of Holy Trinity, leased to the said John Eustace, the small tithes of Castlemartyn and Kynegh appertaining to Kilcolyn, for 6 years; rent 10s., and to maintain a priest in Castlemartyn for the tenants of it and Kynegh, saving mortuaries and other duties to the Prior and convent.
Witnesses, Sir William Englande, canon, John Haroll, Peter Wolff and Thomas Wodhorn, clerks. (Partly English).
Dated 1512.

400. (330.) Thomas Plunket of Dunsoghly, gent., grants to Holy Trinity church, his crops in Dunsoghly, co. Dublin, viz.—wheat, oats, barley, beans and peas, for the purpose in No. 396 supra.
Dated 1 June, 5 Henry VIII. 1513.

401 (332.) Patrick Bermyngham, chief justice of the King's Bench, and Berthelmew Dillon, chief baron of the Exchequer, arbitrators in a suit between Richard Skyrett, prior of Christ Church, Dublin, and Sir John Chashell, prior of St. John's, Athirde, award that the Prior and convent of Christ Church should release to the Prior and convent of St. John's aforesaid, the lands of Blakiston, co. Louth, for 10s. rent, a year.
Dated 8 May, 6 Henry VIII. (1514.) (English.)

402 (333). John Cashell, prior of the House of St. John the Baptist of Athirde, grants to Holy Trinity Church, 10s. yearly rent from Blakeston, co. Louth.
Dated 20 Nov., 6 Henry VIII. (1514.)

403 (334). Exemplification of grant (No. 364 deed (c) supra) to Prior and convent of Christ Church, enrolled in Chancery, 7 Henry VIII.
Witness.—William Preston, lord viscount Gormanston.
Dated 14 March, 7 Henry VIII. (1516).

404. Margaret Mychell, widow, grants to Holy Trinity Church, her messuages and lands in Langton, Cornebill, and Conryhyllys, in co. Kildare.
Dated 28 March, 7° Henry VIII (1516).

405 (336.) The Prior of Holy Trinity church binds himself in £100 to William Talbott, of Dublin, merchant, and Jenate Stanyhurst, his wife, to abide the award to be made by Patrick Bermyngham, chief justice of the King's Chief Place, Mr. Richard Delahyd, chief justice of the Common place, and Sir Bertholome Dillon, chief baron of the Exchequer, with reference to Pasavaunt's lands, and Clark's lands, in the city of Dublin, provided the award be made by Thursday before the feast of St. Valentine the martyr prox. (Partly English).
Dated 25 Jan., 8 Henry VIII. (1517).

406 (335.) William, archbishop of Dublin, exemplifies No. 288 *supra.*
Witnesses.—Alexr. Plunket, principal official of Armagh, Sir Thaddeus
Madyne, lawyer, Sir Thos. Pomyk, rector of Lyons, in the diocese of
Kildare, and Thomas Walsh, notary public.
Dated Monday, 10 Feb., 1516 (1517.)

407 (337.) Exemplification of a recovery suffered before Richard
Delahyde, Easter Term 9 Henry VIII., of messuages in parish of St.
James, Dublin, in parish of St. Nicholas the Bishop within the walls,
in the Skyner Row, in the Fysshe shamlis, in the parish of St. John
Evangelist, *alias* in the Bothe st., called the Toure of Dublin, on the
" Key," and in Ship strete, Passannts lands, messuages called gardeyns
in St. Francis street, messuages in parish of St. Audoens, in parish of
St. John the Evangelist at the city crans, on the " Key," in St. Michael's
lane, in Brigo strut, called Clerkis landis ; in a suit wherein Richard
Talbot, of Dublin, son of Richard Talbot, and John Pers, chaplain, son
of Thomas Pers, were complainants, Richard Skyrret, prior of Holy
Trinity Church, Wm. Dongh, merchant, and Agnes, his wife, defor-
cients, Stephen Warr, tenant, and Barnabas Fitzhenry, vouchee.
Dated 24 May, 9 Henry VIII. (1517).

408. Edmund Walsh of Carykmane, at the request of William
Hazard, sub prior of Holy Trinity Church, renounces his claim in the
lands called Ketingsland and Priouresland near Carykmoyne.
Witnesses—Thomas Doyng, prior of the Augustine priory, Sir John
Canlane, chaplain, Patrick Wogan, friar, Wm. Langton, regular canon,
Maurice Black, Denis Morghowe, John Clerk and Thomas Walsh,
clerk, notary public.
Dated 21 Feb., 1519.

409 (336.) Sir Edward Plunkett, knight, lord of Donnawny, and
Amy Bermyngham his wife, Christopher Plunket of Donsoghly, gent.,
and Katherine Bermyngham, his wife, release to William Hassard, prior
of Holy Trinity Church, Dublin, and the convent thereof all actions
which they have against them.
Witnesses—Patrick Whit and Henry Cowyll, chaplain.
Dated 5 July, 13 Henry VIII. (1521).

410 (339.) Wm. Hassard, prior of Holy Trinity, guardian of the
spiritualities of the sees of Dublin and Leighlin, the archbishop of
Dublin being absent, and the see of Leighlin vacant by the death of
Thomas the late bishop, delegates the episcopal jurisdiction of Leighlin
diocese to Karole [abbot] of Dowyshe, chancellor, and Cornelius, dean of
Leighlin, and appoints them sub-custodians of the see during his pleasure.
Dated at Holy Trinity, 3 Feb., 1522.

411. Nicholas Nangle, chaplain, survivor of William Whyte, chaplain,
grants to Holy Trinity Church, the lands granted them by Juliana Sprote,
widow, in Clony and Powrtan, parish of Dunboyn, co. Meath.
Dated 20 Oct., 15 Henry VIII. (1523).

412. Release of premises in No. 411, *supra.*
Dated, 21 Oct., 15 Henry VIII. (1523).

413 (340.) James White, archdeacon of Armagh, grants to Holy
Trinity Church, a messuage, with garden annexed in Dalkey, co.
Dublin.
Dated 20 Oct., 16 Henry VIII. (1524).

414 (340*.) Grantor in No. 413, *supra*, appoints James Rochford of Dublin, yeoman, to deliver seisin of premises therein.
Dated 20 Oct., 16 Henry VIII. (1524).

415 (341*.) Release of No. 413, *supra*.
Dated 22 Oct., 16 Henry VIII (1524).

416 (341b.) Anna Bartholome, daughter and heiress of Johanna Waryng, widow of Peter Bartholome, grants to James Whitt, chaplain, her lands in Dalky, co. Dublin, to the use of Holy Trinity church.
Witnesses—James, archdeacon of Armagh, Henry Gawran.
Dated 11 Dec., 17 Henry VIII. (1525).

417. The Prior and convent of Holy Trinity church reduce to 6s. 8d. the rent of 16s. payable by Sir Nicholas de St. Laurence, lord of Howth, out of a stone messuage in Oxmantown, near the bridge, opposite the chapel of the St. Mary, and situate between the land of Thomas Tyve on the north, the Lyffy on the south, the highway on the east, and the garden of the said Thomas on the west; for 59 years.
Dated (5) day of April, 1526.

418 (342.) George Dondall, prior of the House of St. John the Baptist of Athirle, co. Louth, grants to Holy Trinity church, 10s. rent from lands in Blakeston, co. Louth.
Dated at Athirle, 20 Oct., 18 Henry VIII. (1526).

419 (343.) William Donowt, citizen and merchant of Dublin, bequeaths his body to be buried in the tomb of his ancestors in Holy Trinity church, and his dwelling-house to the said church, on condition that his anniversary be observed, and a yearly sum of 10s. paid towards the building of the parish church of St. Michael in High-street.
To Richard Roche he bequeaths his wood called Irishwood, and appoints William Hassard, prior of Holy Trinity church, and Catherine Cole, his executors.—*Circa* 1530.

420 (344.) Inquisition taken at Lucan, before Thomas Bermyngham, seneschal there, on Thursday after the feast of St. Barnabas the Apostle, 24 Henry VIII., by Richard Hyll, Patrick Lay, Richard Geres, James Bryan, Pers Brenan, John Lang, Richard Holms, Patrick Wade, Thomas O'Mᶜke, James Jordan, William Wale, and James Gryffyng, all of Lucan, finds that the boundary between the land of Holy Trinity church and that of Sir Nicholas Horpor or Harpol, chaplain, lies between the hole made in the wall of the barn of the said Nicholas on the south, and a hole made in the wall of the churchyard of Lucan on the north.
Dated 13 June, 1532.

421 (345.) Henry VIII., on the security of Donald O'Cullan and Andrew Walshe, of the co. of Dublin, husbandmen, grants to Richard Savage, of Chapel Ysold, a custodiam of St. Lanus ye lands in co. Dublin, during pleasure.
Dated at Dublin 24 Aug., 24 Henry VIII. (1582).

422 (346.) Walter Cusak, treasurer of St. Patrick's and official of Dublin, exemplifies No. 193 *supra*.
Witness—Master William Power, canon of St. Patrick's, John Walsh, literate, George Allen, and Hugh Holgrane, notary public.
Dated 27 Oct., 1533.

H

423 (347.) Richard Freman of Cottrelleston, husbandman, grants to Patrick Cromall, chaplain, to the use of the Prior and convent of Christ Church, land in Cottrelleston, in Wycston, parish of Balmadon, and in Jordaneston, parish of Clonmethan, co. Dublin, the gift of William Bysset and Olyff Ray his wife.

Dated 4 May, 26 Henry VIII. (1534).

424 (347*.) Grantor in No. 423 supra, appoints John Ball, yeoman, to deliver seisin of the premises therein.

Dated 4 May, 26 Henry VIII. (1534).

425 (348). Patrick Cromall, chaplain, grants to Holy Trinity church, the premises in No. 423 supra.

Dated 10 May, 26 Henry VIII. (1534).

426. William Hassard, late prior of Christ Church, having resigned during a suit between him and Walter Kerdyff of Shallon regarding the lands of Muche Cabbraghe, co. Dublin, the convent of Christ Church and Walter agreed to abide the award of Gerald Allmer, chief justice of the King's Bench, and Patrick Fynglas, chief baron of the Exchequer. Master Arland Ussher and Thomas Stephyns having given their bond that the Prior and convent should abide this award, George, archbishop of Dublin, undertakes that the new Prior shall bind himself to abide the award and release the said Arland and Thomas.   (English).

Dated Trinity Term, 29 Henry VIII., 1537.

427 (349). William Power, archdeacon of Dublin, declares that, in pursuance of a mandate from George, archbishop of Dublin, he has installed Robert Paynewyke, late canon of the monastery of Lanthony, as Prior of Christ Church.

Witness—Nicholas Bernet, notary public.

Dated 4 Jul. 1537.

428 (350.) Nicholas Hancoke of Dublin, merchant, Genet Stancst (or Stanhurst), his wife, late wife of William Talbot, mayor of Dublin, and Christopher Talbot her son, executors of the will of the said William, grant to Henry Gawran, Patrick Tothe, and Robert Molan, chaplains, master and wardens of the fraternity of "Corpus Christi" at the altar of St. Katharine in the church of St. Michael the Archangel, Dublin, William Browne's messuage in High st., Dublin, lying between the messuage of John Sarsvell on one side, and that of Christopher Plunket of Donshoghle now inhabited by David Rochforde on the other, to maintain a priest to celebrate for the souls of Wm. Talbot, his wife and relatives.

Witness.—William Mowshurst, registrar of the court of Dublin.

Dated 10 Oct. 30 Henry VIII. (1538).

429 (351). Exemplification of a petition, writ of dedimus potestatem, and the examinations thereunder. The Prior of Christ Church, Dublin, stating that John Kerdyff sold Mocha Cabhraghe, co. Dublin, to justice Plunket, who granted it to Holy Trinity church, and that Walter Kerdyff, son of the said John, now second justice of the King's Common Place, sues the occupiers thereof; prays a writ of dedimus potestatem to examine Christopher Plunket of Dunsoghly, son and heir of the said justice Plunket. On the 6th July, 31 Henry VIII., Christopher Plunket of Dunsoghly deposed that Edward Caddell of Harbartstown and Richard Pentney informed deponent that the said John had sold Mocha Cabhraghe to his father, the justice, and that Sir Richard Rogers

chaplain, in the priest's chamber in Dunsoghly where he was at school, had stated to him that his father had purchased 20 nobles a year. Deponent further stated that archbishop Rouskesbe was informed by justice Plunket that all his lands had been purchased truly. (*English*). Dated at Dublin 10 July, 31 Henry VIII. (1539).

430 (352). Rental of Holy Trinity church prepared by brother Christopher Rathe, canon of the said church, in the year 1539. (*English*.)

431 (351ᵃ). John Alen esquire, chancellor, George, archbishop of Dublin, William Brabazon, esquire, sub-treasurer, ordain that Holy Trinity church, having been secular at its foundation, its ministers shall in future be regarded as secular priests and wear secular habits; that it shall have a dean, precentor, chancellor, and treasurer, like St. Patricks; that Robert Paynswicke *alias* Castoll, the prior, shall be dean, and that he and his successors shall enjoy Clankene for his dignity, and the church of Glasnevin for his prebend, with the temporalities in Glasnevin and Clonmell, tithes being excepted, Dromconragh, with its tithes, Clankey, Dalkeya, Killeny, Balliloghan, and Hayhurter, Ballybrenan, Ballytipper, Dallyogan, Ballymoghan, Farnicoast, Kylmahyoke, the spiritualities in Ballyfinch and Ballycheor, the temporalities of Balscaddon and Smotherowurt, Priorsland and Ketingesland near Carrickmoyne and the churches of Carrickmayne, Tullaghe, Stalorgan, Clonkyne, Kylmahyoke, Dalkeya, Kilkeny, Ballyleghan, Rocheston, Cornelacourta, Kylbegote, Stalorgan, and Newton, with their chapels and tithes, and the Pole mylle without the Pole gate of Dublin; that Richard Ball the sub-prior be precentor of the church and have the church of Ballgriffyn, now created a prebendal church, and the churches of Ballgriffyn and Drumsallan, with their tithes and lands, one half the tithes of Glasnevin, one half the small tithes of Dromconragh, and lands in Cowlocke; that Walter Whyte, seneschal and precentor, be chancellor and enjoy the church of Kilcullen erected into a prebendal church, the tithes of Galmorstown, Castlemartin, Kinnegh, and Blakroth in said parish, the other half of the tithes of Glasnevin, the other half of the small tithes of Dromconragh, tithes of Kyrolenall, lands in Roganstown, Lespopyll, Mynystown, Dundalke, Dromcarr, and Carlingford; that John Mosse, sub-precentor and sacrist, shall in future be treasurer, and that he and his successors shall enjoy the church of Balscaden erected into a prebendal church with the great tithes thereof, lands in Ponchestowne, and the water mill of Glasnevin; that the said dignitaries, like those of St. Patricks, shall reside in the church; that, saving the dean, one of them shall celebrate second mass daily, and the mass of the B.V.M. and High mass on festivals proper to the same; that eight regular canons and four choristers shall be known as the vicars choral, £53 13s. 4d. being yearly assigned for the vicars and £6 13s. 4d. for the choristers, such sums to be realised from the rents of lands in Grangegorman and Oxmantown Greene, the £20 from the fee farm of Dublin, the great tithes of Kilcullen, the tithes of Rathole and Ballycor, the great tithes of Nicholstowne and Gilgoone, the lands of Athird, Delverstowne, Cloonia, Porterstown, and Kilcullen, and the tithes of fish in the Liffey; that John Ourragh, priest, the first of the vicars choral, be sub-dean and have a place in the chapter and a voice in the election of archbishop and dean, and that the parish church of St. Michael, Dublin, now erected into a prebendal church, with its tithes, be assigned to him, together with £4 from the above sum for a stipend; that

H 2

one of the vicars choral shall be succentor, whose office shall be to
instruct the choristers, and that the church of St. Michan, erected
into a prebendal church, be assigned to John Kerdyff as such succentor
with like privileges as the sub-dean; that the chancellor shall have a
vicar choral to correct the Latin of the choir books; that Christopher
Rathe be appointed to such office as minor canon, and that the church of
St. John the Evangelist be assigned to him, together with a stipend of
4 marks Irish from the sum aforesaid; that the treasurer shall have a
vicar choral, and that Oliver Graunt be appointed to such office, as
minor canon, with a stipend of 5 marks Irish as aforesaid; that the
other vicars choral shall each have £3 6s. 8d. for stipend; that the
archdeacon of Dublin shall have a stall in the choir, a place in the
chapter, and a prebend in the church; that vacancies be filled and duties
performed in manner prescribed; that a clerk learned in music and
organ playing shall teach the boys, perform at mass, and have the office
of beadle with a stipend of £6 13s. 4d., and a moristan and a third clerk-
be appointed to ring the bells, &c., that the building and repair of the
church and refectory be maintained from the issues of the lands of
Kinsale, Ballydoude, Cromlen, Mapestown, Drogheda, Athboy, Brenes-
toune, Donboyne, Oabroghe, Ballymore, Rathmoore, Stagobbe, in the
Maginneeshes, the chief rents and tithes of Kyllcatar, the chapel of
Phillipstowne Nugant, the woods myll, gardens in Oxmantown, without
the gate of St. Nicholas, Dublin, near the church of St. Andrew, and
without the Pole gate; and that a syndic steward or proctor be elected
to manage the affairs of church and chapter.
Dated 12th day of December, 31 Henry VIII. (1539).
Calendared from the Novum Registrum.

432 (353.) The Prior and convent of Holy Trinity church petition
Henry VIII. for letters patent to change them into the Dean and
chapter of Holy Trinity church, and that Robert Castell *alias* Payneswyke, the prior, and Richard Ball, Walter Whyte, John Mosse, John
Curraghe, John Kerdiffe, Christopher Rathe, Oliver Graunt, William
Owen, and Nicholas Owgaan, late canons thereof, should become secular
priests; that Robert Castell *alias* Payneswyke should become dean,
and Richard Ball, Walter Whyte, and John Mosse, precentor, chancellor and treasurer, respectively; that they should have power to
allocate their lands for salary amongst themselves, and fill the offices of
precentor, chancellor, or vicar choral, when vacant; that the archdeacon of Dublin should have a stall in the choir and participate in the
acts of the chapter; that they should individually pay, in lieu of
twentieths, sums to be imposed by a new commission, or, as a body, a
twentieth part of the clear yearly value of their possessions; that first
fruits should be payable on every promotion, and that the dean and
chapter should enjoy such portions of their possessions as were allocated
to them by John Alen, Esq., chancellor of Ireland, George, archbishop
of Dublin, and William Brabaston, Esq., sub-treasurer, by virtue of
Royal Commission.—*Circa* 1540.

433 (354.) The Dean and chapter of Holy Trinity ratify the allo-
cation of their possessions to the dean, precentor, chancellor, treasurer
and vicars choral, as made by the Royal Commissioners, in No. 431 *supra*
by their deed of the 12 September, 31 Henry VIII.
Dated 11 July, 34 Henry VIII. (1542).

434 (355.) Account of the economy rents of the Cathedral church of
the Blessed Trinity in the year 1542, by John Mos the proctor; sets out

the receipts, from the city of Dublin, in the Hie street, the Trynyte lane
Saynt Myghillis lane, the Wyne Taverne, the Fyshe street, Saint Warburge's street, the Skynner rowe, Saint Nicholas street, the Rochell lane,
the Bridge street, upon the Key, the Coke street, Saint Patrikis street,
Saint Fraunces street, Saint Thomas street, Oxmantown, the Fysher lane,
the Ship street and Saint George's lane; from lands in the country,
in Kyllestre, Stagub, Rallymore, Maplistown, Drenestown, the Col-
bragha, Kynsalye, Athboy, Rathomore, Ballydowd and Bakyr, Drogheda,
Ballicanlor, Dunboyne, Phyllippstowne Nugent, Cromlyugo; and from
the church, viz. The Knellis, the month's minds of "Ben," the twelve-
month's minds, the Funerals, the Obligations, and the "Compos." Amongst
the payments occur, 8 stone of cast lead 9s. 4d., a quire of paper 4d., 5
stone of resin 5s. 10d., a carpenter for 5 days 5s., his servant 3 days
2s., 40 lbs. wax 20s. 8d., rushes to our Lady chapel 2d., casting 24
stone of lead 4s., fire wood for same 1s., glasier 5 days 5s., 2 panes
colored glass to the chapter house window 2s., 20 carnocks of lime
16s. 8d., six dozen quarter boards 6s., 43 quarts of oil 14s. 4d., thirteen
dozen tallow candles 13s., the haller (tiler) 9 days 6s., his servant 8
days 4s., washing 7 amyttis and 2 chalice cloths 4d., 5 carts haller sand
2s. 0d., 4 matts to the quires 2s. 6d., 2 chalice cloths and making 10d.,
the mason and his servant one day tiling the church 1s. 4d., a thousand
mass breads 1s. 8d., a thousand lath pins 4d., washing the choristers'
surplices 2 towels and 2 rochets 0d., 2 loads of turf 4d., a "bawderken"
8s., a thousand lath nails 1s. 8d., a dozen of Christs 2s., 200 tiles 2s.,
washing 2 albs 2 surplices 2 rochets and 5 amytts 0d., 2 sconces to the
quire, 8d., marking 2 towels 0d., a key to the quire door 3d., Peter
Doher for punishing a thief 4d., the brawderer (embroiderer?) 1 day 1s.,
2 ounces verdigris 4d., for torches 3 lb. tallow 8d., 5 girdles for albs 4d.,
for the Lord's supper 1½ quarts of oil 1s. 0d., a surplice cloth and
making 4s., at mass a quart of mustard 0d., 4 lb. solder 2s., cleaning
the eagle and both pair of great candlesticks 1s. 6d., 7 pair of gloves for
the ringers 1s. 0d., rushes to the rood loft and my lord Kildare's chapel
2d., a quire of paper for songs 6d., 3 locks to the wax chest 1s.,
brooms 3d., a pint pot to the church for wine 6d., a chaping pot to the
church for water 4d., 2 barrows 4d., 2 carts of stones, 6d., a dozen
shrouds 2s., 3 dozen ditto 5s., 1½ dozen large ditto 4s. 0d., 2 wall plates
1s. To Sir John Mos for his pains 40s. (Some other items in this
account are set out in Mr. Gilbert's History of the City of Dublin, pp. 110
and 143 vol. 2.) (English).

1542.

(Calendared from Novum Registrum.)

435. George, archbishop of Dublin, informs William Carde, vicar
of St. Dulacin, that the chapel of Balgryffyne with its minor tithes
has been united to his vicarage.

Dated 7 April, 34 Henry VIII. (1543).

436. (356.) Walter Kerdyffe, of Shallon, gent., second justice of the
Kings Common Bench, and John Kerdyffe, of Shallon, gent., bind them-
selves, in 200 marks, to Thomas Lokwode and the chapter of Holy
Trinity church, to abide the award of the Right Honorable Sir Anthony
Santleger, K.G., lord deputy, John Alone, lord chancellor, William
Brabazon, vice treasurer of the Exchequer, Sir Gerald Aylmer, chief
justice of the chief place, Sir Thomas Luttrell, chief justice of the
common place, James Bathe, chief baron of the Exchequer, Sir Thomas
Cusake, master of the rolls, and Thomas Howth, second justice of the

Kings chief place, concerning Mychie Cabhraghe, co. Dublin. *(Partly English.)*
Dated 6 Nov., 36 Henry VIII. (1544).

437 (357.) Henry VIII. commands Thomas Lockewode and Edward Basnot, deans of Christ Church and St. Patricks, respectively, to levy the subsidy granted by parliament, held 27 April, 35 Henry VIII., for ten years, for defence of the kingdom, and pay same into the Exchequer.
Dated, 12 Nov., 38 Henry VIII. (1546).

438 (358.) Edward VI. directs Edward, bishop of Meath, Thomas Lockwod, dean of Holy Trinity, William Bynaley, L.B., master in chancery, and Ludwig Tudor, L.B., rector of Rosslare, to hear the appeal of John Fyan *alias* Feth, rector of St. Himer of Killare, diocese of Meath, from George, archbishop of Armagh.
Dated at Dublin, 16 March, 1 Edward VI. (1547).

439 (359.) Edward VI. grants 10 marks yearly, each, to Christopher Rathe, John Herman, and Nicholas Dardyse, priests, to perform Divine service in Christ Church, Dublin. Sir Anthony Sentleger, K.G., P.C., lord deputy of Ireland, Sir Richard Rede, chancellor, Sir William Brabazon, vice-treasurer, Sir Thomas Lutrell, chief justice of the common bench, James Bath, chief baron of the Exchequer, and Sir Thomas Cusak, master of the rolls, commissioners, having recommended an increase of six priests and two singing boys.
12 July, 1 Edward VI. (1547).

440 (360.) George, archbishop of Dublin, releases to the dean and chapter of Holy Trinity church, Dublin, 40s. (portion of 46s. 8d.) yearly, out of the proxies of the churches of St. Michael Archangel, St. John Evangelist, St. Michau, Clonakeyne, Stalorgan, Dalkey, Kylleuen, Tullaghe, Whitchurche, Balgriffen, Balscadan, and Glasnevyn, co. Dublin, for the maintenance of the vicars choral.
Dated 16 Sep., 1 Edward VI. (1547).

441 (361.) George, archbishop of Dublin, with the consent of the chapter of Holy Trinity church, grants to Edward de St. Laurence *alias* Houthe, lord Houthe, John Eustace of Conffe, John Plunket of Donsoghly, Reginald Talbot of Belgarde, Thomas Fitzwilliam of Baggotrath, Edward Barnewall of Dromnaghe, Christopher Lottrell, son and heir of Sir Thomas Luttrell, of Luttrellston, chief justice of the Common Bench, John Bathe, son and heir of James Bathe, chief baron of the Exchequer, Christopher Barnewall, son and heir of Patrick Barnewall of Gracedieu, Richard Dyllon of Soryne, and Patrick Fynglas, son and heir of Thomas Fynglas of Werpalleston, the advowsons of Ballybough, Boyesion, Templebodan, and Uske ; in trust that the grantees shall, whenever a living is vacant, present one of the vicars choral of Holy Trinity church thereto, and assign the whole, should royal licence be obtained, to the dean and chapter there. *(Partly English.)*
Dated 20 Sep., 1 Edward VI. (1547).

442. Similar to No. 441 *supra*, granting the churches therein named.
Dated, 20 Sep., 1 Ed. VI. (1547).
[In dorso] Witnesses to the livery of saisin, Walter Trott, vicar of Rathmore, Thomas Long of Hertwell, Richard Ewstace of Newland, gent., Remond Estyng, gent., Garrott McDonaghe galoclaghe, Fylyme O'Berne, Maloghyng Kelly, and Edmond O'Malowny.

Sir Edmonde Ewstas attorne for the spiritualities of Ouske in presence of John Kyelly, curate of Kylcollyng, James Flangan, vicar of Donaday, Dannes Stanton, and Wm. O'Collynnan, clerks of Clogoyswod.

Sir Edmond Ewstas, yearly tenant of the spiritual tithes of Ballehoght near Ballymore, co. Dublin, attorns in presence of Fergus McEocha.

Ferrall McKeho, tenant of the temporalities of Ballehoght, attorns in presence of Fergus McEocha mac Fergus, Sir Edmond Ewstas, parson of Ouak, and Laghlen Keila.

Almad MakEohe attorns for the spiritualities of Boystona.

(*Attornments partly in Irish.*)

443 (362.) George, archbishop of Dublin, grants to the Dean and chapter of Holy Trinity church, for his life, 6s. 8d. yearly, for proxies as in No. 440, *supra.* (*English.*)

Dated 20 Sep., 1 Edward VI. (1547).

444 (363.) George, archbishop of Dublin, unites the churches of St. Brigid of Stalorgan and Kylmohude to the church of St. Fintain of Clonkeyne, the union, if there be any, of Kylmohude with the church of St. Mary of Donabroke, being first revoked.

Dated 8 Aug., 1551.

445 (364.) Martin Stanton, official of the metropolitan court of Dublin, in a suit between Thomas Lockwode, dean of Holy Trinity, Dublin, and rector of Clonkene, of the one part, and James Goodman of Balyloghan, and James Goodman of Cornelliston, gentleman, parishioners of Clonkene, of the other part, decrees that the election of minister or parish clerk of Clonkene belongs to the dean.

Dated 20 Nov., 1552.

446 (365.) Philip and Mary grant licence to Richard Talbots of Dublin, John Caddell of Nell, and Michael Goldyng of Tartayna, gentleman, to convey to the Dean and chapter of Holy Trinity, the rectory of Kyllmahud, co. Dublin, notwithstanding the statute of mortmain.

Dated 8 Nov., 1 and 2 Philip and Mary (1554).

447 (366.) Philip and Mary require the dean and chapter of the Metropolitan church, Dublin, to elect Hugh Curren, LL.D., to be archbishop of Dublin. (*English.*)

Dated at Westminster, 18 Feb., 1 and 2 Philip and Mary (1555).

448 (368.) Philip and Mary confirm the grant of Edward VI., that the establishment of Holy Trinity church should be increased by six priests and two chorister boys, 10 marks to be paid each priest, and 4 marks to each boy, and that their nomination be vested in the dean and chapter.

Dated at Dublin, 20 May, 1 and 2 Philip and Mary (1555).

449 (367.) Mary charges the dean and chapter of Christ Church, Dublin, to obey the archbishop of Dublin lately appointed (*English.*)

Dated at Greenwich, 16 Sep., 2 and 3 Philip and Mary (1555).

450. Patrick Cromall, chaplain, grants to Thomas FitzWilliams of Baggotrath, William, son and heir of John Bathe of Athearn, John, son and heir of James Bathe of Drumnaghe, and Christopher Barnewall of Graceslewe, land in Cottrelston, co. Dublin, land in Wieston, parish of

Balmadon, and land in Jordanston, parish of Clomothan, co. Dublin, granted to him the 4th May, 36 Henry VIII., by Richard Froman of Cottralston; and appoints Matthew Hamlinge, yeoman, to deliver seisin thereof.

Witnesses—John Plunket, Thomas Alen.

Dated 4 Nov., 2 & 3 Philip and Mary (1555).

Present at the delivery of seisin—John Herman, clerk, Matthew Hamlen, clerk, Richard Dillon, husbandman, Richard Cowgmr.

[Indorse] Grantor declares that the premises were granted to him by Richard Freman, to the use of the prior and convent of Christ Church, and the feoffees are to be seised thereof to the same use.

451 (369.) Thomas Loverousa, dean, and the chapter of St. Patrick's, release to the dean and chapter of Holy Trinity church, their goods, chattels, musical instruments, &c., in the possession of the latter.

Dated 27 April, 1558.

452. The Dean and chapter of Holy Trinity, by William Magrane their attorney, having presented their bill to the Right Honorable William Gerrard, lord chancellor, against Thomas Heiwarde of Malahide, John Husborne of Rogerston, Thomas Terrell, Patrick Carre, Thomas Carrs of Houth, and Patrick Managhan of Clontarff, fishermen, to recover tithes of fish, especially herrings, taken in the river Lyffy between Isold fonte and the Barrefoote, Dublin, Thomas Heward answered that the common custom of Ireland was to give half of such tithes to the parish church where they land the fish, and the other half to the parish where the fishers dwell. The lord chancellor decreed in favour of complainants. (English.)

Dated 23 June, 19 Elizabeth. 1577.

453. The Lord Deputy and Council, at the instance of the Dean and chapter of Christ Church, Dublin, declare that the town and land of Glasnevyn should be exempt from cesses of subsidy and carriage. Signed by H. Sydney, lord deputy, T. Armagh, Adam Dublin, H. Meath, W. Darcy, H. Bagnal, John Challonor, Lucas Dillon. (English).

Dated 16 June, 20 Elizabeth (1578).

Enrolled in Chancery by Robert Byrne, 22° Elizabeth.

Entered in the Book of Acts, 8 Sep., 1643.

454 (370.) John Garvey, dean, and the chapter of Holy Trinity church, appeal for aid to repair the church, and request offerings to James Walsh, precentor, or to Peter Calf, his substitute.

Dated 1583.

455. John Garvey, bishop of Kylmore and dean of Holy Trinity, appoints Henry Whyte, clerk, or in his absence William Taffs, to be seneschal of Balscadden, county Dublin, on the condition that they shall find horsemeat and man's meat for the dean and his company when they keep court there, and yearly present a dish to the dean as the custom hath been. (English.)

Dated 12 December, 1586.

456. Jonas Whelan, dean, and the chapter of Holy Trinity appoint John Hamnett, of Dublin, yeoman, their attorney, to take possession of the parsonage of Kilkullen, co. Dublin, the messuages and lands in Mynstowne, in the possession of widow Hamlyn, those in Roganston in the possession of Patrick Saunders, "Gyfford's" farm in Cromlyn in

the possession of Thomas Chambers, and the wood in Cromlyn called Gifford's Grove, in the tenure of the widow Malone. (*English.*)

Dated 17 May, 38° Elizabeth (1590.)

457 (371.) Rents due to the house of the Petie canons of St. Patrick's, Dublin, amounting to £6 6s. 3d (*English.*)

17 Oct., 1609.

458 (372.) A clause from the will of Nicholas Weston of Dublin, alderman, directing his body to be buried in Christ Church, and leaving to it 0s. 8d. yearly out of Mr. Brice's house in the corn market, for a lamp to hang in the body of the church, his son, William Weston, to be executor, and Sir John King, knight, Walter Sedgrave, Matthew Handcoke, and Edward Ball of Dublin, alderman, overseers. (*English.*)

Dated 8 Jan., 1617.

(*Calendared from Novum Registrum.*)

459 (373.) Pope Urban VIII. directs the Bishops of Ossory, Ferns, and Cork, or their vicar-generals, to hear the complaint of Patrick Cahil, priest of the diocese of Meath, rector of the parish church of St. Michael, Dublin, and master in theology, against the Archbishop of Dublin, who had ordered him to depart from the city and diocese within 15 days, and suspended him under the pretence that he was author of certain perverse publications concerning the office of the Holy Inquisition.

Dated at St. Mary major, Rome, v. Kal. Sep. 9 Urban VIII. (28 Aug., 1631.)

460 (374.) Order in Council, that, in the cause of the Dean and chapter of Christ Church, and the inhabitants within its precincts, against the Mayor and citizens of Dublin, in the chief place, the parties not being able to agree on an indifferent jury to determine whether the Liberty within the precincts was within the city or not, the Lord Chancellor shall name 48 knights and gentlemen of note in the county, or strangers sojourning in the city, from whom a jury may be impannelled. The premises meanwhile to pay cess, but the prebendal houses to have exemption. (*English.*)

7 Nov., 1633.

(*Calendared from Novum Registrum.*)

461 (877.) Order of Council that no cellar or vault under Christ Church or house adjoining be used as tavern, tippling house, or tobacco shop ; the Archbishops of Armagh, Dublin, and Tuam, to view all erections against the walls which stop up light, disgrace or darken the church, and all encroachments; and removal of same to be ordered on their certificate. No person to put on his hat until the preacher have read his text ; none but the Lord Deputy and his lady to use curtains before their seats ; none to commit nuisance against the walls, or to walk and talk in the aisles during Divine service. (*English.*)

28th Nov., 1633.

(*Calendared from Novum Registrum.*)

462 (376.) Orders as to the Vicars choral in the performance of Divine service, as to their not talking, their kneeling, sitting, standing, &c., and especially as to the order of the service ; any vicar transgressing to forfeit 40s., for a second offence £1, and for a third, to be deprived of his place.

As in K. Edward VI. time, the vicars should be presbyters. John

Jewet is directed by next ordination to take deacon's orders, and Wm. Ballard and Wm. Betney within six months. (*English.*)

Dated at the Chapter House, 10 Jan., 1634.

(*Calendared from Novum Registrum.*)

463 (875.) A clause in the will of Arthur Champen, of Christ Church yard, Dublin, merchant, bequeathing £40 to the Dean and chapter of Christ Church for maintaining morning prayer in Christ Church for ever, they entering into good security for performing the trust.

Also £300 to the same, to provide 2d. worth of bread, 1 lb. of beef, and 1d. to be given every sabbath day to twenty poor and aged Protestants, the poor of each parish to be relieved in turn ; security to be given, and if not, then said sum to be left with the Mayor and sheriffs of Dublin for the like purpose : if they refuse, then to be bestowed for such pious purposes as the Provost of Trinity College and his overseers should think fit.

Appoints Stephen Stephens, gent., and Wm. Bladen, stationer, both of Dublin, and Edward Aldrich, of Clonnis, co. Monaghan, gent., overseers, and his wife Alice, executrix. (*English.*)

21 Jan., 1684.

(*Calendared from Novum Registrum.*)

464 (379.) Heads of a bill to incorporate the Dean and chapter of the Holy Trinity, Dublin, proposing that they shall be one body corporate, shall have all the possessions belonging or granted to the late Prior and convent, shall make laws to govern themselves, shall distribute their possessions amongst their members, shall maintain the choir and repair the church, and shall grant leases of their houses and lands. The clerk of parliament states that he could not find that it had passed into law. (*English.*)

Transmitted 29 Sep., 16 Charles I. (1640.)

(*Calendared from Novum Registrum.*)

465 (876). Petition of the Dean and chapter of Christ Church to the Lord Lieutenant and Council, presenting two drafts of Acts of Parliament for confirming the translation of the Prior and convent into a Dean and chapter of the cathedral church of the Holy Trinity, and confirming tenants in their legal estates, with order of council referring it to the judges. (*English.*)

Dated 19 March, 1644.

(*Calendared from Novum Registrum.*)

466 (880). Pope Innocent X. directs the Archbishop of Dublin, and the Bishops of Leighlin and Ferns, or their vicars general, to admit Patrick Chaell, vicar of St. Michael's, Dublin, to the office of Dean of Holy Trinity church, vacant by the death of William Bearrex.

Dated at St. Peter's, Rome, iii. Non., Nov., 1° Innocent X. (3 Nov. 1644.)

467. Sir Joshua Allen disclaims all intention of passing letters patents for any lands belonging to the Dean and chapter of Holy Trinity, in Stillorgan, particularly the ruinous church, and land commonly called "church land," now in their possession.

Witnesses.—Gilbert Nicholson, notary public, Maurice Watson. (*English*).

Dated 3 Sep., 1684.

Appendix VIII.

Index to Deputy Keeper's Reports, Sixteenth to Twentieth Inclusive.

[References are by Roman Numeral to Report, and Arabic Cipher to page.]

Abstract of Decrees of Court of Claims, (State Paper Office),	xix.	39
		41
Abstracts and Statements of Title, (Longfield), L. E. C., arranged,	xx.	12
Abstracts and Statements of Title, (Registrar), L. E. C., arranged,	xx.	12
Accountant-General's (Chancery) Orders, 1784-1880, arranged, &c.,	xvi.	7
Accountant-General's (Chancery) Orders, 1784-1838, stamped, &c.,	xix.	11
Accountant-General's (Chancery) Powers of Attorney, arranged,	xvii.	8
„	xix.	11
Accounts, Constabulary, 1829-35, (State Paper Office),	xviii.	30
„ „ Reports on, 1826-31, „	xviii.	20
„ Excise, (1858-62), Index to, „	xvii.	25
„ Guardians' and Receivers' (Chancery), Index to,	xix.	13
„ Lunacy, (1843-50), indexed,	xvii.	10
„ Military, (State Paper Office),	xviii.	19
Act of Settlement, Records relating to, (State Paper Office),	xix.	35
Addresses to the King, (1682-6), (State Paper Office),	xvii.	28
„ „ „ Index to „	xvii.	25
Administration Bonds arranged, &c.,	xviii.	10
„ „ Index continued,	xx.	13
„ „ (Ardagh), Draft Index completed,	xix.	12
„ „ (Ardfert), „ „ „	xix.	12
„ „ (Cashel and Emly), Index to,	xvi.	7
„ „ (Cloyne), Draft Index completed,	xix.	12
„ „ (Consistorial Court, Dublin), 1792-1858, arranged,	xviii.	10
„ „ (Cork), Draft Index completed,	xix.	12
„ „ (Elphin), „ „ „	xix.	12
„ „ (Ferns), „ „ „	xix.	12
„ „ (Killala), „ „ „	xix.	12
„ „ (Killaloe), „ „ „	xix.	12
„ „ (Kilmore), „ „ „	xix.	12
„ „ (Leighlin), „ „ „	xix.	12
„ „ (Limerick), „ „ „	xix.	12
„ „ (Lismore), „ „ „	xix.	12
„ „ (Meath), arranged,	xix.	11
„ „ „ Draft Index completed,	xix.	12
„ „ (Ossory), arranged,	xvi.	7
„ „ „ Draft Index completed,	xix.	12
„ „ (Prerogative), 1832-46, flattened, &c.	xviii.	10
„ „ „ arranged,	xix.	12
„ „ (Raphoe), arranged,	xix.	11

Administration Bonds (Raphoe), Draft Index completed, . xix. 12
    „   „   (Tuam), Draft Index completed, . xix. 12
    „   „   (Waterford and Lismore), arranged, xix. 11
    „   „   (Waterford), Draft Index completed, . xix. 12
Admiralty Papers, Arrangement of miscellaneous, . xx. 12
Affidavits, (Landed Estates Court), arranged, . xx. 11
  „ (Lunacy), 1843-63, indexed, . xvii. 10
  „ of Service of Orders of Council, 1661-88, (State Paper Office), . xx. 21
  „ of Service of Orders of Council, 1682-88, Index to, (State Paper Office), . xvii. 25
Almanacks and Directories, Dublin, (1734-1870). . xvi. 11
    „   „   „ Further addition to, xviii. 12
    „   „   „   „ xix. 14
Appearances, Certificates of, L. E. C., arranged, . xx. 12
Appointments and Vacancies, . xx. 11
Ardagh Administration Bonds, Draft Index completed, xix. 12
    „   „   Index completed, . xx. 18
  „ Will and Grant Books, (1702-1802 and 1838-58), Draft Index to, . xx. 13
Ardfert Administration Bonds, Draft Index completed, . xix. 13
    „   „   „ Index completed, . xx. 13
  „ Inventories arranged, &c., . xix. 12
Armagh Diocesan Records flattened, . xviii. 10
  „ Testamentary and Diocesan Cause Papers arranged, . xix. 12
Army Account Books, 1829-31, (State Paper Office), . xvii. 26
  „ and Militia Returns, Ireland, 1603-6, (State Paper Office), . xvi. 11
  „ States, 1728-61, (State Paper Office), . xviii. 19
Arrangement and Sorting of Papers, (1883), . xvi. 0
    „   „   „ (1884), . xvii. 0
    „   „   „ (1885), . xviii. 9
    „   „   „ (1886), . xix. 11
    „   „   „ (1887), . xx. 11
Assessments and Assignments, 1648-9, (State Paper Office), . xx. 28
Assistant Deputy Keeper, Appointment of Mr. W. M. Hennessy as, . xix. 3
Athy and Harristown, Oaths of Burgesses and Returns of M.P's, . xvi. 6
Attainders, Records of, (Queen's Bench), . xvii. 4
Attendance Book, 1881, Military Department, Chief Secretary's Office, (State Paper Office), . xviii. 20
Barrack Books, 1816-1831, (State Paper Office), . xvii. 26
  „ Correspondence, 1703-1793, indexed, (State Paper Office), . xx. 22
Basement of Record Treasury, concreting completed, . xvii. 9
Battersby, Mr. George, Presentation of Index to Rental (1613) by, . xx. 13
Bays in Record Treasury, Diagram of State of, 31 Decr. 1883, . xvi. 7
Bays in Record Treasury, Diagram of State of, 31 Decr., 1884, . xvii. 9

Bays in Record Treasury, Diagram of State of, 31 Decr.
1885, ... xviii. 9

Bays in Record Treasury, Diagram of State of, 31 Decr.,
1886, ... xix. 11

Bays in Record Treasury, Diagram of State of, 31 Decr.,
1887, ... xx. 11

Berry, Mr. H. F., Appointment as First Class Clerk of, xix. 8

Bills of Indictment of Grand Juries, William and Mary,
(Queen's Bench), ... xvii. 15

Blue Coat School, Dublin, Charter of, deposited, xx. 10

    "   "   "   Warrant for deposit of Charter
of, ... xx. 34

Bonds (see " Marriage Licence " and " Administration "
Bonds).

Bookbinding and Repairing, Work done in 1883, . xvi. 8

  "   "   "   " 1884, . xvii. 10

  "   "   "   " 1885, . xviii. 11

  "   "   "   " 1886, . xix. 13

  "   "   "   " 1887, . xx. 12

Books of Entry, Car. I., (Queen's Bench), . xvii. 14

Brigade Major's Book, Yeomanry, 1828-31, (State Paper
Office), ... xvii. 28

Calendaring, Progress in, 1883, . . . xvi. 7

  "   "   1884, . . . xvii. 10

  "   "   1885, . . . xviii. 10

  "   "   1886, . . . xix. 13

  "   "   1887, . . . xx. 12

Carte Papers, Purchase of additional volumes of, xx. 10

Cashel and Emly Diocese, Index made to Administration
Bonds, ... xvi. 7

Cause Papers, Armagh Testamentary and Diocesan,
arranged, ... xix. 13

  "   Chancery, (Master Murphy), stamping
completed, ... xvi. 7

  "   Chancery, (Receiver-Master), stamping
completed, ... xvi. 7

  "   Equity Exchequer, interpolations among, xix. 11

  "   " placed in boxes, . xviii. 10

  "   Lunacy, Index to, . . . xviii. 11

  "   Prerogative, Arrangement of, . xvi. 7

  "   "   completed, . xvii. 10

  "   " Index completed to, xvii. 10

  "   Probate Division, Arrangement of, xix. 11

  "   "   " xx. 12

Certificates of Appearances, L. E. C., arranged, xx. 12

Chancery, Cause Papers, (Murphy), stamping completed, xvi. 7

  "   " (Receiver-Master) " xvi. 7

  "   Detailed Index continued, . . xx. 13

  "   " completed, . . xvii. 10

  "   Enrolled Decrees, Nos. 401–500, Indexed, xix. 13

  "   Flattening, &c., of Records, . xviii. 9

  "   Index to Receivers' and Guardians' Accounts
continued, ... xx. 12

  "   Indexes, List of Additional, . xvi. 8

  "   Land Judge, Memorandum on Records from, xix. 16

Chancery, Land Judge, Records removed from, (1886), .   xix. 6
  "   "   Removal of Deeds Boxes from, .   xx. 10
  "   "   Rentals, (1881-2), removed from,   xvi. 6
  "   Lunacy Office, Papers, (to 1843), arranged and
                indexed,   .   .   .   xvi. 7
  "   "   Records removed from,   .   .   xvi. 4
  "   "   "   .   .   .   xx. 10
  "   Petitions, Cross reference Index to, completed,   xix. 12
  "   "   (to March, 1843), Index to, .   xvi. 7
  "   "   "   "   .   .   xviii. 10
  "   "   (1843-59),   "   .   xix. 12
  "   "   "   "   engrossed,   xx. 18
  "   Order permitting recall of Records to Land
                Judge, ...   xix. 18
  "   Patent Rolls, (1860-76), Index copied,   xvii. 10
  "   Receivers' and Guardians' Accounts, Index to,   xviii. 10
  "   "   .   .   .   .   xix. 12
  "   Record and Writ Office, Records removed
                from, 1883,   .   .   .   xvi. 3
  "   Record and Writ Office, Records removed
                from, 1884,   .   .   .   xvii. 8
  "   Record and Writ Office, Records removed
                from, 1885,   .   .   .   xviii. 6
  "   Record and Writ Office, Records removed
                from, 1886,   .   .   .   xix. 4
  "   Record and Writ Office, Records removed
                from, 1887,   .   .   .   xx. 4
  "   Rejoinders and Replications arranged,   xix. 12
  "   Warrant for removal of Records from Land
                Judge, ...   xix. 17
Chief Constables, Entry of Letters to, 1881-2, (State Paper
                Office), ...   xviii. 20
  "   Secretary's Office, Records removed to State Paper
                Office from,   .   .   .   xviii. 20
  "   Secretary's Office, Records removed to State Paper
                Office from,   .   .   .   xix. 40
  "   Secretary's Office, Letters from, 1701-1834, in-
                dexed, (State Paper Office),   .   xx. 22
  "   Secretary's Office, Letters from, 1760-1831, indexed,
                (State Paper Office),   .   .   xx. 22
Christ Church Deeds, Arrangement and Calendaring of,   xvi. 8
  "   "   Calendar of portion of, printed, . {   xx. 18
                                                        86
  "   "   covered,   .   .   .   xx. 12
Circular Letter, &c., Book, Yeomanry, 1831-3, (State
                Paper Office),   .   .   .   xvii. 28
Civil Establishments, Royal Commission on; Queries
                replied to,   .   .   .   xx. 11
  "   Petitions, 1818-39, (State Paper Office), .   xvii. 28
Claims, Abstract of Decrees of Court of, (State Paper {   xix. 39
                Office), ...   41
  "   L. E. O., arranged,   .   .   .   xx. 12
Clerk of the Crown, Green-street, Records removed from,
                flattened, &c.,   .   .   .   xix. 12

Clogher Administration Bonds, Draft Index to, . xviii. 10
    ,,   ,,   ,,   Index completed, . xx. 13
    ,, Diocesan Records flattened, . . xviii. 10
Clonfert Administration Bonds, Draft Index to, . xviii. 10
    ,,   ,,   ,,   Index completed, . xx. 13
    ,, Marriage Licence Bonds arranged, . xix. 11
Cloyne Administration Bonds, Draft Index completed, . xix. 12
    ,,   ,,   ,,   Index compared, . xx. 13
    ,, Diocese, Church Papers flattened, . xx. 13
    ,,   ,,   Records flattened, . . xviii. 10
Commissariat Police Correspondence, 1828-35, (State
    Paper Office), ... xviii. 20
Commissary General and Constabulary General, 1824-30,
    (State Paper Office), . . . xviii. 20
Commission Book, 1819-21, (State Paper Office), . xvii. 28
    ,, Irish Land Act, 1886-7, Records of, (State
    Paper Office), ... xx. 93
Commissioners of Inquiry, Reports of, 1806-13, (State
    Paper Office), ... xviii. 20
Commissions of Inquiry, William and Mary, (Queen's
    Bench), ... xvii. 16
    ,, Prerogative, (1847-57), flattened, &c., . xviii. 10
    ,,   ,,   arranged, covered, &c., . xix. 11
Common Pleas Division, Amalgamation of Queen's Bench
    Division with, ... xx. 8
    ,,   ,,   ,,   detailed Index continued, . xx. 13
    ,,   ,,   ,,   flattening, &c., of Records in 3 G
        from, ... xvi. 6
    ,,   ,,   ,,   Records removed from, 1883, . xvi. 4
    ,,   ,,   ,,   ,,   ,,   1884, . xvii. 6
    ,,   ,,   ,,   ,,   ,,   1886, . xix. 5
    ,,   ,,   ,,   ,,   ,,   1887, . xx. 6
    ,,   ,,   ,,   Records, (1866-1876), Request and War-
        rant for removal of, . . xx. 19
    ,,   ,,   ,,   Records, (1866-1876), transfer of, . xx. 3
Concordatum Lists, 1824-33 (State Paper Office), . xvii. 28
Connor Administration Bonds, Draft Index to, . xviii. 10
    ,,   ,,   ,,   Index compared, . xx. 13
Consents, Chancery, Arrangement of, 1884, . xvi. 9
    ,,   ,,   ,,   1885, . xvii. 9
    ,, L. E. O., arranged, . . . xx. 13
Consistorial Court, Dublin, Administration Bonds,
    1792-1858, arranged, . . . xviii. 10
Consistorial Court, Dublin, Draft Index to Grant Books
    commenced, ... xvi. 7
Consistorial Court, Dublin, Draft Index to Grant Books
    continued, ... xvii. 10
Consistorial Court, Dublin, Draft Index to Grant Books
    continued, ... xviii. 10
Consistorial Court, Dublin, Draft Index to Will Books of, xix. 12
    ,,   ,,   Indexes, List of Additional, xvi. 9
    ,,   ,,   Records removed from, . xx. 9
Constabulary Accounts, 1829-85, (State Paper Office), . xviii. 20

Constabulary Accounts, Reports on, 1826-31, (State
        Paper Office),   .   .   .   xviii. 20
    „   County Expense Blotter, 1827-35, (State
        Paper Office),   .   .   .   xviii. 20
    „   „   Expense Book, 1829, (State Paper
        Office),   .   .   .   xviii. 20
    „   Establishment Ledger, 1824-30, (State
        Paper Office),   .   .   .   xviii. 20
    „   Finance Letter Book, 1824-5, (State Paper
        Office),   .   .   .   xviii. 20
    „   General and Commissary General, 1824-30,
        (State Paper Office),   .   .   xviii. 20
Conveyances, Draft, (Hargreave), L. E. C., arranged,   .   xx. 12
    „   „   (Longfield),   „   „   .   xx. 11
    „   „   Miscellaneous,   „   „   .   xx. 12
Copinger, W. A., Esq., Donation from,   .   xix. 14
Cork Administration Bonds, Draft Index completed,   .   xix. 12
    „   Marriage Licence Bonds arranged,   .   xix. 11
Council Office Collection, Report on, (State Paper Office),   xx. 23
    „   „   „   Volumes Indexed, (State Paper
        Office),   .   .   .   xx. 22
Country Letters, 1827-35, (State Paper Office),   .   xvii. 28
    „   „   Yeomanry, 1825-35,   „   .   xvii. 28
County Corps, 1809,   .   .   .   xviii. 20
Court of Claims, Abstract of Decrees of, (State Paper {   xix. 39
        Office), ...   41
    „   of Claims, Extract from Minutes of Proceedings of
        (1663), (State Paper Office),   .   xvii. 19
    „   of Claims, Portions of Minutes of, removed from
        Hanaper Office,   .   .   .   xvii. 6
    „   of Delegates, Transmisare to, arranged, &c.,   .   xix. 11
Cromwellian Period, Historical material for,   .   xviii. 8
Crown, Clerk of the, (Dublin), Records removed from
        office of,   .   .   .   xviii. 4
    „   Clerks of the, Queries addressed to,   .   xviii. 20
    „   Clerks of the, Summary of Returns made by,   .   xviii. 23
    „   Deeds, Deposit of,   .   .   .   xx. 11
    „   Office, Queen's Bench, Records removed, 1884,   .   xvii. 5
    „   „   „   „   „   1887,   .   xx. 6
    „   „   „   „   „   unremoved, 1884,   xvii. 6
    „   and Peace, Condition of Records of Clerks of,
        (Ireland),   .   .   .   xviii. 8
    „   and Peace Office, Dublin, Order in Council for
        removal of records of,   .   .   xviii. 15
    „   and Peace Office, Dublin, Records of, abstracted
        and recovered,   .   .   .   xviii. 3
    „   and Peace Records, Ireland, removal contem-
        plated,   .   .   .   xviii. 8
    „   „   „   „   Kildare, Order dealing with, {   xx. 8
                                20
    „   Rental (1613), Index Nominum, presented,   .   xx. 13
Custom House detailed Index continued,   .   xx. 13
Customs' Book, 1827-31, (State Paper Office),   .   xvii. 28
Declarations of Title, L. E. C., covered,   .   xx. 12

Decrees of Court of Claims, Abstract of, (State Paper Office).   xix. 39, 41

„   Enrolled, Chancery, Nos. 401–500, indexed,   xix. 13

Deeds Boxes, Landed Estates Court, Arrangements for recall of,   xix. 6

„   Landed Estates Court, Removal of,   xx. 10

Deputy Keeper, Appointment of Mr. J. J. Digges La Touche as,   xix. 3

„   Death of Sir S. Ferguson,   xix. 3

Derry Administration Bonds, Draft Index to,   xviii. 10

„   and Raphoe Marriage Licence Bonds arranged,   xix. 11

Deserters' Books, 1834–35, (State Paper Office),   xviii. 20

Destruction of Records, Act for the, recommended,   xviii. 9

Detailed Indexes continued,   xx. 13

Diocesan Registries, (Land Commission), Removal of records of,   xx. 8

Directories and Almanacks, Dublin, (1734–1870),   xvi. 11

Disentailing Deed Rolls, Progress in Calendar of, 1883,   xvi. 8

„   „   „   „   1884,   xvii. 10

„   „   „   „   1885,   xix. 13

Domestic Letters, Lord Lieutenant and Council, (1667–89),   xvii. 28

„   „   „   „   „ Index to,   xvii. 20

Donations, 1883,   xvi. 12

„   1884,   xvii. 13

„   1885,   xviii. 13

„   1886,   xix. 14

„   1887,   xx. 16

Down Administration Bonds, Draft Index to,   xviii. 10

„   „   „   Index compared,   xx. 13

„   Connor and Dromore Marriage Licence Bonds arranged,   xix. 11

„   Diocesan Records flattened,   xviii. 10

Drakestown Parish Register, Return by Mr. Fuller of,   xvi. 12

Drogheda, Records from, flattened,   xviii. 10

Dromore Administration Bonds, Draft Index to,   xviii. 10

Dublin Almanacks and Directories, (1734–1870),   xvi. 11

Dublin Consistorial Court, Administration Bonds (1702–1858) arranged,   xviii. 10

„   „   „   Draft Index to Grant Books,   xvi. 7

„   „   „   „   „   „   xvii. 10

„   „   „   „   „   „   xviii. 10

„   „   „   „   „   Will Books,   xix. 13

„   „   „   Records removed,   xx. 9

„   Crown and Peace Records abstracted and recovered,   xviii. 3

„   „   „   removed,   xviii. 3

„   Marriage Licence Bonds arranged,   xix. 11

„   „   „   „   1840–52,   xx. 12

„   „   „   „   1718–46, Draft Index to,   xix. 12

Eccles-street Collection, (Clerk of the Peace Records),   xviii. 6

Ecclesiastical Affairs, 1777–1831, (State Paper Office),   xviii. 19

Elphin Administration Bonds, Draft Index completed,   xix. 12

English Departmental Correspondence, Yeomanry, 1803–28, (State Paper Office),   xvii. 28

Entries, Books of, (State Paper Office),   xviii. 19

„   Volumes of „   „   xvii. 25

Equity Exchequer Cause Papers, interpolations among. . xix. 11
  ,,   ,,   ,, placed in boxes, . xviii. 10
  ,,   ,, detailed Index continued, . xx. 13
  ,,   ,, Records, flattening, &c., (1885). . xviii. 9
Exchequer Division, Records removed, 1883, . xvi. 5
  ,,   ,,   ,,   ,, 1885, . xviii 7
  ,,   ,,   ,,   ,, 1887, . xx. 7
  ,,   ,,   ,,   ,, without warrant, . xvi. 6
Excise Accounts, 1658-62, (State Paper Office), . xvii. 28
  ,,   ,,   ,, Index to, (State Paper Office), xvi. 15
  ,,   ,,   ,,   ,,   ,, xvii. 25
  ,, Book, 1824-32 ,,   ,,   ,, xvii. 28
Exigents and Returns, William and Mary, (Queen's Bench), xvii. 17
Fane Collection, (Letters of Lord Westmoreland &c.), . xvi. 13
  ,,   ,, Supplemental Letters to, . . xvi. 14
Fees remitted, 1886, ... xix. 14
  ,,   ,, 1887, ... xx. 16
  ,, Table of, 1883, ... xvi. 11
  ,,   ,, 1884, ... xvii. 11
  ,,   ,, 1885, ... xviii. 12
  ,,   ,, 1886, ... xix. 14
  ,,   ,, 1887, ... xx. 10
Ferguson, Sir Samuel, Death of, ... xix. 3
Ferns Administration Bonds, Draft Index completed, . xix. 12
Fetherstonhaugh, Mr. A. J., Appointment of, . . xx. 11
Fiants, Charles I., Index progressing, . . . xvi. 7
  ,,   ,, completed, . . . xvii. 10
  ,, Charles I. and II., cleaned, numbered, &c., . xvii. 10
  ,, Elizabeth, Calendar completed, . . xviii. 11
  ,,   ,,   ,, of, 1580-1596, . { xvi. 7 / 17
  ,,   ,,   ,,   ,, 1596/8-1601, . { xvii. 10 / 29
  ,,   ,,   ,,   ,, 1601-3, . . xviii. 27
  ,,   ,,   ,, Index proceeding, . . xix. 13
  ,,   ,,   ,,   ,, . . xx. 12
  ,, George III., ,, placed in portfolios, xviii. 9
Fireproof Bays, Progress in, 1883, . . . xvi. 6
  ,,   ,,   ,, 1884, . . . xvii. 9
  ,,   ,,   ,, 1885, . . . xviii 9
  ,,   ,,   ,, 1886, . . . xix. 11
  ,,   ,,   ,, 1887, . . . xx. 11
First-class Clerk, Appointment of Mr. H. F. Berry as, . xix. 3
Forty-nine Officers' Records connected with, (State Paper Office), . xix. 30
French Huguenot Statements and Declarations, Memorandum on, . xviii. 24
  ,, Military Pensioners, Statements and Declarations of, . xviii. 11
Fuller, J. F., Esq., Return of Drakestown Parish Register by, . xvi. 12
Government Correspondence, 1822-35, (State Paper Office), . xvii. 28
Grand Juries, Bills of Indictment of, Wm. and Mary, (Queen's Bench), . xvii. 15

Grant Book, Prerogative, (1692–7), indexed,   .   .   xix. 12
  ,,   Books, Consistorial Court, Dublin, Draft Index
      continued, ...   xvi. 7
  ,,   Books, Consistorial Court, Dublin, Draft Index
      continued, ...   xvii. 10
  ,,   Books, Consistorial Court, Dublin, Draft Index
      continued, ...   xviii. 10
Green-street, Records removed from Clerk of the Crown,
  flattened, &c., ...   xix. 11
Hanaper Office, Chancery, flattening, &c., of Records from,   xvi. 8
  ,,   ,,   ,,   .   .   xviii. 10
  ,,   ,,   Records removed, 1884,   .   xvii. 6
Harristown and Athy, Oaths of Burgesses and Returns of
  M.P's, ...   xvi. 8
Hennessy, Mr. W. M., Appointment as Assistant Deputy
  Keeper of, ...   xix. 3
Huguenot Statements and Declarations, Memorandum on,   xviii. 24
Incumbrance Rolls covered, ...   xviii. 10
  ,,   ,, , linen-lined paper wrappers for.   xvii. 9
Incumbrances, Schedules of, L. E. O., covered,   .   xx. 12
Index to 16th–20th Reports formed,   .   .   .   xx. 14
Indexes, List of additional, ...   xvi. 8
Indexing, Progress in 1883, ...   xvi. 7
  ,,   ,,   1884,   .   .   .   xvii. 10
  ,,   ,,   1885,   .   .   .   xviii. 10
  ,,   ,,   1886,   .   .   .   xix. 12
  ,,   ,,   1887,   .   .   .   xx. 12
Indictment, Bills of, Wm. and Mary, (Queen's Bench),   .   xvii. 16
Indictments of Treason, Index to, Wm. and Mary, (Queen's
  Bench), ...   xvii. 19
Inquisitions, Wm. and Mary, (Queen's Bench),   .   .   xvii. 16
Intern Arrangements, 1883, ...   xvi. 6
  ,,   ,,   1884,   .   .   .   xvii. 9
  ,,   ,,   1885,   .   .   .   xviii. 9
  ,,   ,,   1886,   .   .   .   xix. 11
  ,,   ,,   1887,   .   .   .   xx. 11
Inventories, Ardfert, arranged, &c.,   .   .   .   xix. 12
  ,,   Limerick,   ,,   .   .   .   xix. 12
  ,,   Ossory,   ,,   .   .   .   xix. 12
  ,,   Prerogative, ,,   .   .   .   xix. 13
Iron Chest, (Queen's Bench), Report on contents of,   .   xvii. 13
Iron Fittings, 1883, ...   xvi. 6
  ,,   ,,   1884, ...   xvii. 9
  ,,   ,,   1885, ...   xviii. 9
  ,,   ,,   1886, ...   xix. 11
  ,,   ,,   1887, ...   xx. 11
Judgments, Registrar of; Records removed, 1886,   .   xix. 9
  ,,   ,,   ,,   1887,   .   xx. 9
Kildare Co., List of 40 shilling freeholders,   .   .   xvi. 6
  ,,   ,, Oaths before Commissioners of Array,   xvi. 6
  ,,   Crown and Peace Records, Order dealing
     with, ...   xx. 3
       12
  ,,   Marriage Licence Bonds arranged,   .   xix. 11
Kilkenny Confederates—Orders on Process—1644-9, Index
  to, (State Paper Office), ...   xvi. 15

Kilkenny Confederates — Orders on Process — 1644-9,
    Index to, (State Paper Office), . . xix. 40
    „ Confederates Records, (State Paper Office), . xviii. 17
    „ Confederation, 1644-9, „ . xx. 21
Killala Administration Bonds, Draft Index completed, xix. 12
    „ and Achonry Administration Bonds, Index com-
    pared, ... xx. 13
    „ and Achonry, Grants of Administration, 1800-57,
    indexed, ... xx. 13
Killaloe Administration Bonds, Draft Index completed, xix. 12
Kilmore Administration Bonds, „ xix. 12
    „ Will and Grant Book, 1853-7, indexed, . xix. 12
    „ and Ardagh Marriage Licence Bonds arranged, xix. 11
King's Letters, 1793-1827, (State Paper Office), . xviii. 19
    „ „ (1817-20), „ . xvii. 28
    „ „ Military, 1714-1824, (State Paper Office), xvi. 16
    „ „ Military, 1714-1824, Index to, (State
    Paper Office), . . . xvi. 15
Land Act, 1886-7, Records of Commission on, (State Paper
    Office), ... xx. 22
Land Commission, Conditions of Loan of Landed Estates
    Court Rentals (O'Brien collection) to, xix. 88
    „ „ Records removed, 1886, xix. 9
    „ „ Records of Diocesan Registries re-
    moved, . . xx. 8
    „ „ Rentals, (O'Brien collection), lent to, xix. 10
    „ Judge, Chancery, Memorandum on records from, xix. 19
    „ „ „ Order permitting recall of records to xix. 18
    „ „ „ Records removed from, 1886, xix. 6
    „ „ „ Removal of Deeds Boxes, xx. 10
    „ „ „ Warrant for removal of records, xix. 17
Landed Estates Court, Arrangements for recall of Deeds
    Boxes to, . . . xix. 6
    „ „ „ Papers arranged, xx. 11
    „ „ „ Records of, Detailed Index to, . xx. 13
    „ „ „ Rentals (O'Brien collection), con-
    ditions of Loan to Land Com-
    mission, . . xix. 88
LaTouche, Mr. J. J. Diggs, Appointment as Deputy
    Keeper, ... xix. 3
Law Exchequer, detailed Index continued, . xx. 13
LeFanu, T. P., Esq., Transfer to Chief Secretary's Office, xvii. 3
Leighlin Administration Bonds, Draft Index completed, xix. 12
Leinster, Presentation of Records by Duke of, xvi. 6
Letters, Domestic, Lord Lieutenant and Council, 1667-89, xvii. 28
    „ „ „ „ Index to, xvii. 28
Limerick Administration Bonds, Draft Index completed, xix. 12
    „ Diocese, Church Papers flattened, xx. 12
    „ Inventories arranged, &c., xix. 12
Lismore Administration Bonds arranged, xix. 11
    „ „ „ Draft Index completed, xix. 12
Literary Inquiries, 1883, . . . xvi. 12
    „ „ 1884, . . . xvii. 12
    „ „ 1885, . . . xviii. 12
    „ „ 1886, . . . xix. 14

Literary Inquiries, 1857, . . . xx. 17
Littledale, W. F., Esq., Donations to Office by, . xvi. 11
   „   „   „ Further donation by, . xviii. 12
   „   „   „ . xix. 14
Lopdell, Mr. John, Resignation of, . xx. 11
Lunacy Accounts, 1843–50, Index to, . xvii. 10
  „ Affidavits, 1843–65, „ . xvii. 10
  „ Cause Papers, (to 1843), arranged and indexed, . xvi. 7
  „   „   „ Index to, . xviii. 11
  „ Petitions, 1850–63, „ . xvii. 10
  „   „   „ . xviii. 11
  „   „ and Reports, 1813–50, Index to, . xvii. 10
  „ Registrar in, Chancery, Records removed, . xvi. 4
  „   „   „ . xx. 10
  „ Reports and Accounts, 1850–63, Index to, . xvii. 10
  „ Writs in, Index revised, . xx. 13
Marriage Licence Bonds, Clonfert, arranged, . xix. 11
  „   „ Cork,   „ . xix. 11
  „   „ Derry and Raphoe, arranged, . xix. 11
  „   „ Down, Connor and Dromore, arranged, . xix. 11
  „   „ Dublin, arranged, . xix. 11
  „   „   „ 1840–53, . xx. 12
  „   „   „ Draft Index to, 1718–46, . xix. 12
  „   „ Kildare, arranged, . xix. 11
  „   „ Kilmore and Ardagh, arranged, . xix. 11
  „   „ Meath, arranged, . xix. 11
  „   „ Ossory, „ . xvi. 7
  „   „ Tuam, „ . xix. 11
Masters' Certificates, Chancery, Arrangement of, . xviii. 0
M'Ghee, Mr. Thomas, Retirement and death of, . xix. 4
M'Kenna, P. Esq., Londonderry, Donation to Office by, . xvi. 11
Meath Administration Bonds arranged, . xix. 11
  „   „ Draft Index completed, . xix. 12
  „ Marriage Licence Bonds arranged, . xix. 11
  „ Miscellaneous Diocesan Papers flattened, . xix. 13
  „ Records, (Diocesan), 1744–36, . xviii. 8
  „ Will and Grant Book, 1667-1731, Draft Index to, . xx. 13
Military Accounts, (State Paper Office), . xviii. 19
  „ Certificates, 1684-1774, indexed, (State Paper Office), . xx. 22
  „ Commissions, 1715-1763, indexed, (State Paper Office), . xx. 22
  „ Contracts, 1710-1760, indexed, (State Paper Office), . xx. 22
  „ Correspondence, 1686-1776, indexed, (State Paper Office), . xx. 22
  „ King's Letters (See King's Letters).
  „ Notifications, 1702-1767, indexed, (State Paper Office), . xx. 22
Militia Book, 1835-30, (State Paper Office), . xvii. 28
Minutes, Civil Department Chief Secretary's Office, 1802–35, (State Paper Office), . xviii. 19
Miscellaneous Papers, Arrangement of, (State Paper Office), . xvi. 15

Miscellaneous Papers, Arrangement of, (State Paper Office), xvii. 23
,, ,, ,, ,, ,, xviii. 16
,, ,, ,, ,, ,, xix. 39
{ 40
,, ,, ,, ,, ,, xx. 21
,, Collections, Detailed Index continued, xvi. 7
,, ,, ,, ,, xvii. 10
,, ,, ,, ,, xx. 13
Murphy, (Minor in Chancery), Cause Papers stamped, xvi. 7
Musters, Rolls of, 1741-80, (State Paper Office), xviii. 19
O'Brien Rentals lent to Land Commission, xix. 10
,, ,, Supplemental Index to, xvi. 7
Official Papers, 1854-86, Draft Index to, (State Paper Office), xx. 23
Order in Council dealing with Crown and Peace Records, Dublin, xviii. 15
Order in Council dealing with Crown and Peace Records, { xx. 3
Kildare, } 20
Orders, Accountant-General's, (Chancery), 1784-1880, arranged, &c., xvi. 7
Orders, Accountant-General's, (Chancery), 1784-1838, stamped, &c., xix. 11
Orders in Council, Affidavits of Service of, 1661-88, (State Paper Office), xx. 21
Orders in Council, Affidavits of Service of, 1682-8, Index to, (State Paper Office), xvi. 13
Orders in Council, Affidavits of Service of, 1682-8, Index to, (State Paper Office), xvii. 25
Orders, Parliamentary, 1832-3, (State Paper Office), xviii. 20
Orders on Process, 1644-9, Kilkenny Confederates, (State Paper Office), xx. 26
Orders on Process, 1644-9, Kilkenny Confederates, Index to, (State Paper Office), xix. 40
Ordnance Books, 1817-31, (State Paper Office), xviii. 20
Ossory Administration Bonds, Draft Index completed, xix. 13
,, Bonds, arrangement of, xvi. 7
,, Inventories arranged, &c., xix. 13
Parish Registers, Changes in places of deposit of, 1883, xvi.279
,, ,, ,, ,, 1882-4, xvii.277
,, ,, ,, ,, 1886, xix. 80
,, ,, ,, ,, 1887, xx. 15
Parliamentary Orders, 1832-3, (State Paper Office), xviii. 20
Parochial Records Acts, Proceedings under, 1883, xvi. 10
,, ,, ,, ,, 1884, xvii. 11
,, ,, ,, ,, 1885, xviii. 11
,, ,, ,, ,, 1886, xix. 16
,, ,, ,, ,, 1887, xx. 14
,, ,, Change in mode of collecting, xx. 14
,, ,, Distribution of, 1883, xvi. 11
,, ,, Table of, corrected to April, 1886, xviii.151
Passes for Ships, 1677, (State Paper Office), xvii. 26
,, ,, Index to, (State Paper Office), xvi. 15
,, ,, ,, ,, xvii. 25
Patent Rolls, Chancery, 1860-76, Index copied, xvii. 10
,, ,, James I., Index to Calendar, xvi. 7

Patent Rolls, James I., Index to Calendar, . . xix. 13
Paymaster's Certificates, L. E. C., covered, . . xx. 12
Peace, Clerk of the, Dublin, Records removed from, . xviii. 4
  " " " " (Eccles-st.), . xviii. 6
  " Clerks of the, Queries addressed to, . xviii. 30
  " " " Summary of Returns made by, . xviii. 23
Pensioners, Memorandum on Statements of French
          Huguenot, . . . xviii. 24
  " Statements and Declarations of French
          Military, . . . xviii. 11
Petitions, Chancery, Cross Reference Index to, com-
          pleted, . . . xix. 12
  " " to March, 1843, Index to, . xvi. 7
  " " " " . . xviii. 10
  " " (1843–50), " . xix. 12
  " " " " . . xx. 13
  " L. E. C., arranged, . . . xx. 12
  " Copy, L. E. C., arranged, . . xx. 12
  " to Lords Lieutenant and Council, (State Paper
          Office), . . . xvii. 28
  " Lunacy, Index to, . . . xvii. 10
  " " " . . . xviii. 11
  " (State Paper Office), Index to, . { xvii. 32
                                        25
  " " " " . . . xviii. 16
  " and Reports, Lunacy, 1843–50, Index to, . xvii. 10
Portarlington, St. Michael's Parish, Register missing, . xx. 14
Powers of Attorney, Accountant General's Office,
          Chancery, arrangement of, . . xvii. 9
Powers of Attorney, Accountant-General's Office,
          Chancery, arrangement of, . . xix. 11
Prerogative Administration Bonds, arrangement of, . xix. 12
  " " " flattened, &c., . xviii. 10
  " Cause Papers, arrangement of, . xvi. 7
  " " " " . . xvii. 10
  " " " Index to, . xvii. 10
  " Commissions arranged and covered, . xix. 11
  " " flattened, . xviii. 10
  " Grant Book, 1692–7, indexed, . . xix. 12
  " Inventories, arrangement of, . . xix. 12
  " Miscellaneous Records, flattened, . { xviii. 9
                                          10
  " Wills, 1811–1858, Index to, . . xvi. 7
  " " " . . . xviii. 10
  " " " and Intestacies, 1847–9, Index re-copied, . xx. 13
Private Official Correspondence, Yeomanry, 1812–15,
          (State Paper Office), . . xvii. 28
  " " Letter Book, Yeomanry, 1816–33, (State
          Paper Office), . . . xvii. 28
Probate Division, Cause Papers arranged, . . xix. 11
  " " " " . . . xx. 12
  " " Certificate for retention of Records in, . xix. 17
  " " " " " . . . xx. 35
  " " No increment received from, 1884, . xvii. 9
  " " Records removal, 1886, . . xix. 6

Probate Division, Records unremoved, 1887, . . xx. 10
Queen's Bench, Crown Office, Records removed, 1834, . xvii. 5
   "   "   "   "   "   " 1887, . xx. 6
   "   "   "   "   " unremoved, 1886, . xvii. 5
   "   "   Detailed Index continued, . xx. 13
   "   "   Division, Amalgamation of Common Pleas
     Division with, . . . xx. 3
   "   "   Flattening of Records of, 1885, . xviii. 0
   "   "   Iron Chest, Report on contents of, . xvii. 13
   "   "   Records removed, 1884, . . xvii. 4
   "   "   "   " 1888, . . xix. 5
   "   "   "   " 1866-70, . . xx. 35
   "   "   Request and Warrant for removal of
     Records of, 1866-1876, . . xx. 19
Queries addressed to Clerks of the Crown and Peace, . xviii. 20
Raphoe Administration Bonds arranged, . . xix. 11
   "   "   Draft Index completed, . xix. 12
Rebellion of 1641, Records in relation to, (Queen's Bench), xvii. 13
   " 1888,   "   "   " xvii. 16
Receiver Master, Chancery, Cause Papers stamped, . xvi. 7
Receivers' and Guardians' Accounts, Chancery, arrangement of, ... xvii. 9
   "   "   "   "   " xviii. 10
   "   "   "   "   " xix. 12
   "   "   "   "   " xx. 12
Record Publications, Donations of, 1883, . . xvi. 12
   "   "   " 1884, . . xvii. 12
   "   "   " 1885, . . xviii. 12
   "   "   " 1886, . . xix. 14
   "   "   " 1887, . . xx. 16
   "   Tower, Catalogue of Books, Papers, &c., in, xvi. 15
   "   "   Detailed Index continued, . xx. 13
   "   "   Papers received in, 1883, . xvi. 15
   "   "   "   " 1885, . xviii. 20
   "   "   "   " 1886, . xix. 40
   "   "   "   " 1887, . xx. 32
   "   "   Records removed, 1883, . { xvi. 6 / 18
   "   "   "   " 1884, . { xvii. 0 / 27
   "   "   "   " 1885, . xviii. 8
   "   "   "   " 1886, . xix. 9
   "   "   "   " 1887, . { xx. 8 / 32
Record and Writ Office, Chancery, Records removed, 1883, xvi. 3
   "   "   "   " 1884, xvii. 3
   "   "   "   " 1885, xviii. 6
   "   "   "   " 1886, xix. 4
   "   "   "   " 1887, xx. 4
Recruiting Correspondence, 1614-34, (State Paper
   Office), ... xvii. 28
Registrar of Judgments, Records removed, 1880, . xix. 9
   "   "   " 1887, . xx. 9
   " in Lunacy, Chancery, Records removed, . xx. 10
Rejoinders and Replications, Chancery, arranged, . xix. 12

Rentals, 1861-2, removed from Land Judge's Court, Chancery, ... xvi. 4
  ,, Duplicate, L. E. C., arranged, . . xx. 12
  ,, (O'Brien collection), compilation of Supplemental Index to, ... xvi. 7
  ,, Landed Estates Court, (O'Brien collection), xix. 10
Loan to Land Commission, . . . 88
Repairing and Bookbinding, Work done in 1863, xvi. 8
  ,,   ,,   ,, 1884, xvii. 10
  ,,   ,,   ,, 1885, xviii. 11
  ,,   ,,   ,, 1886, xix. 13
  ,,   ,,   ,, 1887, xx. 12
Replications and Rejoinders, Chancery, arranged, xix. 12
Reports and Accounts, Lunacy, 1850-63, Index to, xvii. 10
Returns to Writs of Exigent, Wm. and Mary, (Queen's Bench), ... xvii. 17
Revenue Exchequer, Sheriffs' Constats, 1630-47, Index to, ... xix. 18
Rolls of Musters, 1741-80, (State Paper Office), xviii. 19
Routes, 1737-64, (State Paper Office), xviii. 19
Royal Commission on Civil Establishments; Queries replied to, ... xx. 11
Rural Deans' Reports Returned, . . xx. 12
St. Luke's, Cork, Safety of Registers of, . xx. 14
Sales, L. E. C., Index to, . . . xvi. 11
Schedules of Incumbrances, L. E. C., covered, xx. 13
Sheriffs' Constats, 1630-47, (Revenue Exchequer), Index to, xix. 13
Shipping, 1630-8, (State Paper Office), . xx. 21
Ships and Vessels belonging to Irish Ports, 1792-4, (State Paper Office), . . xvii. 28
Sorting and Arrangement of Papers, 1883, xvi. 6
  ,,   ,,   ,, 1884, xvii. 9
  ,,   ,,   ,, 1885, xviii. 9
  ,,   ,,   ,, 1886, xix. 11
  ,,   ,,   ,, 1887, xx. 11
Staff, Changes in, 1884, . . . xvii. 3
  ,, 1886, . . . xix. 3
  ,, 1887, . . . xx. 11
State Paper Office (see Record Tower).
State Papers, Keeper of, Report of, 1883, xvi. 13
  ,,   ,,   ,, 1884, xvii. 21
  ,,   ,,   ,, 1885, xviii. 16
  ,,   ,,   ,, 1886, xix. 35
  ,,   ,,   ,, 1887, xx. 21
Statements and Abstracts of Title, (Longfield), L. E. C., arranged, ... xx. 12
Statements and Abstracts of Title, (Registrar), L. E. C., arranged, ... xx. 12
Surrenders, (Geo. IV. to Vic.), placed in portfolios, xviii. 9
Tapestry, Irish House of Lords, History of, xvii. 24
Taxing Office, Records removed from, 1885, xviii. 6
Testamentary detailed Index continued, xx. 13
  ,, Indexes, List of Additional, xvi. 9
Tipperary, Palatinate of, List of Additional Indexes, xvi. 10
Tithe Owners' Relief Fund, 1833, (State Paper Office), xviii. 30

K

Title, Declaration of, L. E. O., covered, — xx. 12
Transmission to Court of Delegates arranged, &c., — xix. 11
Treason, Indictments of, Index to, Wm. and Mary, (Queen's Bench), — xvii. 19
Treasury Letters, 1793–1627, (State Paper Office), — xviii. 19
    ., Payments under Acts of Parliament, 1833–7, (State Paper Office), — xviii. 20
    .. Votes, &c., 1833–4, (State Paper Office), — xviii. 20
    .. Warrant Book, 1631–4, .. — xvii. 28
    .. Warrants, Yeomanry, 1814–31, .. — xvii. 28
Tuam Administration Bonds, Draft Index completed, — xix. 12
    " " " Index compared, — xx. 13
    " Marriage Licence Bonds arranged, — xix. 11
Unregistered Miscellaneous Papers, arrangement, &c., (State Paper Office), — xlix. 40
    " Miscellaneous Papers indexed, (State Paper Office), — xx. 31
Vacancies and Appointments, — xx. 11
Vice-Treasurer's Book, 1820–1831, (State Paper Office), — xviii. 20
Visitation Papers flattened, — xx. 12
Waterford and Lismore Administration Bonds arranged, — xix. 11
    " " " " Draft Index completed, — xix. 12
    " " " " Index compared, — xx. 13
Will Books, Dublin Consistorial Court, Draft Index to, — xix. 12
Wills, Prerogative, 1811–58, Index to, — xvi. 1
    " " " — xviii. 10
Wood, Herbert, Esq., Appointment on Staff of, — xvii. 3
Wool Licences, 1699, Index to, (State Paper Office), — xvi. 15
    " " — xvii. 35
Workmen, Services, Appointment of, — xx. 11
Wright, Rev. W. B., Donation from, — xx. 16
Writs of Capias, Car. I., (Queen's Bench), — xvii. 14
    of Exigent and Returns thereto, Car. I., (Queen's Bench), — xvii. 13
    " in Lunacy, Index to, revised, — xx. 13
Yeomanry Brigade Major's Book, 1828–31, (State Paper Office), — xvii. 28
    .. Circular Letter, &c., Book, 1831–3, (State Paper Office), — xvii. 28
    .. County Letters, 1826–35, (State Paper Office), — xvii. 28
    .. English Departmental Correspondence, 1803–28, (State Paper Office), — xvii. 28
    " Private Official Correspondence, 1812–15, (State Paper Office), — xvii. 28
    .. Private Official Letter Book, 1818–33, (State Paper Office), — xvii. 28
    " Treasury Warrants, 1814–31, (State Paper Office), — xvii. 28

DUBLIN: Printed for Her Majesty's Stationery Office,
By ALEX. THOM & Co. (Limited), 87, 88, & 89, Abbey-street,
The Queen's Printing Office.

STATE OF BAYS

on

EAST AND WEST SIDES OF RECORD TREASURY,

31st DECEMBER, 1857.